YO-CKN-113

AMERICAN LABOR

FROM CONSPIRACY
TO
COLLECTIVE BARGAINING

ADVISORY EDITORS

Leon Stein *Philip Taft*

LABOR AND THE EMPLOYER

Samuel Gompers

ARNO & THE NEW YORK TIMES
NEW YORK 1971

Reprint Edition 1971 by Arno Press Inc.

© 1920 by E. P. Dutton & Co.
Reprinted by permission of E. P. Dutton & Co., Inc.

Reprinted from a copy in
The U.S. Department of Labor Library
LC# 79-156413
ISBN 0-405-02921-7

American Labor: From Conspiracy to Collective Bargaining—Series II
ISBN for complete set: 0-405-02910-1
See last pages of this volume for titles.

Manufactured in the United States of America

*LABOR MOVEMENTS AND
LABOR PROBLEMS IN AMERICA*

LABOR AND
THE EMPLOYER

LABOR MOVEMENTS AND LABOR PROBLEMS IN AMERICA

LABOR AND THE EMPLOYER

BY
SAMUEL GOMPERS
PRESIDENT OF THE AMERICAN FEDERATION OF LABOR
VICE-PRESIDENT OF THE NATIONAL CIVIC
FEDERATION

COMPILED AND EDITED BY
HAYES ROBBINS

NEW YORK
E. P. DUTTON & COMPANY
681 FIFTH AVENUE

COPYRIGHT, 1920,
BY E. P. DUTTON & COMPANY

All Rights Reserved

Printed in the United States of America

FOREWORD

Since the first volume of this compilation was prepared the industrial situation in the United States has grown more acute and the essential labor issues more sharply defined. During the war, workingmen and employers gave to the Government a loyal and united service, in shop and mine no less than on the field, which promised to lay broad foundations for an era of good-will and coöperation during the reconstruction and in peace-time relations for years to come. But in the period since the end of hostilities three factors especially have conspired to disappoint or at least postpone these hopes. There has been a continuing pressure of high living costs, where relief was anticipated; an unwillingness of various employing interests to extend to labor in industrial dealings the recognition accorded, at least tacitly, in the many plans and programs jointly undertaken and worked out during the war, and, on the other side, a renewed, widespread and determined effort of radical elements to capitalize the ideas and emotions of the war upheaval for revolutionary propaganda. All three of these factors have affected the mood of labor in many quarters, and lent new force for the time being to the "boring from within" tactics of socialist and syndicalist factions in the trade-union movement.

In such a situation, the views of the chief authoritative exponent of American trade-unionism on the outstanding topics discussed in the present volume are at this moment directly to the point. The issues are literally those around which industrial unrest for the most part centers. Thereby the volume adds an immediate practical interest to the permanent educational value which thoughtful students of the unfolding movements of the time will readily see in it.

The first volume, *Labor and the Common Welfare*, embodies Mr. Gompers' interpretation of labor's relation to the well-being of the whole community. The present volume goes to the heart of the ever-present concrete problems of employment relations.

From the root questions of wages, working hours and unemployment the range of discussion brings us to the challenging issues of strikes, boycotts, the so-called "closed shop," arbitration, collective bargaining, profit-sharing, and the labor view of a true democratization of industry. Whether one agree or disagree with Mr. Gompers' views is of course beside the mark: the issues are too broad and the situation too serious to omit candid consideration of the salient points in any position so interwoven with the industrial fabric and so inseparable from it, if not in one form then in another, as that of labor organization.

It should be stated that the preparation of these volumes has been made possible only by the initiative foresight and care, extending over many years, of Mr. Gompers' secretary, Miss R. Lee Guard, in collecting and preserving copies of all publications in which his writings, addresses or testimony have appeared, since the early years of the American Federation of Labor; the sources ranging from the daily newspapers and labor press to government reports and official documents and economic reviews, and including some privately reported matter which has probably never before appeared in print.

As in *Labor and the Common Welfare,* a portion of the selections from earlier years, on subjects more fully worked out in Mr. Gompers' recent writings, are nevertheless placed in the record because of their interesting revelation of consistency in the central ideas advocated throughout the whole period, and by reason also of their historic place in the development of the American labor movement.

HAYES ROBBINS.

TABLE OF CONTENTS

		PAGE
I.	THE AMERICAN FEDERATION OF LABOR	1
	History, Objects and Methods	1
	Progress by Evolution, not Revolution	32
II.	EMPLOYERS AND EMPLOYERS' ORGANIZATIONS	38
III.	ECONOMICS AND ETHICS OF HIGH WAGES	58
IV.	THE SHORTER WORKING DAY	81
V.	THE UNION SHOP AND THE "OPEN" SHOP	108
VI.	CHILD LABOR AND WOMEN IN INDUSTRY	118
VII.	UNEMPLOYMENT, INSURANCE AND COMPENSATION	133
VIII.	SOME EVERY-DAY PROBLEMS AND CRITICISMS	161
	Organization of the Unskilled	161
	The "Color Line" in Labor	166
	"Limitation of Output"	170
	The Union Label	175
	Jurisdiction Disputes	178
IX.	INDUSTRIAL WARFARE	185
	Strikes	185
	The Boycott	203
	Picketing	217
	Violence and "Graft"	218
	Restrictions on Labor Activities	232
X.	INDUSTRIAL AGREEMENT	259
	Arbitration—Voluntary and Compulsory	259
	Compulsory Investigation	266
	Incorporation of Trade Unions	272
	Collective Bargaining	278
XI.	THE LABOR VIEW OF PROFIT-SHARING, "EFFICIENCY" MANAGEMENT AND INDUSTRIAL DEMOCRACY	290
	Profit-Sharing and Co-operation	290
	"Efficiency" Experiments	294
	The True "Democratization of Industry"	303

LABOR AND THE EMPLOYER

LABOR AND THE EMPLOYER

I

THE AMERICAN FEDERATION OF LABOR

HISTORY, OBJECTS AND METHODS

We, the defenders of the young but rapidly developing trade union movement in America, should be comforted and inspired by the knowledge that we do not stand alone and unsupported in the struggle to secure better conditions for the working classes. The formation and rapid development of the American Federation of Labor have been hailed with the heartiest expressions of joy and hope on the part of many trade unionists in other lands. In this connection it is particularly agreeable for me to state that the first official tender of sympathy and coöperation was made by the *Federation Francaise des Travailleurs du Livre,* the Typographical Union of France. While I am now speaking there are numberless gatherings of men and women, in many cities, in many lands, on several continents, speaking in many languages, but all converging to one idea and filled by the same aspiration. On the continent of Australia, and several of the adjacent islands, trade unions have taken deep root in the affections of the people, and the eight-hour work-day has for many years been the unwritten but effective law of the land. On the continent of Europe the trade union movement is slowly but none the less surely leading the more advanced minds from the dark valley of anarchical, revolutionary class hatred to the upper region of a truly organic system. In Great Britain and Ireland, the cradle of our now universal movement, the Twentieth Annual Trade Union Congress unanimously adopted a resolution, "To bring about united action on questions directly affecting the interests of labor," by means of an International Congress. It is almost needless to say that it is my earnest desire that America shall be worthily represented at said Congress. . . .

Owing to the fact that the Constitution only went into effect on March 1st I found myself in a peculiar predicament, charged with the duty of immediately after the convention entering upon the duties of the office of president, and devoting my efforts to the Federation. There was no money in the treasury to buy stationery, pay salary or publish the official journal, the payments of organizations having mostly been made during the latter part of the year. I, however, set to work in the best way possible under the circumstances.

In June last I issued the official journal which per resolution of the Executive Council was named the *Union Advocate.* As its editor I have studiously avoided the publication of objectionable matter, and while there has been no attempt at elegance, I have endeavored to make it what the Constitution calls for and its name signifies, an advocate of trades unions.

It would be obviously unjust were I to close this report without mentioning the fact that being placed in the position above indicated, Cigarmakers' Union No. 144, of New York city, cheerfully assisted me by giving me an office in their establishment for the whole year free of charge, and placing all their facilities at my disposal.—*From annual report to A. F. of L. convention, Baltimore, Md., December, 1887.*

Let us concentrate our efforts to organize all the forces of wage labor and, within the ranks, contest fairly and openly for the different views which may be entertained upon the different steps to be taken to move the grand army of labor onward and forward. In no organization on earth is there such toleration, so great a scope, and so free a forum as inside the ranks of the American Federation of Labor, and nowhere is there such a fair opportunity afforded for the advocacy of a new or brighter thought. . . .

The trades union! That takes the individual, oftentimes careless of his obligations to his fellow-man, ignorant of the very causes of the evils under which he labors and works within him a revolution; fans to life the good that lies dormant in his nature, that moral sense which all possess; that makes of him an enthusiast—a man—with new views, greater aspirations and

nobler desires; a loftier purpose, a grander conception of society and life; that shows things in a different light, and awakens him to the fact that no matter what his occupation, how low his station, he is entitled to an opportunity to earn an honest livelihood, and no other can justly call himself master, notwithstanding wealth, gifts of birth—a generated spirit of independence and self-reliance that is the trade union's pride and honor, and which is the hope and safeguard of all civilization. True patriotism; not that hybrid brand too often sung to-day by the very class that persecuted the patriots of old, who would make slaves of freemen here. The trade union is right; and it is this sense of right that has defied the decrees of kings and priests in the past, and which, while suffering, defies the rulings of courts, judges and blacklisting corporations to-day. It lives both because of and in spite of them, and it will continue to live when its enemies sleep. Justice is its goal, and it seeks not a definition of that holy word in musty statutes and befogged legal opinions. It opens its eyes and sees the word written on the very face of things, so that he who runs may read, and it decorates the thought in becoming, simple attire, truth in terms, fair play in action, "Do unto others as you would be done by."
—*From pamphlet, "The Trade Union," 1894.*

It is now generally admitted by all really educated and honest men that a thorough organization of the entire working class, to render employment and the means of subsistence less precarious, by securing an equitable share of the fruits of their toil, is the most vital necessity of the present day.

To meet this urgent necessity, and to achieve this most desirable result, efforts have been made, too numerous to specify, and too divergent to admit of more than the most general classification. Suffice it to say, that those attempts at organization which admitted to membership the largest proportion of others than wage-workers were those which went the most speedily to the limbo of movements that won't move; while, of the surviving experiments, those which started with the most elaborate and exhaustive platforms of abstract principles were those which got the soonest into fatal complications, and soonest became exhausted.

In the face of so many disastrous failures to supply the undoubtedly existing popular demand for a practical means of solving the great problem, the question naturally suggests itself to many: "Which is the best form of organization for the people, the workers?"

We unhesitatingly answer: "The organization of the working people, by the working people, for the working people—that is, the trade unions."

The trade unions are the natural growth of natural laws, and from the very nature of their being have stood the test of time and experience. The development of the trade unions, regarded both from the standpoint of numerical expansion, and that of practical working, has been marvelously rapid. The trade unions have demonstrated their ability to cope with every emergency—economical or political—as it arises.

It is true that single trade unions have been often beaten in pitched battles against superior forces of united capital, but such defeats are by no means disastrous. On the contrary, they are useful in calling the attention of the workers to the necessity of thorough organization, of the inevitable obligation of bringing the yet unorganized workers into the union, of uniting the hitherto disconnected local unions into national unions, and of effecting a yet higher unity by the affiliation of all national and international unions in one grand-federation, in which each and all trade organizations would be as distinct as the billows, yet one as the sea.

In the work of the organization of labor, the most energetic, wisest, and devoted of us, when working individually, can not hope to be successful, but by combining our efforts *all* may. And the combined action of all the unions when exerted in favor of any one union will certainly be more efficacious than the action of any one union, no matter how powerful it may be, if exerted in favor of an unorganized or a partially organized mass.

We assert that it is the duty, as it is also the plain interest, of all working people to organize as such, meet in council, and take practical steps to effect the unity of the working class, as an indispensable preliminary to any successful attempt to eliminate the evils of which we, as a class, so bitterly and justly complain. That this much-desired unity has never been achieved is owing in a great measure to the non-recognition of the autonomy, or the right of self-government, of the several trades.

The American Federation of Labor, however, avoids the fatal rock on which previous organizations, having similar aims, have split, by simply keeping in view this fundamental principle as a landmark, which none but the most infatuated would have ever lost sight of.

The rapid and steady growth of the American Federation of Labor, arising from the affiliation of previously isolated, together with newly-formed, national unions; the establishment of local unions of various trades and callings where none before existed; the spontaneous formation of federal labor unions, composed of wage-workers following various trades in places where there are too few persons employed at any particular one to allow the formation of local unions of those trades, thus furnishing valuable bodies of auxiliaries and recruits to existing unions upon change of abode; the central labor unions, trade assemblies, the citadels of local power; the States' federations for State legislative advancement, this steady growth is gratifying evidence of the appreciation of the toilers of this broad land of a form of general organization in harmony with their most cherished traditions, and in which each trade enjoys the most perfect liberty while securing the fullest advantages of united action.

And now, in conclusion, you will permit us to express our acknowledgment of the very moderate amount of governing which has fallen to the lot of those who have the honor to address you. While much of this good fortune must be attributed to the nature of the federal form of our organization, our task has been immeasurably lightened by the assistance of a body of organizers, who, without hope of reward, except the consciousness of performing a sacred duty to their fellow-workmen, have carried the propaganda of trade unionism into the remotest parts of the continent.—*From circular, "Labor Omnia Vincit," to "All Wage-Workers of America," issued 1894.*

American Federation of Labor endeavors to unite all classes of wage-workers under one head, through their several organizations to the end: (1) That class, race, creed, political and trade prejudices may be abolished; (2) that support, moral and financial, may be given to each other. It is composed of international, national, State, central and local unions, representing the great bulk of organized labor in the United States and Canada; it gives to any organization joining its ranks recognition in the labor field in all its phases; it secures in cases of boycotts, strikes, lockouts, attentive hearing before all affiliated bodies, and it renders financial aid to the extent of its ability; it is not a moneyed institution. It allows each organization to control its own funds, to establish and expend its own benefits without let or hindrance; it aims to allow—in the light of experience—the utmost liberty to each organization in the conduct of its own affairs consistent with the generally understood principles of *labor;* it establishes inter-communication, creates agitation, and is in direct and constant correspondence with a corps of representative organizers throughout the country; it watches the interests of the workers in national Congress; it endorses and protests in the name of *labor,* and has secured vast relief from burdensome laws and government officials; it is in communication with reformers and sympathizers in almost all classes, giving information and enlisting their coöperation; it assembles once a year all classes of wage-earners, in convention, to exchange ideas and methods, to cultivate mutual interest, to secure united action, to speak for *labor,* to announce to the world the burdens, aims and hopes of the workers; it asks—yea, demands—the coöperation of all wage-workers who believe in the principle of *unity,* and that there is something better in life than long hours, low wages, lack of employment, and all that these imply.

Its existence is based upon economic law, to wit: That no particular trade can long maintain wages above the common level; that to maintain high wages all trades and callings must be organized; that lack of organization among the unskilled vitally affects the organized skilled; that general organization of skilled and unskilled can only be accomplished by united action. Therefore, *federation.* Again: That no one particular locality can long maintain high wages above that of others; that to maintain high wages all localities must be organized; that this can best be done by the maintenance of national and international unions; that any local union which refuses to so affiliate is inconsistent, non-union, and should be "let alone"; that each national or international union must be protected in its particular field against rivals and seceders. Therefore, *federa-*

tion. That the history of the labor movement demonstrates the necessity of a union of individuals, and that logic implies a union of unions—*federation.—Circular issued in 1894.*

The Denver convention elected Mr. John McBride, of the United Mine Workers of America, president of the American Federation of Labor. As a consequence my term of office expires this day, and having been so long officially associated with the trade unionists of America, it does seem to me not entirely inappropriate to bid all a direct and official good-by.

I do not ask the readers of this magazine nor my fellow-unionists to imagine for a moment that in leaving the office of president of the American Federation of Labor I sever my connection with the labor movement, for as a matter of fact, even if I so desired, I doubt that I should be enabled to carry it out. I am now nigh upon forty-five years of age, and have been in the labor movement for more than thirty years. Of this, actively more than twenty-six, hence the labor movement and the labor cause have grown to be part of my existence, part of my very nature. To speak for it, to write for it, to work for it has been my highest hope, my inmost aspiration. Beyond it I have seen nothing, and success outside of it has seemed to me to be impossible.

At all times advocating the cause of the wage-workers who were struggling for ameliorative measures and emancipation, and at times speaking in defense of those who perhaps had neither the courage nor the opportunity to speak for themselves, and perhaps even again pleading for some who, in their demoralized condition, have been forced to repudiate the authority to speak in their name, hence it is not presuming too much when I repeat that the labor movement and the labor cause are part of my very being, and from which it is difficult, if not impossible, to depart.

Of course I have made enemies. I expected to when I first entered actively in the struggle, and any man who imagines for a moment that he could be in active participation in this combat for the right without incurring the enmity and ill-will of some, better not enter the arena, for if any such thought is entertained it were better both for the beginner as well as the movement that his attentions be directed to another and less controversial channel.

To always act for the right without fear or favor or as to personal consequences is to run counter to schemes of all kinds. Having set the maxim and watchword the truth and the right for my guidance, it is but natural that I should have come in conflict with the weak-kneed, the trickster as well as those who have well formed but different opinions.

I have always held that every trade unionist should have one of two elements in his makeup, and which seemed to me were necessary essentials to success. The first was a thorough knowledge of the trade union movement, its history, its struggles, its tendencies, and for what it stands, or in the absence of this knowledge that it required absolute faith in the ability of the trade unions to accomplish the amelioration in the condition, and the final emancipation of labor. Talk as one will, but if either one of these two characteristics is not the dominating influence of a trade union leader or member success is an impossibility.

It is therefore not unnatural that men who lack the knowledge of the trade union movement, and who have no faith in it, but who look upon it as a secondary consideration in the struggles of labor, merely to be used for personal or ulterior purposes should have felt dissatisfied with me, recognizing that I was always ready and anxious to prevent the use or abuse of our movement by those who appeared either under the mask of friendship, or as its open and avowed enemies.

For office in the movement I care and cared nothing. To me the movement was greater than any man or set of men, and believing as I did and do, that the trade union movement is the natural class organization of the wage-workers in which they must seek present improvement as well as future disenthrallment, I have dared to fearlessly express my convictions regardless of whom it hurt or benefited.

No one can truthfully say that I have ever entered into any caucus for any purpose whatsoever. I never entered into any deals, or bargains or combinations, either to elect myself or any other man to office, or to even advance legislation or propositions which I favored or to defeat men or measures to which I was opposed. I stood for a cause, and was willing at all times to bear the full brunt of antagonism and opposition that could be manifested against it or myself.

I have not been reëlected, and can fairly say that I have no regrets to express. I feel the consciousness of having performed my duty to the very best of my ability and with a single purpose, to benefit my fellow-wage-workers. There is nothing that I have done in the cause that I would seek to undo, or words that I have expressed that I would unsay, except to do and say them with greater force and emphasis.

I beg to assure my successor as well as all unionists that I shall, so far as in me lies and opportunities present themselves, help to place our organization and our movement upon a higher plane of advantage and success, in the sincere hope that the day of labor's emancipation may be so much nearer at hand.—*American Federationist, January, 1895.*

Presumably, it is but proper to say a word to my friends and fellow-unionists upon resuming the duties of the presidency of the American Federation of Labor, after an absence from that office for a year.

Many may mistake the real point involved in my election to that office and count it as squelching and annihilating a certain school of thought in the ranks of the American Federation of Labor. I would say that nothing can be farther from the purpose than that. I recognize as fully as any one what was intended to be accomplished by my election. But it is only fair to say that, as I have ever been in the trade union movement, and in all matters connected with my life, I believe in the fullest opportunity for thorough discussion and proper presentation of all schools of thought in the labor movement. My only insistence has been, and is to-day, that a man shall be true to his trade union in season and out of season, in spite of friend or foe, and that, apart from that, it is his province to believe in and advocate any reform which, in his judgment, is calculated to best advance the whole line of the trade union movement.

I have ever believed that the trade union platform was the broadest of any in existence. There is room enough for the most radical as well as the ultra-conservative—in fact, I have always regarded the existence of both these elements as essential to the success of our movement.—*American Federationist, February, 1896.*

It is a strange fact that the history of the labor movement demonstrates, daily, that those unions of workers which have provided themselves most surely with substantial treasuries are those in which the members are more highly respected, whose wages reach the highest point, whose hours of labor are the lowest, whose conditions of employment are the most reasonable and fair, and whose requests are more generally heeded, and who are required less often than all other workers to resort to a strike in order to obtain the redress of a grievance or the granting of some new concession, while on the other hand the workers unorganized or poorly organized, or who even when organized have neglected the first essential—the payment of high dues in the union and an accumulation of a good fund—are those who are compelled to work the longest hours for the lowest wages under the most onerous conditions, and whose tenure of employment is such as to be only subject to the will or whim of some petty boss or understrapper. . . .

A peculiarity noted by all active participants in the labor movement is this fact, that the unions which have failed to make timely provisions for protection and defense usually make up these defects by hysterical shrieks and so-called "radical" demands; while on the other hand the unions which have taken time by the forelock and manifested the good sense of contributing fair dues to the union, are the modest in bearing, yet most successful in maintaining the rights of their members and defending their wages and hours, gradually securing concessions and improved conditions. . . .

Stripped of all verbosity, there is more true, hard common sense than sentiment and ranting, and yet more successful results, among the workers who count with existing conditions and prepare to battle for their rights to-day.—*From "Cheap John Unions," American Federationist, February and March, 1896.*

As to the walking delegate, who has been the object of caricature for years, he is in reality the counsel of the labor organizations, and it is through him they act. Despite all talk to the contrary, his position is also the hardest of all, for he not only has to combat with the employers, but in turn has also to fight with his own organization to prevent their taking hasty action. In many cases he alone has prevented what would otherwise have been most serious strikes. We must have some one to present our case for us, for should an individual laborer attempt to argue with his employer it would be as the meeting between the lion and the lamb, and in the end the lamb would have disappeared. The arbitrators must be of equal power.—*From address in Wesley Chapel, Cincinnati, Ohio, December 20, 1896.*

The workers have suffered in all times, and they have naturally sought, in all times, a remedy for their misfortunes. In the recent past, when the right of combination was denied them, even in the most advanced countries, the workers had little hope of relief in periods of misfortune save in the grudging and meager dole of charity. Since the complete break-up of the old system of hand production and the massing of vast numbers of workers in manufacturing centers, however, the workers have found themselves comparatively free to take united action, and dating from that time we have witnessed a growth of working class organization that bids fair to soon assume irresistible proportions. This growth has been hampered, it is true, not only by many short-sighted holders of capital, but also by a host of charlatans, who have promised with sublime impudence to free the workers from all their sufferings by some magical process, to be effected by a mere wave of the hand. It is creditable to the courage and devotion of the organized workers that they have almost invariably repulsed the onslaughts of their declared capitalistic enemies; and it is also creditable to the strong common sense distinguishing them, resulting, as this trait does, from the practical habits formed by their daily vocations, that the great bulk of the toilers have turned a deaf ear to all the chimerical schemes advocated by would-be social revolutionists, and that they have steadily persevered in their efforts to alleviate their sufferings little by little, as their power of mutual helpfulness gradually increased with time. Thus, during the half-century now drawing to a close, we have seen a revival of the trade union form of organization and its steadily increasing adaptation to the demands of modern social necessities.

Previous to the commencement of the period referred to, the unions had been more or less temporary coalitions formed with the object of removing some specific abuse, which if not removed by the employer, the workmen struck and were supported by passing the hat among their fellow-craftsmen in the immediate vicinity. But the funds raised in this precarious manner were never sufficient to sustain a long struggle; and it was not until the workmen had been taught by the bitter experience resulting from frequent defeats that permanent unions came into vogue. Even then, and for many long years afterward, the unions were strictly local bodies, embracing only those working in a certain town, and were supported by very small weekly or monthly contributions devoted almost exclusively to strike purposes, with occasional assessments for burials or for relief of extreme cases of distress. If a union man, of no matter how long standing, went to another town to ply his craft, he was regarded as a non-unionist and was required to undergo another initiation. Thus, the old system of isolated local unionism not only impeded the spread of the only then existing type of union, but it also formed a formidable obstacle to the development of trade union efficiency by preventing the establishment of any regular system of insurance against the vicissitudes of a workman's life. As a consequence of the recognition of these shortcomings by unionists engaged in industries which extended over an entire country, the first national unions were formed; and the greater number of these unions of unions soon realized the necessity of establishing adequate funds for benevolent purposes, as the former isolated unions had previously striven to provide for strikes and lockouts. There were, however, several national unions that deliberately refused to establish such funds on the plea that the proposed extension of operations was "foreign to the objects" for which they had been formed. It would not be difficult to prove that such refusals have reacted very injuriously on the several unions concerned, seeing that the greater part of these have been unable to stand the strain resulting from loss of membership in adverse times, or when they have survived they have failed to adequately elevate the standard of their crafts in periods of general prosperity. We are not yet in possession of American trade union statistics covering a sufficiently long period to fully show the evil effects of the neglect to establish high dues and proper benefits, but we have fortunately at our disposal perfectly reliable figures furnished by our British trade union brothers which fully sustain our contention.—*American Federationist, January, 1900.*

THE AMERICAN FEDERATION OF LABOR 13

Through the pages of written history runs the thread of the organized struggle of the workers for the attainment of justice. Those who studiously search may learn that in the effort of the workers to remedy wrongs and establish rights, the trade union has been the factor by which concessions have been forced from existing society. With the beginning of the nineteenth century, and almost with the initiation of our own Government as an independent nation, an immense impetus was given to the movement of labor; but from the fact that ours was entirely an agricultural country, the trade unions were sparse and fragmentary.

Industry was incapable of full development, so long as chattel slavery existed; hence, the formation of national unions could not be effectually achieved. The abolition of chattel slavery paved the way for larger industrial development, and conjointly with it the greater growth and expansion of trade unionism upon a national basis. Now, as industries are frequently merged and concentrated, we present to the world the best federation of organized labor which has been recorded by history.

It is not within the province of this report to review the industrial history of the century, or the attempts of the workers of our country to form a general federation of labor. At another time, and by more competent hands, should this be recorded; but it is not this which we have to bear in mind. Previous attempts at concentration of the organized workers' efforts were made, in all of which the failure to recognize the true functions of such a movement proved the fatal rock upon which they foundered, went to pieces, and strewed the débris of distrust and discouragement until it not only injured and destroyed the unions, but weakened the faith and the confidence which the workers had in organized effort to abolish injustice, and to attain redress.

Nor is it out of place to call attention to the fact that, though our federation was formed in 1881, the records demonstrate that a large preponderance of those who were in attendance were not its friends; for, though there were a large number of delegates, who were authorized to attend by the peculiar term of the call, yet at the convention immediately succeeding there were but nineteen delegates in attendance. But though few in numbers, the men of that and subsequent conventions, realizing that the time would come when the necessity for a broad and comprehensive federation would be generally recognized, hewed strictly and closely to the line.

The movement for the establishment of the eight-hour day in 1886, though hampered by a most unfortunate event, still had wakened the toilers to a realization of their duty to such an extent, and had accomplished so much, that that year brought a greater recognition of the true worth of our Federation, and the adoption of the present title.

The history of the struggle made by the few men (upon whom were imposed the duties and sacrifices, without compensation of any kind and with scarcely a dollar to prosecute the work of organization and education) during the five years of 1881-86 to maintain the Federation, has not been, and perhaps never will be, written. The beginning of this new era of our Federation gave the toilers new hope and new courage; for they saw that our movement was founded upon correct principles, and that its affairs were placed in the hands of men who desired above all things the promotion of the interests of the toilers and the achievement of their rights.

I affirm without fear of successful contradiction, and in spite of the insinuations and slanderous charges of the enemies of our cause, that our movement has been freer from dishonest and faithless men than any institution, organization, or movement in our own, and perhaps in any other country.

The American Federation of Labor has not indulged in any exhaustive or elaborate platform of abstract principles. It recognizes that the best organization for the working people is an organization of the working people, by the working people, and that is the trade union; to assure and insure the right of the trade unions to self-government, and yet to insist that the toilers in each union shall appreciate the interdependence of organizations, and by the federation of all to present a solid phalanx of the workers of America.—*From annual report to A. F. of L. convention, Louisville, Ky., December, 1900.*

Let me tell you just what the Federation is. It is a central labor body bearing the same relation to national and international unions that the Federal Government bears to the states of our Union, and the same relation to local unions not identified with national unions that the Federal Government bears to one of our territories.

The local union looks after most of its own affairs, just as a municipality of California looks after most of its affairs. Some functions, some powers are reserved for the national and international bodies, however, just as some functions of government are vested in the state rather than in the municipality. In the same way there is a division of authority between the national and international unions and the American Federation of Labor.

Local unions of a given trade are grouped into the State and national and international bodies, which together constitute the Federation.

Within our own time there have been earnest advocates of a very different system of trade unionism—the conglomerate system—a system banding all local unions into one central body, without intermediate grouping of trades. A conspicuous example of this was the National Labor Union, which expired in 1868, after going into politics to the extent of nominating David Davis for President. Another example is the Knights of Labor, an organization which has clearly proved the system to be unsound.

As the Federation is constituted, it cannot be overwhelmed by its growth. The national and international unions of the various crafts relieve the central body of danger and leave it free to do what can be done with safety and advantage for the common welfare.—*American Federationist, September, 1902. (From address on western tour.)*

Mr. Parry says that if the organizations of labor taught their members some things that were of use to them it might count to the credit of the unions, but he says they do not.

I have in my possession a list of the official journals of our international unions in America, a list containing the names of 74 official trade journals, and wherever there is any technical work to be done those trade journals not only give drawings and sketchings, but lessons that teach the men the work they were not taught and are not now being taught in the industry on account of the improved tools and new machines. These official journals offer prizes and other inducements to incite the interest of the members in doing good work and knowing how good work should be done.—*From Labor Day address, 1903, Indianapolis, Ind.*

Our opponents talk of men losing their individuality when they join a union labor organization. That is absurd. As soon as a workman enters a modern industrial plant he has lost his individuality. No longer is he a whole workman in the sense of the position he occupied some years ago. He is simply one little cog in the great wheel of industry. He is one atom in the great aggregate of employees who furnish the finished product. If the workman of to-day expects to regain something of his individuality as a man and a workman which he has lost as an artisan in his trade or craft, it is necessary for each and all to unite in order for them to represent the makers of the whole produced article, the finished product.—*From testimony before U. S. Senate Committee on Education and Labor, 1904.*

The most of the labor leaders are not in the business for money. Take our salaries! The highest of them, outside of the heads of the railroad unions, is not more than $3,000 a year, and many men receive only $1,000 or $2,000 and some less. Nearly every one of them could make more outside of the labor organizations, and if they were corrupt they could enrich themselves where they are. There are bad men in all ranks of life. Sam Parks was notoriously such, but Sam Parks is not typical of the labor movement in any respect.

I have been president of the American Federation of Labor for more than 20 years. For the first five years I received no salary and worked at my trade to support myself, doing my union work at nights and on holidays. At the end of that time I gave up cigarmaking and devoted my energies to the American Federation of Labor, receiving $1,000 a year. As time went on my salary was gradually increased until it reached $2,100, and it is only within the past year that it has been $3,000. I think I may say honestly that I am not in the work for the money. I do it because I love it. I have no amusements or anything outside of it, and my happiest hours are when I work the hardest.
—*From interview with Frank G. Carpenter. (American Federationist, April, 1904.)*

To the opponents of labor I will defend the labor movement, even for its mistakes, and when I can not find a defense I will try to make the best excuse I can, but to my own fellow-trade unionists I propose pointing out their follies and weaknesses, with the hope that they will find the right and that they will fight for true trade unionism, and protect not only their own interests, but the interests of trade unionists generally. . . .

In the case of the American Federation of Labor, the decision of the Executive Council has neither police nor militia, army nor navy to enforce it. As a consequence it must depend upon something else. What is that something else? It must be confidence in the intelligence and the good-will of the affiliated organization toward those who compose the Executive Council. I grant you that should you or I be hurt we may feel resentful, perhaps vindictive; may want to mete out punishment to those who have done us ill; but, brothers, we must bear in mind that care is to be observed in selecting the method by which a penalty shall be imposed upon those who do us ill, and particularly is this true in the labor movement. . . .

Suppose that you should declare that you will withdraw from the American Federation of Labor now, and within a month or two or three or six months you should carry out your resolution to withdraw. What then? I want you to consider it. What then? Would that action be likely to increase your power, your influence, the membership of your brotherhood? Would it likely do any good to the labor movement, to your fellow-workmen? Would it likely maintain the wages and hours that you have fought for and obtained? Would it likely secure an increase in wages or a reduction of the hours of labor? Would it likely bring a little more sunshine into your homes? Would it likely make the life of the fireman in his work and during the time when he is not working brighter? Would it make his work less irksome? I leave those questions for you to answer for yourselves.

Of course, there is nothing on earth—no power outside of your own good judgment—that would prevent you withdrawing, or that could prevent you should you decide to withdraw. Should you withdraw, is it not likely that some other organization, feeling that it also had not secured all that is desired, would say: "Well, the Brotherhood of Firemen has withdrawn and so will we." And others would say: "Well, so will we." Is it not likely that some of your own locals would say: "We are no longer a part of the international labor movement; the strength of the brotherhood is not what it once was"? Then one local after another would go, and in the last analysis, reaching your own membership, you would be obliged to say: "The international no longer exists; it is no part of the labor movement; no longer it presents the great solid front that it once presented, a front that, like the rock of Gibraltar, withstood all assaults."

Then, instead of concentrating all our judgment, all our fealty, all our loyalty, to a great, glorious cause, we would disintegrate, and each organization would, like unto a little grain of sand beaten by wind and storm, be driven from pillar to post by our worst enemies.—*From address to convention of International Brotherhood of Stationary Firemen, Washington, D. C., August, 1904.*

He serves himself best who serves his fellowmen. No man can live alone. The idea of talking about a man's individuality! How can a man who is compelled to sell his labor at any price, how can that man be said to have an individuality? Individuality means not simply acting as an individual, but the *power* to act as one, the ability to act as one; having some reserve force by which that individuality can take shape and form to the advantage of its possessor. This has been lost in the modern industrial plants, and it is only by the unity of these individuals, the unity of the working people who have lost their single individuality, that they gain their collective social importance.—*From address at Fort Edward, N. Y. (American Federationist, October, 1904.)*

At the last meeting I quoted Heine as saying, "Freedom! Freedom is bread. Bread is freedom." I am in entire accord with Heine. He did not mean simply the piece of bread, such as this in my hand, that one may eat, but all that the term implies. Liberty can be neither exercised nor enjoyed by those who are in poverty. Material improvement is essential to the exercise and enjoyment of liberty.

Any one may say that the organizations of labor invade or deny liberty to the workmen. But go to the men who worked in the bituminous coal mines twelve, fourteen, sixteen hours a day for a dollar or a dollar and twenty-five cents, and who now work eight hours a day and whose wages have increased 70 per cent. in the past seven years—go tell those men that they have lost their liberty and they will laugh at you. Go to the wives who have received the benefit resulting from this higher wage and the companionship of their husbands; go to their children and compare them with the children who were deprived from going to school and have grown up to become miners and miners' wives, and see the difference in the standard of education and of morals. Say to these miners' wives and children to-day that their husbands and fathers have lost their liberty by joining the union! Go to the bricklayers, who worked formerly ten hours a day, but who for the past several years have enjoyed the eight-hour work day, with higher wages, with greater comforts, with larger enlightenment and social activity —tell these bricklayers that their liberties have been invaded! Go to the workers in the clothing trades who worked in the sweatshops, whose very homes, even whose bedrooms, were the factories where they toiled, and who organized and fought and won, and lost and won, and lost again and again, until that healthier public judgment was formed that abolished sweatshops—go to them and tell them that their liberties have been invaded by the unions.—*From address before The National Civic Federation, New York City. (American Federationist, June, 1905.)*

The advocacy of the accumulation of funds, the establishment of benefit features, and the necessity of higher dues in order to insure the payment of such benefits, will, of course, lay us open again to the taunt of trade union opponents that we establish "dues-paying" institutions; but the failure of any of our unions to render every financial assistance requisite, and for which the members in their organization have neither paid nor contributed, is taken advantage of by these self-same opponents, exaggerated, flung in our faces as a taunt of trade union ineffectiveness.

Organized wage-earners are not averse to the payment of reasonably higher dues to their unions, providing they can be guaranteed and feel assured that their interests as workmen will not only be protected and promoted, but that they may lean upon their fellow-workmen in union to stand by them in all the ills of life; lean upon them and receive their support, not as a charity doled out to them, but as a right received and toward which they themselves have contributed. The failure of a union to be of such substantial support to the workmen is to them sufficient cause to lose faith and confidence in organized effort.

It is a notable fact that unions which make least provision for benefits are those which suffer most through reduced membership resulting from either a trade decline or the loss of a strike, are the last to recover, and consequently the least effective in protecting the interests of their craftsmen.

Unions adopting these benefit features should be admonished in the beginning against making large promises which they may possibly be unable to fulfill. Nothing can contribute so much to the loss of the workers' confidence in a union as its failure to fulfill its promises. Almost any other association may close or suspend the payment of benefits to its members; a union, never. Time and experience may demonstrate that the union is able to pay higher benefits than promised in the beginning, when the change can then be made.

It is gratifying to be enabled to state that much progress has been made by our international unions in the establishment of general beneficial features, the accumulation of funds, and the requirement of the payment of higher dues by their membership; but the advance is not satisfactory; it is not general; it is the duty of all to make it so, and thus insure the success, permanency, and continuity of our movement, make it of constant increasing advantage to our fellow-workers, and a still greater benefit to all mankind.—*From annual report to A. F. of L. convention, Pittsburg, Pa., November, 1905.*

Permanent changes and progress must come from within man. You can't "save" people—they must save themselves. Unless the working people are organized to express their desires and needs and organized to express their will, any other method tends to weaken initiative.—*From pamphlet, "The Workers and the Eight-hour Workday," 1905.*

Here, in seven counts, is Professor Laughlin's indictment of the modern union:

1. The unions have stimulated rather than attempted to remove the antagonistic class feeling between the employer and the employee.
2. The unions have encouraged the theory of a right to ownership in the product made by labor, capital, and management. So long as great fortunes are made in the United States, the fact itself is taken as proof that labor is not receiving its due share of the results of production.
3. The unions feed their members chiefly on socialistic and un-American literature. In the main, the literature of socialism and unionism is indistinguishable.
4. They have approved the mistaken policy of "making work" by a limitation of output. With most laborers there is a belief that work, or employment, is limited, and if a particular job is prolonged they get so much more out of the employer.
5. The unions have wrongly based their whole course of action on the principle of a monopoly of the supply of laborers in a given occupation.
6. The outcome of such an attitude has been a series of acts of violence which have shocked the civilized world.
7. Wrong-headed leaders are the inevitable consequence of a wrongly devised theory of unionism.

Before commenting on these counts we may say that Professor Laughlin's alternative or substitute for the whole unionist system is—what? nothing more nor less than "increased productivity."

Does a workman feel that his pay is insufficient? Instead of demanding an advance, instead of leaving or threatening to leave in case of a refusal, he should increase his output! Then the employer would meet him with open arms and say: "My dear friend, you have done well by me, and you shall have a raise." (Perhaps a hoist.)

What is true of the individual is true, of course, of the mass. Let workmen organize, by all means. Let them form unions, hold meetings, and study the ways and means of improving their condition. But, instead of thinking about strikes, collective bargaining, union labels, education and agitation, they should think of but one thing—the increase of productivity "Let us work more and the employer will pay us more," should be the grand, wise motto of all labor organizations. . . .

We would ask Professor Laughlin whether he really thinks that increased productivity would necessarily, in all cases, bring increased wages. We used to hear a good deal about the duties of enlightened self-interest. Self-interest is ever present, but, alas! the enlightenment is seldom perceptible. Increase the output to any extent that you please in order to obtain proper compensation, it will still be necessary to form unions, to strike or be in a position to strike, and to use the lawful weapons of organized coöperation generally.

Has our learned professor heard of piece-work? Has he heard of manufacturers who reduce the rate of pay when they see that their employees "work too much"? In these cases you have increased productivity with the result of less, rather than more, pay.

Finally, is "increased productivity" a simple theory? Does it depend on labor alone? What about inventions, machinery?

Suppose the employer claims that the entire increase of the output is due to patents and new processes he has introduced, and refuses to advance wages?

We have said enough to show that Professor Laughlin's substitute is of the quack order. It means nothing. It seems simple, but in reality it is a formula which goes to pieces at the slightest attempt at analysis. If the professor had spoken of increased productivity as *one* of the factors of the situation, no one could have taken exception to his statement, but there would have been nothing new or wonderfully original about it, and it would not have affected the question of union policy. . . .

Now, we may take up the points of the above indictment of trade union policy and briefly comment.

1. The unions have not sought to stimulate antagonistic class feeling. They have sought legitimate objects, and are not responsible for the "feelings" of employers. They have not been free from mistakes. What class has? Are the employers always wise, virtuous, and tactful?

2. The unions have encouraged no theory save the one that labor is entitled to reasonable pay, a reasonable work-day, and humane conditions of labor. They seek to secure better treatment by exercising their legal and moral rights. The fact of great fortunes may well be taken into account in considering the question of labor's just share.

3. Trade union literature is not socialistic. Ask the socialist leaders. It is not, however, individualistic, in the plutocratic

sense of the term. It rejects many of the pseudo-scientific propositions of the capitalistic economists. Who does not, nowadays?

4. Unions have not generally limited output, but they have tried to check practices which selfish and greedy employers have resorted to in the effort to get an unconscionable amount of work out of their employees. They object to "the pace that kills," to driving labor at a rate that results in mental and physical collapse at the age of 40 or 45.

5. The unions have sought to diminish competition in the supply of labor. Can believers in "supply and demand" object to this? What principle forbids the substitution of collective for individual bargaining?

6. Violence is not the "outcome" of this "attitude." Unfortunately, no great movement has been free from violence.

But it is as absurd to condemn unionism, even on account of a certain amount of violence, if it occurs, as it is to condemn competition on account of fraud, adulteration, and misrepresentation.

A great movement must be judged by its general results, not by mere incidents which history rightfully always forgets.

Human nature is what it is. In the meantime, union leaders are doing all that they can to discourage violence and foster the spirit of dignity, and to acquire confidence and encourage reliance on purely moral and economic means.—*American Federationist, July, 1906.*

In no institution on earth is the controlling power so completely in the hands of the rank and file. Many national and international unions have the initiative and referendum, not only as it affects laws, rules, resolutions, strikes, lockouts, and the like, but also as to the nomination of candidates and elections of officers.

The very day that any union official departs from the path laid down by organized labor his representative position in it is put in jeopardy. The bonds existing between the members and officials are mutual confidence, obedience by the representatives to the mandates of their constituents, continual unity in purpose, and responsiveness to the cause which has brought all together.

The pretense by critics that any leader of American labor

follows the bent of his own vagaries, dictates a course of action to a set of blind followers, or makes rules and regulations to suit his own ambitions, is to be taken no more seriously than vaudeville horse-play. The assertions that the members of organized labor are not themselves fully responsible for their movement is insulting to American manhood.—*American Federationist, May, 1910.*

A profound and striking social truth is recognized as one's mind dwells on the special and indeed unique schooling to which a representative of labor in the course of his duties is necessarily subjected. He must, if he is to be successful, faithfully interpret the spirit as well as the demands of the members of his union, and in addition he must study the reasoning of the employers in order finally to make the best of his own cause. His views must be at least as broad as the practical labor situation which bears upon his international union, and they ought to be broader, taking in not merely the needs and plans of all organized labor but even in a more remote way all labor. His methods can not be those of a man who, like the average employer, fights merely for benefits to be enjoyed by a single firm, or company, or locality, or even industry. General principles must be his guide. Business can not be his foremost care; his concern is human beings. Yet in his methods of promoting the aims of his union his business precepts necessarily include system, good faith in keeping contracts, and the general maintenance of financial probity.

The representative of labor speedily learns responsibility, or else he fails. When, through carelessness, or deceit, or instability, he has lost a hold upon the employers with whom he has occasion to confer, he quickly finds that he has also undermined his influence with his fellow-union members. The man fully qualified for the position of a labor official dealing with employers has learned to control himself—speaking in conference only when necessary, confining himself to relevant matters, and permitting his opponent to have the questionable satisfaction of uttering opprobrious epithets or bursting into fits of temper. The late Bishop Potter, who assisted in numerous arbitration and conciliation labor cases, repeatedly said that a most impressive thing to him was the creditable, earnest demeanor of

labor committeemen when in consultation with employers.—
American Federationist, November, 1910.

What do they see? [Visitors at American Federation of Labor conventions.] What is the "show"? What is it that converts their mere curiosity into interest or, perhaps for the hour, into antipathy; later resulting in inquiry, sympathy, and then advocacy? . . . The gallery visitor will hear, to his surprise, prominent statesmen express appreciation of the achievements of the trade unions far more favorable than are commonly found in print outside labor publications, following up their general statements with details of good work to which their experiences enable them to testify. The visitor will also note that representatives of various professions, faiths, or organizations are present to give honored recognition to union labor. However, if skeptical, he may hold his own approval in abeyance. He has not yet penetrated to motive, purpose, limits, possibilities, and, finally, moralities.

But should the visitor happen in at an hour when reports are being made and resolutions for human betterment and common uplift are discussed, he will be most apt to catch the spirit of our movement, to feel the earnestness of our delegates, and to have convincing proof of the vitality, practicability, power, and, above all, the righteousness of our now world-wide institution—trades unionism.

The point at issue may affect one small trade or twenty occupations embracing a million men. It may involve the principles of liberty and justice. In any case, delegates one after another exhibit familiarity with the subject, straightforwardness in statement, directness of vision, practical purpose, and an aim to benefit mankind.

Who can look on at such work, done in such a way, hour after hour, day after day, with the subjects changing as resolution after resolution is discussed, and remain uninstructed and unmoved?

We declare that no man can possibly follow these deliberations and not be affected by them. He may possibly be prejudiced against unions, and seek to confirm his prejudgments; but he will be stirred up, roughly. He may perhaps become suddenly conscious of the world of thought and action that the unions encompass, little to the ken of their fellow-countrymen in general. He may pass out of the hall, go to his own affairs, for the time being not wholly sensible of the change wrought in his being. But he can not remain exactly the same man. Something has passed before his vision that will, in its good time, engage his thought, enlist his sentiment, and direct his judgment.—*American Federationist, November, 1912.*

The American Federation of Labor is formed of a number of different affiliated organizations—about 118 national unions of trades and industries. They are sometimes called international, and include the United States, Canada, and the American possessions of the United States. There are about 38 State federations of labor and slightly more than 600 central or federated bodies in various cities; about 800 federal labor unions, composed of various trades and callings, for which there are no national unions in existence.

The purposes of the Federation, from the beginning, have been to relieve the workers, the working people, from burdensome long hours of toil; to protect them in their work, their lives, their health; to improve their material, social, moral and political standing; to bring about a better condition for the toilers of our country as a reward for the services they render to society.

The Federation was organized in Pittsburg in 1881. It was after the panic of 1877, which found the working people of our country in a very demoralized and a practically impoverished condition. There were small organizations throughout the country. There was little cohesion, little common purpose or action. At a preliminary meeting in Terre Haute about the middle of the year 1881, a general convention was called to be held in Pittsburg in November of that year, for the purpose of devising ways and means to bring about a more general federation or concert of action among the workers, to protect them from the continual downward tendency in their material condition. I could, by reference to the proceedings of that first convention, enumerate some of the measures for which that convention declared. It declared for a shorter workday; for increased wages or, at any rate, a protest against the continual decreases in wages which had been imposed upon the workers from 1877; for a Federal law that would regulate and limit and finally stop the Chinese immigration. I think that substantially covers the declarations of the Federation at this meeting, which have been gradually enlarged and increased and developed.

Among the first efforts was the establishment by law of a limitation of the hours of labor of women and children, and in our first efforts we were quite content to limit the hours to twelve per day; then to sixty hours per week; then to fifty-eight hours, to fifty-four, and to forty-eight.

At every opportunity we had, and we often created the opportunity, we endeavored to have legislators, both national and state, introduce measures which we helped frame or approved or helped in any way we could for their enactment. . . .

I may say this, that by reason of the fundamental system of the organization of our Federation, our advice is sought and is of considerable influence. We have tried to make our organization as fundamentally democratic as it is possible to organize any institution to-day. There is no power vested in the officers of the Federation. They can act in an advisory capacity; they can suggest; they can recommend. But they can not command one man in all America to do anything; they can not order him to do anything. Under no circumstances can they say, "You must do so and so," or, "You must desist from doing so and so." And this is true in the governmental affairs of the local organizations anywhere on the continent of America, industrially and politically. Following this line of thought, this demarcation, in our political campaigns, the final determination of any course is lodged in the authorities in the locality.

The per capita is 8 cents per member per annum for all members of organizations affiliated to the American Federation of Labor; and it is out of this 8 cents per member we provide for all the activities of the American Federation of Labor in its organization work, in its agitation work, in its legislative work, and in its publications. Even though it may not be appropriate under the resolution adopted by the House for the committee to consider what I am about to say, I would like to have the opportunity of saying this: That outside of all its work—political work—we are engaged in the work of enlightening the working people of the country upon their life conduct and conservation of their lives and their health. We have printed millions of copies of a document on tuberculosis.

The constitution provides the amount of per capita required of each organization. There was a time when the per capita from internationals was one-quarter of a cent. In the course of time that was increased to one-third and then to one-half; it is now two-thirds. It is now 8 cents a year, and the organizations are required to pay monthly two-thirds of a cent for each member in good standing in their organization. . . .

The American Federation of Labor is not an incorporated body. Our proceedings are open to the public. We usually have a large hall, and the delegates are provided with seats and desks, right in front on the platform are the officers, the president and secretary, and also the official stenographer. There is a whole row of seats and desks provided for correspondents, newspaper men; stands and galleries are open. Any one is welcome as a visitor or an observer. Copious minutes of the proceedings of one day are taken, and during the night they are printed and are laid on the desk of each delegate and newspaper man in the morning.

Detective agencies send circulars over all the country saying that these proceedings are secret, and obtain fees from business men for supplying them with information about the proceedings of this Federation, which are open to the whole world. It is a piece of bogus detective work. Associations in different parts of the country do that, notoriously one in Cleveland, and a number of others.

The last executive session that I remember in a convention of the American Federation of Labor was over twenty years ago. None has been held since. I think it would have been better if there had never been any executive sessions.

The proceedings of the Executive Council, which meets from time to time, are not published in their entirety, because they would be too bulky. In the *American Federationist*, we publish some matters important to the public and the most important actions of the Executive Council meeting.

Legislative expenses are published in the monthly accounts in the *American Federationist.—American Federationist, December, 1913. (Abstract of testimony before House Lobby Investigation Committee.)*

THE AMERICAN FEDERATION OF LABOR

I did not have the good fortune to be born in the United States. I came here when I was a mere boy of 13, but strongly imbued with the sense of injustice—I was a factory boy when I came here with my parents. I became impressed with the possibilities of human endeavor in the United States, the possibilities of working out the best conception of human justice and human liberty. In my early manhood a coterie of men, including myself, determined that under no circumstances should we be diverted from the purpose of devoting our efforts to the accomplishment of the best that could be secured in our time; that no allurement of office or emolument of business or speculation of any sort in which one solitary dollar was involved should lure us from devotion to human uplift and the best conception of American ideals.—*From abstract of testimony before House Lobby Investigation Committee, Washington, D. C., December, 1913.*

The labor movement did not begin with my advent into it. The labor movement is as old as the ills of humanity. The labor movement is the result of the ills of humanity and a constant protest against those ills. It is a demonstration of protest against every wrong which exists and which has been long endured; it is a demand for every right to which the toilers are entitled and which they have not yet achieved.—*From address before Operative Plasterers' convention, Washington, D. C., September 28, 1914.*

In the conventions of the American Federation of Labor no proposition submitted, whether by any delegate or officer, is evaded, avoided or suppressed; and whether a resolution has merit or has none, a report upon it to the convention is made after a committee has given it its careful consideration; and a delegate, even though his proposition be reported adversely, has the opportunity to present his views thereon. In addition, only within the last busy hours of the generally busy convention, was a limit of time placed upon any delegate for the expression of his views. There is no freer forum than the conventions of the American Federation of Labor anywhere in the world.—*American Federationist, January, 1915.*

All the predatory forces that menace the welfare of wage-earners do not come from employers. There exists among the workers and in the labor movement an element which is either misguided or is so depraved that it is willing to lead workers into unnecessary suffering and useless misery.

There are both extremes in this element. Its highest fringe contains the irreconcilable impossibilists who think that nothing but revolution and destruction can right the wrongs of workers.

Its lowest depths are those who are in the pay of corporate and employers' class interests to lead workers into the morasses of ill-advised action and thus fritter away their opportunities to make real progress.

There are those who go among the workers, whose present wrongs are great enough to appeal to the compassion of any human being, and lead these workers into strikes and then urge them to employ the methods of revolution, to refuse to enter into agreements with employers, or to accept any improvements because the full rights to which they are entitled are not granted at once.

Wage-earners have a right to inaugurate a revolution if they think such action is justified, but no leaders have a right to involve workers in revolutions under guise of strike. A strike is something very different from a revolution. A strike is for the purpose of gaining some definite, concrete improvement in working conditions. The strike movement succeeds or fails in proportion to its effectiveness in accomplishing the purpose for which it was inaugurated. If a strike results in tangible benefits, those benefits are definitely formulated in the agreement by which the contest ends and industrial peace is restored.

These industrial contracts between workers and employers are the mile-stones of industrial progress. They clinch each forward movement in a tangible form and become a new basis for future demands and movements for greater progress.

An economic movement to be successful must be under the control of directors who understand the technique of the labor movement and who know the effectiveness of every move. It is a very dangerous thing in time of strike to advise workers to "raise hell." If that leader does not know what to do with the "hell" after strikers have raised it, he has embroiled those workers in a very dangerous condition—a condition that may endanger the whole movement.

Efforts to put "the fear of God" into the hearts of those who have no regard for human rights may have a place in the movement for human progress, but how, what, and by whom? There's the rub.

The hope of the workers lies in definite, persistent, intelligent and constructive action along lines that lead to definite, beneficial results to the workers—to the masses of the people—hence, to the glory and perpetuation of our great Republic.—*American Federationist, November, 1916.*

I have to meet here a thought—if I may use the term—a thought thoughtlessly expressed, as to the percentage of the working people of the United States that are organized. We usually find it stated: "Why, there are only about 10 per cent. of the people of the United States who are organized." And then they proceed to argue upon the basis of that small number.

As a matter of fact, in the American Federation of Labor we have unions which in total number nearly 4,000,000 members. The four railroad brotherhoods represent some 500,000. That means approximately 4,500,000. That is not 10 per cent. of the population of the United States; it is less than 5 per cent; but the fact usually overlooked is that nearly every one of these four and a half million people have wives and children, and counting the American quota as usually five to a family, these four and a half millions represent about 23,000,000 people, or, in other words, very nearly a quarter of the population of the United States.—*From address before National Industrial Conference, Washington, D. C., October 17, 1919.*

There is developing very rapidly a public demand that every worker shall be provided with a decent, sanitary and comfortable home. The wage-earners of America are deserving of this new conception of living and are entitled to no less. This, then, is the inspiration, the motive of one of the ultimate objects of the American Federation of Labor.

The demand of the wage-earners is not only for sanitary and fit houses to live in, but that a sufficient number of houses shall be available so that they may be freed from the evils of high rents, overcrowding and congestion. The ordinary method of supplying houses through their erection by private capital for investment and speculation has rarely, if ever, been adequate. Nearly all of our workmen's habitations are built on a system of exploitation. Most of the houses built for the wage-earners are built to sell. This system of exploitation does not permit of proper housing facilities and adequate upkeep.

Our present practices and policies for housing the workers are unjust. We demand that every wage-earner shall be afforded the opportunity of living in a healthful, wholesome dwelling and environment which shall tend to uplift and not debase. The safety of the republic is not promoted, nor its standard of citizenship elevated, by the streams of persons reared in slums and unsanitary tenements.—*From "Labor Standards After the War"; Annals of the American Academy, December, 1919.*

PROGRESS BY EVOLUTION, NOT REVOLUTION

With the growth and extension of our Federal Labor Unions, we occasionally find a difficulty which is increasing and one which requires constant correspondence and attention. Through a false notion inculcated during the existence of the Knights of Labor, it is difficult, in some instances, to convince our members of Federal Labor Unions of the absolute necessity to maintain the clear-cut character of our movement as a wage-earners' movement. Often through expressions of kindly feelings, employers, superintendents, foremen, and business men of the localities are accepted as members. It has occurred that when the enforcement of the laws and the policy of the Federation has been insisted upon, it was assumed that an injustice was practiced. Experience shows that workmen, when others than wage-earners are members of the union, are often reluctant in expressing their true sentiments or are prevented from taking such action as would tend to protect them against any wrongs inflicted upon them by their employers, in a word having been placed practically in their unions in the same defenseless position as they are in their employment. Again, business men, for the simple purpose of advancing their own business interests, have joined the union, and, consequently, created divisions and schisms and diverted the purpose of the organization. Of course, it does not necessarily follow that because a business man may join that it is simply for the advancement of his own interests, but in order to avoid the possibility of wrong in this line, the laws and policy of our organization exclude them from membership. If an employer, superintendent, foreman, business man, etc., is favorably inclined toward our fellow workers, and our movement, there are ample opportunities for such manifestations without his membership in our unions. It has required constant vigilance and caused a good deal of annoyance to prevent a wider spread of the danger referred to.—*From annual report to A. F. of L. convention, Nashville, Tenn., December, 1897.*

If a Western labor union is a logical movement, so is a Northern and Southern and Eastern federation of labor. Our employers do not divide on sectional lines and stop at state boundaries. I have heard of some men who have declared for international socialism, and yet in the next breath for the division of the national labor movement.

Let us have unity at home first.

The Western Labor Union has taken a new tack and has taken the American continent as its field. If it was right at first it is wrong now. If it was right to have a Western labor union, then why abandon the Western field?

I now address myself to this question of the ballot-box. What is to be remedied—the economic or social or political life? If it is the economic life that is to be remedied, then it should be done through the economic life and through no other medium.

Some tell us that the solution of this question is the coöperative commonwealth. But is that the final solution of everything? You tell us yes. But when you have coöperative commonwealth you admit that some more things will need to be done, the further improvement of the workers. Well, my dear socialists, don't you know we are doing that right now? That we are fighting with hard conditions, trying to improve and elevate the toilers?—*American Federationist, September, 1902. (From address on western tour.)*

History here and elsewhere likewise discloses the indisputable fact that wherever revolutionary policies were pursued, wherever passion supplanted reason and good judgment, wherever progressive measures were displaced by destructive methods, invariably destitution, suffering, ruin and chaos followed in their wake; better things to come were delayed and the hope of a brighter day was dimmed, if not destroyed.

In recent years the American trade union movement has grown by leaps and bounds. Many of its newly admitted members have been urged to become discouraged, and here and there some have become impatient with what is alleged as the apparent slow progress of the movement. Many of these workers hail from foreign lands. They are imbued with ideas and methods not applicable to conditions in our republic. They are totally unfamiliar with the past experiences and present policies of the American labor movement.

There are those among our people, inside as well as outside the labor movement, who are not restrained by conscientious scruples in exploiting this lack of understanding of our foreign workmen and who, to gain temporary leadership and authority, would rush our people into a mad whirlpool of impractical doctrines only to be engulfed in a sea of turmoil, hatred, and possible bloodshed.

We find here and there some persons professing to speak in behalf of the workers preaching into the ears of impatient workers that the American trade union movement is fundamentally wrong; that the labor movement as at present constituted is not controlled by the rank and file. Such persons take particular delight in denouncing international and local trade union officials who expose the real purposes and dangerous results which would follow if the pernicious doctrines and wild vagaries promulgated by these professional hangers-on of the labor movement were enforced.

The one big union idea is the subtle and pernicious plea again resorted to for the purpose of swerving the wage-earners from their orderly and practical course of action. Greater administrative and executive powers in central labor unions is the crafty appeal which is made to these organizations to undermine the confidence and authority of local and international trade unions. When this appeal is not heeded, the most cowardly and dastardly methods are resorted to in the hope of controlling and dominating the policies of such organizations.

THE AMERICAN FEDERATION OF LABOR

The one big union idea is not new to the men in the American labor movement. It has been tried time and again and in every instance it has been found wanting. The American wage-earners have not yet forgotten the disastrous experiences of the Knights of Labor, the American Railway Union and the American Labor Union. The monument of folly erected on the remains of all these movements indicates the fate of the one big union idea as clearly as the midday sun defines an unclouded sky.—*American Federationist, April, 1919. (From editorial by Matthew Woll, republished by mutual consent as expressing the views of Mr. Gompers.)*

American labor views with heavy heart the terrible curse of bolshevism forced by the gun and bayonet on the people of Russia and sincerely hopes for the success of their brave and valiant fight to eradicate it forever from their sore ridden land.

No more monstrous or degrading government ever was set up anywhere in the world. Its entire existence has been one of terrorism, tyranny and brutal slaying of those who are seeking for a just government. For the bolsheviks have proved more tyrannous than ever were the Czar and his brutal officials. They have brutalized Russia and used every means to throttle freedom by joining Germany in its efforts to enslave the world.

The wage earners of America, through the American Federation of Labor, have declared their abhorrence of bolshevism. They have indorsed and earnestly hoped the people of Russia would establish a democratic government through freely chosen members of a constituent assembly. They desire of all things that the people of Russia will free themselves from this yoke of oppression.

The convention of the American Federation of Labor held in June, 1919, declared:

This convention refuses to indorse any government in Russia until the people of that country through a constituent or other form of assembly, representing all the people, through popular elections shall have reëstablished a truly democratic form of government.

That declaration was unanimous and came from the very hearts of the workers.

The wage earners of America desire most earnestly the people of Russia to know, and with the greatest emphasis possible, that they are anxiously awaiting the certain victory over the oppressors of that country. For there is no greater foe to the best interests of the workers, to right, justice and equality, to the freedom of the Russians than the poison of bolshevism.

But the right will surely triumph. Bolshevism must and will be forever eradicated and the world will owe a debt of gratitude to the loyal sons of Russia who accomplish that glorious end.

It is, therefore, the hope of American labor that those struggling for the right to life and happiness in a democratic nation will never give up until they are absolutely free of the bolshevik curse.—*From statement prepared for publication in "Struggling Russia," October 1, 1919.*

Singular testimony to the fundamental democracy of the trade union movement and its effectiveness as a destroyer of the autocratic idea is furnished by Herbert Hoover, former United States Food Administrator. In a newspaper interview, Mr. Hoover had this to say regarding the Bolshevist extermination in Budapest:

We could take another example of bolshevism in the efforts of Bela Kun and his colleagues in Budapest. The distinction between this situation and Russia is that they were dealing with a population of much higher intelligence, of much higher average education, and it required but three months for the working people of Budapest to realize the fearful abyss into which they had been plunged. It was solely due to the efforts of the trade unions of Budapest that the bolshevists were thrown out of Hungary.

The *American Federationist* has declared and the officers of the American Federation of Labor have declared that had there been a well organized trade union movement in Russia there would never have been a Bolshevist success in that country. What Mr. Hoover has to say after having been on the ground in Europe is proof of what American trade unionists knew was bound to be the fact. The best safeguard of any nation against autocracy and dictatorship, whether of an organized plutocracy or a misguided section of the working people, is a strong, intelligent and well organized trade union movement. The United States possesses that best of all forms of insurance and the blind hopes of certain employers for its destruction will avail nothing.—*American Federationist, December, 1919.*

The trade union movement is a progressive movement to secure some of the advantages which have come by reason of the great production of wealth; to secure a normal workday; to secure a wage that shall bring comfort into the home, that shall afford an opportunity to the workers to give advantages to their children and their dependents, that these children may have the opportunity of going to the schools, the colleges and the universities; that they may be taken out of the factories, the workshops, the mills and the mines and given an opportunity to run, to play in God's sunshine, and that they may grow up into the manhood and the womanhood of the future upon which our Republic and our institutions depend.

The American labor movement is not at war with society. It seeks to overthrow nothing. It is as loyal and devoted to the ideals of our Republic as any group or individual in all America can be. And it is not fair to the men and the women in the American labor movement to attempt now to place them in the position of disloyalty or failure to appreciate and to give service to this ideal of the world's government, the Republic of the United States of America.

Not only during the war but before the war occurred there was no institution in any part of the world that did more for the cultivation of the best, most kindly and fraternal spirit between the English-speaking peoples of all the world than the much misrepresented and misunderstood American Federation of Labor. . . .

I am proud to have the opportunity of saying to you that on last Sunday there was a meeting of the Executive Committee of the League to Enforce Peace and a committee of the American Federation of Labor, a committee of the groups which had taken action in favor of the ratification of the treaty, to see how helpful we could be in order that we may have the pleasure of knowing that at last the war has come to an end officially and that we may do our share in carrying out our hope and our prayer that war among the nations of the world will never come again.—*From address by invitation before Chamber of Commerce, Boston, Mass., January 8, 1920.*

II

EMPLOYERS AND EMPLOYERS' OR-GANIZATIONS

Recently the movement among the corporate and employing classes to combine has taken more rapid strides than ever before.

We frequently hear of the formation of organizations among them with the avowed purpose of antagonizing and thwarting the efforts of the working people. This movement has not only been going on in one country, but the efforts have been directed to give it an international character. Many an expression have I heard of fear of such a growing power, and it becomes my duty to call attention to the fact that, as wage-workers, we have nothing to fear from such combinations, providing we have the intelligence, the energy and the courage to meet the combinations of our employers with the organizations of labor.

There is no greater power to deal with the exactions or to curb the tendency to injustice of corporations than the well disciplined and prepared grand army of organized labor.—*From annual report to A. F. of L. convention, Detroit, Mich., December, 1890.*

No one will deny that we not only have competition among workers and workers, but also among employers and employers; and so long, at least, as our present industrial and social system shall obtain it is doubtful that this will cease or lessen in acuteness. Is there, however, an employer who is at all inclined to be fair to his employees, who has not felt the awful and degenerating influence which some of his unscrupulous—commonly known as "cut throat"—competitors have wrought in the business by contemptible methods of hiring the lowest priced labor and demanding the longest hours of labor?

In most things, except cost of labor, employers are fairly on an equality. They can usually buy their material in the same market and at the same prices. Machinery, rent, etc., are just about the same to all. The difference in prices is in the cost of labor. When contemplating, or "figuring" for a contract or in bidding for the world's market, should there not be some basis, some minimum wage and maximum hours of labor upon which the calculation should be made? Should there not be some line, at least a "living wage" upon which employers could go forth upon an equality in the field of trade? Surely every instinct of justice, not only to the toiler and those depending upon him, not only for the preservation of our race, but also our civilization which hangs in the balance; surely every sense of fair dealing, every regard for progress, success in industry and commerce demands that in labor, above all things, the meanest of employers shall have no unfair advantage over those whose inclinations are in an opposite direction, and who, too often, are forced into the same offensive, reactionary and destructive position. Could industry by any possibility be conducted on the methods of the meanest, unchecked by labor, there is no telling how low down in the industrial world the workers of our country would sink, and how far our civilization would be dragged down with it.—*From "The Eight-Hour Workday," American Federationist, May, 1897.*

In one way or another we have been subject to the annoyance, misrepresentation and brutality of the detective agencies and private armed forces employed by corporations and unfair companies. We have known, too, that detectives have been employed to pry into the affairs of many organizations, information being given to employers as to who are the active men in the movement for the formation of unions, their discharge following frequently, ending in the terrorizing of the members of the organization; and personal spleen has largely entered into such information given to employers. We have known, too, that the supposed "secret" meetings of some organizations have been the means by which the detective agencies have been enabled to concoct stories, having no foundation in fact, to alarm employers as to the radical or revolutionary actions supposed to have been taken by the organization. It requires no great stretch of the imagination to understand that in the absence of facts upon which such reports to employers are based, the imagination of the detectives and the agencies is freely exercised, for, without alarming reports, the uselessness of the agencies is plainly discernible. Quite recently, a correspondence was made public by Mr. James Kilbourne, president of the Kilbourne-Jacobs Manufacturing Co., of Columbus, Ohio, between him and J. K. Turner, manager of the "Manufacturers' Information Bureau," of Cleveland, Ohio, in which the offer was made by the latter to Mr. Kilbourne to furnish a complete report of the "secret sessions" of the convention of the American Federation of Labor now being held. It is to the credit of Mr. Kilbourne that he has given the correspondence to the public press, and in his letter the following language which he employs is worthy of your notice. He says:

The proposition it contains seems to me so infamous that I shall give the letter and my reply to the public press. We have never engaged spies in our business, and certainly shall not do so against the most defenseless class with whom we have to deal.

—*From annual report to A. F. of L. convention, Detroit, Mich., December, 1899.*

In our time we are not, and for the future will not be, called upon to deal with individual employers. Industry has become so developed and wealth so concentrated that we are confronted with the associated interests of the employers. The situation, however, need cause us no alarm, provided we possess the wisdom to unite the forces of labor, and have the fortitude and the courage to meet associated capital by organized labor. Workmen as individuals, in our day, are as much at the mercy of the employing class as is a rudderless ship in a tempestuous sea at the mercy of the waves.—*From annual report to A. F. of L. convention, Louisville, Ky., December, 1900.*

In our industrial system of society I would not have the rights of an employer toyed with nor flagrantly violated. Also, I want to say that I will not tolerate, nor stand by, nor permit, so far as my powers and opportunities may afford, that the rights of the weakest of our fellow-workers shall be trampled upon.

There is in our time, if not a harmony of interests—which I

shall not attempt to discuss at this time, because there is a divergence of opinion upon that subject—yet certainly a community of interests, to the end that industrial peace shall be maintained.

I will not join—I have not joined—in that hue and cry against combinations of capital. I realize that that is a matter of economy and development and strength.

But I do say, and I might say it parenthetically, that I object to the organizations of capital popularly known as "trusts," when they attempt to interfere with the political affairs of our country, and particularly the judiciary. I am speaking of them from an industrial and not from a commercial point of view.

I want to see the organization of the wage-earners and the organization of the employers, through their respective representatives, meet around the table in the office of the employers or in the office of the union, if you please, or, if that be not agreeable to either, then in an office or a room upon neutral ground, there to discuss the questions of wages and hours of labor and conditions of employment and all things consistent with the industrial and commercial success of our country, that shall tend to the uplifting of the human family.—*From address before The National Civic Federation, New York City. (American Federationist, February, 1902.)*

Mr. Harrison Gray Otis refers in his editorials to one point which requires some statement, and that is the risks of employers. He says substantially that the risks of employers imply and involve the necessity to find employment for the worker, to guarantee him wages and good wages. if you please, and for this, and other things, he is entitled to a profit and a large profit.

Now, let me say that of course so long as we shall live in our modern era of industrial society, profit from labor must be conceded; but when the risks of employment, the risks of the employer are taken into consideration, I answer Mr. Otis, *"have you ever considered the risks of the laborer,"* the laborer who begins work even under normal conditions, or best conditions, at twelve or thirteen or fourteen years of age, and works and works and continues to work if not deprived of health or life—continues to work, and after having worked himself out, is dependent upon his family or his friends, or goes to a poor house, or else is left to starve?

Have you ever thought of the risks of labor? Have you ever counted or ascertained or read of the thousands and thousands of railroad men in the country whose lives are lost or who are injured, whose limbs are lost? How about their risks in performing their labor?

In my travels it often occurs that some of our friends, either before or after the meeting, come up and want to shake me by the hand; and I am glad to do it, even when my arm aches, but I feel the short stubs of fingers of the men who have sacrificed their fingers and parts of their hands, hundreds and hundreds of them. Who considers the risks of their labors?

When we read every now and then of the caving in of a mine with fifty, a hundred or more workmen smothered to a horrible death—the mine explosions—did you ever, Mr. Otis, consider these risks of labor? Did you ever notice that in the industries of clothing men and women live a very much lesser time than in other occupations? Do they get a larger wage because they are driven in their trade to a premature death? . . .

Do the trade unions try to take the management out of the employer's hands as Mr. Otis charges? Let me say we do not, but we say that the men and women who give their very lives to their labor, who cannot be distinguished from the labor they perform, ought to have a voice in determining the conditions under which their labor shall be given or sold. The chief merit in the claim of Mr. Otis upon this point is that there is absolutely no truth in it. Witness, if you please, the thousands and thousands of agreements which are made annually between employers and corporations on the one hand and the trade unions on the other.—*American Federationist, September, 1902. (From address on western tour.)*

Organized labor understands that there is organization in capital and among capitalists. You will have to look in another direction for denunciations of the organization of capital than in the annals and the records of organized labor. Our movement regards the organization of capital as the association of our employers. They are good or bad as they are good or bad employers, and the organization *per se* is not the thing which is either good or bad. As a matter of fact, as I see it, as organized labor sees it, we welcome the organization of the employers. We know one thing, that when there is organization founded upon a rational basis there is the greater tendency to agreement between the employers and the employed. We are not hostile to the organization of the employers and if there is any one who desires to advocate the organization of the employer class, we should, perhaps, if not second his efforts, look upon it with entire indifference, but at least we say that no man who undertakes to organize the employers has the right, the moral right, to assail the organizations of labor.—*From address in Buffalo, N. Y., January 9, 1903.*

Mr. Herman Justi, Commissioner of the Illinois Coal Operators' Association and member of the Industrial Department of The National Civic Federation, some time ago delivered an interesting and thoughtful address upon "The Organization of Capital." He distinguished therein between consolidation and organization, and argued that while capital had been consolidating, it had really made no attempt at organizing along the right and economically utilitarian lines. To quote from Mr. Justi's address:

For example, the carpenters have a union—let the builders or contractors have an association; the machinists and molders have their unions—let the manufacturers of machinery and the founders have their associations; the coal miners have their unions—let the coal operators have their associations, and so on through every trade and industry. Let capital pattern after labor—organize. If labor has its chiefs—so also let capital have its chiefs, and let them have their lieutenants; indeed, let capital follow the example of labor even to the extent of employing a corps of "walking delegates." Yes, let them go to the extent even of organizing a Federation of industries to cope or coöperate, as the case may be, with the American Federation of Labor.

What the industrial progress and stability of the country need, taking this view, are the collective wisdom and power both of labor and capital. He does not advocate, suggest, or contemplate futile and stupid and suicidal warfare upon labor organizations. He seeks "to prevent strikes, lockouts, and serious friction, and to insure, as far as may be, peace and harmony in the industrial world." He declares that the purpose of such organization as he proposes is not "to oppress, to repel, to antagonize, to make war, but to deal fairly, to conciliate, to preserve peace, to insure stability."

All this is rational and wholly unobjectionable. Labor, claiming and exercising the right to organize, will not be so short-sighted as to protest against the organization of employers for legitimate purposes. Mr. Justi's sincerity is beyond doubt, and he is consistent as well as sincere. He recognizes the power, influence, and value of union to labor, and he advises the unorganized workmen to join existing unions or form new ones.

But organized capital, unfortunately, has or will have advisers and "defenders" of different type from that to which Mr. Justi belongs.—*American Federationist, March, 1903.*

I was told that an organization of manufacturers held a convention at Atlanta and denounced the trade unions. A convention of what? A convention of manufacturers.

Just think of it! Denounced us, why? Because, as they say, the trade unions deprive the workingman of his liberty. When in the history of the world did the masters fight and make sacrifices for the liberty of their slaves? When did the employer of labor make a fight and make sacrifices for the real liberty of the workingmen? We welcome their organization, but we ask them to follow the path of moderation and reason, the same that they demand of us as workingmen. When they assume a right for themselves, they can not deny that same right to us. They are organizing; organization is the order of the day.—*American Federationist, July, 1905. (From address at Dayton, Ohio.)*

It is only fair to say that the greatest and most enlightened combinations of capital in industry have not seriously questioned the right and, indeed, the advisability of organization among employees. There is economy of time and power and means of placing responsibility in "collective bargaining" with employees which bring the best results for the benefit of all.

Organized labor has less difficulty in dealing with large firms and corporations to-day than with many individual employers or small firms. We have recently seen examples of the bitter antagonism to labor by certain small employers, whose ideas of in-

EMPLOYERS AND EMPLOYERS' ORGANIZATIONS 45

dustry seem to be medieval rather than modern. To some extent they have grasped the idea of organization or association among themselves, but they fail to concede the necessity of organization among wage-workers. In an opera bouffe fashion they emulate the robber barons of the middle ages, whose sole idea of profit was to plunder the individual whom they could find at a disadvantage.

The workers of the country have pretty thoroughly mastered the broad economic truth that organization is the watchword of modern industry. Labor concedes the right of organization among employers. It is perfectly willing to deal with such associations, provided its own rights are not denied or invaded. To put it more strongly, provided its rights are recognized and conceded.—*From address before Chicago Conference on Trusts, The National Civic Federation, October, 1907.*

As an illustration of the methods to be pursued, Mr. Kirby referred to an incident of the civil war in which Governor Seymour, of New York, attempted unsuccessfully to quell with a pacific speech a riot in Troy. "Then," said Mr. Kirby, "a captain wheeled a twelve pound gun into line and the rioters dispersed in every direction. That's my way of dealing with a criminal! The only way to handle that animal" (the organized wage-earner) "is to take him by the horns and shake the cussedness out of him. The labor question involves a great principle that should not be compromised if America is to stay America. . . . We find men of prominence who ought to be ashamed of themselves, harboring the leaders of that organization" (the American Federation of Labor) "and sending them out over the country to address women's clubs. That is the greatest danger we have. If it had not been for that class of people, organized labor of the militant type would be as dead as a mackerel to-day."

Contrast the above with the following utterances:

Said William H. Taft, addressing the annual meeting of The National Civic Federation, last December:

> Time was when everybody who employed labor was opposed to the labor union; when it was regarded as a menace. That time, I am glad to say, has largely passed away, and the man to-day who objects to the organization of labor should be relegated to the last century.

It has done marvels for labor and will doubtless do more. It will, I doubt not, avoid the reduction to a dead level of all workingmen.

Pope Leo XIII, in his Encyclical "On the Condition of the Laboring Classes," advocated the formation of workingmen's unions—

To better the condition, both of families and individuals; 'to infuse a spirit of equity in the mutual relations of employers and employed; to keep before the eyes of both classes the precepts of duty and the law of the gospel

Said Potter Palmer:

For ten years I made as desperate a fight against organized labor as was ever made by mortal man. It cost me considerably more than a million dollars to learn that there is no labor so skilled, so intelligent, so faithful as that which is governed by an organization whose officials are well-balanced, level-headed men. I now employ none but organized labor and never have the least trouble, each believing that the one has no right to oppress the other.

Said the late Bishop Potter:

Organization, coördination, coöperation, are the right of every body of men whose aims are worthy and equitable, and must needs be the resource of those who, individually, are unable to persuade their fellow-men to recognize the justice of their claims and principles. If employed within lawful and peaceful limits, it may rightly hope to be a means of educating society in a spirit of fairness and practical brotherhood.

Said Melville E. Ingalls, chairman of the board of directors of the Big Four Railroad:

For 35 years of my life I have been what you might call a large employer of labor, as a railroad manager. I have seen these modern conditions grow up under my eye. My first experience was in controlling a railroad of 175 miles and three or four hundred employees. I knew every man on the road; I could call him by name and shake hands with him, and we could make all the trade agreements we needed between hours. There was no trouble. If anybody had a grievance he could come in to see the "old man," and the door was always open. When I left the active management of the road we had some 7,000 miles of railroad and some 30,000 employees, and the man who worked on the railroad would have stood just as much chance to see any one with his grievance as he would to get into the Kingdom of Heaven. His only chance was to join an organization and deal through committees. We were always in favor of that; in fact, it seems to me that your trade agreement is just as much a protection to capital as to labor.

Said Wendell Phillips:

I rejoice at every effort workmen make to organize; I hail the labor movement; it is the only hope for democracy. Organize and stand together; let the nation hear a united demand from the laboring voice.

Said the late Senator M. A. Hanna:

Don't organize for any other purpose than mutual benefit to the employer and the employee. Don't organize in the spirit of antagonism; that should be beneath your consideration. If you are the stronger or the abler, much less excuse you have to show resentment, because the other side is simply asking that they have their share. . . . If we can by any method establish a relation of mutual trust between the laborer and the employer, we shall lay the foundation stone of a structure that will endure for all time. . . . It is all wrong to suppose that the laboring element of this country is not ready and willing to join in this movement. I speak from experience. I have found the labor organizations ready and willing to go more than half way.

Said Cardinal Manning:

Labor is capital. Labor has the same right to protect itself by trade unions as any other form of capital might claim for itself.

Said William E. Gladstone:

Trade unions are the bulwarks of modern democracies.

I am sure that I shall not be charged with transgressing the rules of propriety if I suggest that the National Association of Manufacturers should take counsel from and profit by the experiences of the great industrial enterprises of our country, the owners and managers of which work in harmony and coöperation with the organized workmen they employ. On every hand workingmen and employers are seen peacefully at work developing, conducting, and expanding the industrial enterprises in which they are both interested and upon the success and prosperity of which their mutual welfare depends. Unless one's mind is distorted by unreasonable prejudice, unless his eyes be blinded by insatiable greed or passion, unless he be incapable of learning the lesson which history teaches, he will understand that a movement which has done so much to improve the conditions of life and labor, to protect the womanhood and childhood of the nation, to elevate the moral and intellectual standards of the people, and to improve the relations between employer and employed, can not be destroyed or impeded permanently by the irrational and intemperate declarations of men who are in their generation, but not of it.—*American Federationist, August, 1909.*

Nowadays, every branch of organized labor is only too happy when its employers get together. Laborers know that once their bosses can summon the face to look upon one another in council, in presence of the public, those with the meanest faces, trying to hide the cognizance of their base practices toward their employees, will as a rule keep quiet and let those who can with consistency speak up to the level of public expectations of employing-class duty. Besides, a common understanding among employers is sometimes economically beneficial. The justly disposed among them shame their opposites. Consequently, unfair competition is discountenanced. But the principal good reason why laborers like "capitalists" to come together is that the latter organization usually leads to a trade agreement with the laborers. A trade agreement stands for industrial peace.—*American Federationist, August, 1910.*

In general, labor conferees have been severely disciplined in the course of their work. In conference, they usually select a spokesman, his supporters speaking up only in order to prompt him or to add their individual testimony in the matter under consideration. The spokesman, aware of the deep earnestness of the mass of men that he represents and their expectations of him to reflect their ideas and intentions, is straightforward, clear in his statements, and disinclined to enter upon irrelevant questions. On the other hand, a committee of employers are frequently not united in their views and aims, and sometimes have not agreed either upon a spokesman, a common plan, or a clean-cut proposition. And the sorriest exhibition employers make comes sometimes when they have intrusted their case to an attorney-at-law or an association secretary. The moment that the conferees of either side perceive that business-like negotiation has given way to mere "lawyer talk" and paid-for special pleading, the emptiness of the proceedings is "sensed" and the possibilities of satisfactory conclusion diminished. Even such a situation serves in the education of a labor representative. He

EMPLOYERS AND EMPLOYERS' ORGANIZATIONS 49

finds new qualifications for his position in every vexatious experience.

It may be asserted that of the two sides employers are the more inclined to be impatient, exigent, and excitedly emphatic and to resort to an ultimatum. They are also the less familiar with the broader aspects of the labor question. Not infrequently they have but the crudest notions of great modern social problems. Successful employers sometimes labor under the infirmities of character that develop with inherited or otherwise quickly accumulated wealth. Falling readily into the habit of buying at their own wish and command, they grow hotly indignant on having the men they have come to regard as subject to their will interpose the obstacle of a will of their own. That workingmen should have facts, views, perchance theories, and, further, presume to act upon them, is to the capitalist, believing it is he who finds them work, nothing short of disloyalty.

Such employers, of course, fall victims of their own defective development. They must learn through pain and tribulation that times have changed. The feudal age has been left behind by the present century. Labor to-day knows its rights, has developed its methods of asserting those rights, and when organized assumes an equality in the social scheme with every other element, the employing class included.—*American Federationist, November, 1910.*

Let me call your attention to the papers published this morning. You will find a statement made by Mr. Kirby, President of the National Manufacturers' Association, in which he says substantially the following: "In 1907, the American Federation of Labor raised two hundred thousand dollars. There is now but eighty-nine thousand dollars of it left. It would be good to know to whom this money has been paid, whether for dynamiting the Los Angeles Times, and if so, how much?" That is published broadcast and in black face type in all the papers. I prepared this statement in reply:

"Every dollar, to the last cent, received and expended by the American Federation of Labor is published monthly in the American Federation of Labor's official journal—*The American Federationist*—from what source the money is received and for what purposes expended. At the 1907 convention, held at Norfolk, Va., an assessment of one cent was levied, which yielded $16,616.72. This was raised and used to offset the campaign of the Manufacturers' Association to crush out organized labor in Los Angeles and other cities. The detailed report of the income and expenses was published in the official printed proceedings of the conventions of 1908-9 and '10, and can be had, consulted and verified by any one. I invite Mr. Kirby, either for himself or to appoint a committee of three persons, no matter whom he may appoint, to investigate the truth of these statements. I think it but fair that a similar invitation should be extended to a committee whom I might appoint to investigate the receipts and expenditures of the National Association of Manufacturers. I challenge Mr. Kirby to publish the income and expenditures of the National Association of Manufacturers for the past five years. It will disclose whether the war fund of a million and a half dollars raised by the National Association of Manufacturers to war upon organized labor has not been used in the frame-up in Los Angeles and elsewhere, and in the effort to cast odium upon the most humane and altruistic organized effort of our time—the American Federation of Labor. The publication of the National Association of Manufacturers' financial transactions might disclose whether detective agencies, gangs of lawyers and some judges are not on its payroll."

The newspapers did not publish that.—*From address to the class in Economics, Catholic University, Washington, D. C., May 17, 1911.*

Starting in 1902, the Manufacturers' Association began its campaign to deprive organized labor of its primary rights—the right to work or to withhold their labor power (work), and the right to buy from whom they choose; the right of free speech and a free press. These manufacturers have endless means to conduct litigation. By securing a process of judicial legislation, by the perversion of the rightful purposes of injunctions and of contempt proceedings (under which last I am liable myself to be put into prison), they have worked toward the accomplishment of their purpose, and the denial to the working-people of their primary and common rights, rights enjoyed by every other citizen of our country.

The lawyer and the courts have been two of the chief weapons of this band of men organized to destroy labor organizations. A third has been the private detective agencies. The Federation of Labor has protested against the use of the hired detective since its beginning in the '80's. But never has the private detective been used to such an extent, or with such unscrupulousness, as since the campaign of the Manufacturers' Association began. They have been not only private soldiers, hired by capital, to commit violence, and spies in the ranks of labor; they have been and are being used in the capacity of *agents provocateurs*—that is, in disguise as union men, to provoke ill-advised action, or even violence, among workmen. And they have been employed to create evidence, to "frame up" cases against labor, to be used by the lawyers of our enemies in court, and by their publicity agents in creating public opinion.— *From "Gompers Speaks for Labor," McClure's Magazine, February, 1912.*

The National Association of Manufacturers was organized in 1895 to promote trade, commerce and markets, and to eliminate restrictions and barriers; but not until 1900 or 1901 did it adopt its policy of extreme hostility to organized labor under the domination of David M. Parry, who had been elected president. Immediately the organization was diverted to a union-crushing institution. Finding unionism too strongly established in the economic field, the effort to destroy it was carried over into the legislative, judicial, and political. As was indicated in the beginning, big business has depended upon political favors for advantages rather than upon its own superior ability. Big business was made by politics and has always been in politics. Big business owns most of the political bosses, hence the right to dispose of political favors is a natural result.

As a result of this change of policy and purpose of the National Association of Manufacturers, many leading business men who had been prominent in the organization withdrew their membership. Since these hostile employers' organizations had extended their opposition to organized labor to the political field and were bringing every manner of coercion and corruption to bear upon political agents from the highest to the lowest, it was imperative that labor also use its political power. The need was imperative, exigent. By judicial usurpation of authority in the equity courts, labor was embarrassed and harassed when seeking to perform its lawful and necessary duties in protecting workmen and promoting their well-being; by interpreting the Sherman Anti-trust law so that the provisions intended to apply to the manipulation of the material products of labor should also apply to the human workers that produced these things, the very existence of associated action and labor organizations was endangered.

During the year 1907, following labor's avowed intention to use its voting power in behalf of friendly candidates, there was evidence among the ranks of employers' associations of preparations for more unrelenting warfare all along the line. James W. Van Cleave had succeeded Mr. Parry as president of the National Association of Manufacturers. In order to prevent duplication of work and dissipation of energy and to direct and coordinate their efforts most effectively, a number of influential associations of employers had federated in the National Council for Industrial Defense. One hundred and eighty-six national, State and local organizations of business and professional men were banded together against organized labor. In the economic field they prepared to enforce an anti-union policy, to destroy the union shop and union-shop conditions, and to leave workingmen defenseless before the greed and inhumanity of conscienceless employers. A subsidiary organization, the Anti-Boycott Association, organized in 1902, was to institute and prosecute cases against organized labor in the courts. A typical illustration of the work of this organization is the Hatters' case, instituted in 1903 against the Hatters' Union of Danbury, Conn., invoking the Sherman Anti-trust law to prevent the hatters from associating themselves to secure the union shop, and to levy tribute upon trade union funds to the extent of three-fold damages.

The National Association of Manufacturers was tireless in its efforts to prevent the enactment of labor legislation both at the national capital and the State capitals. It brought every manner of influence to bear upon legislators to secure the passage of legislation favorable to the interests. It took an active part in electoral campaigns, assisting its allies and agents both by money and influence. It inaugurated "a comprehensive, vigorous, and intelligent campaign of education" to supplement its other efforts. By right of ownership and through influence it sought to control the public press to the end that organized labor might be discredited. It adopted a policy restraining its membership from advertising in labor publications, intending thereby to withdraw financial support and in that way to suppress the only instrumentality left organized labor of bringing its positions and policies fairly and squarely to the attention of the public. This octopus was the opponent organized labor must face in its fight for human rights—this organization or federation of organizations backed by tremendous financial resources, employing expert advisers and trained skilled experts, not only in touch with, but practically in control of political and social powers, in possession of the organs molding public opinion and creating a subtle but powerful public prejudice. Yet labor continued steadfast in its fight along all lines.

As a part of the campaign to disrupt labor organizations spies were employed to mingle among workmen, join their organizations, report their plans to employers and stir up internal strife and foment quarrels. Fake labor organizations were foisted upon workers with the avowed purpose of advocating the non-union shop and creating harmony between employers and employed—the kind of harmony that exists when the lion and the lamb lie down together, the lamb inside the lion.

Detective bureaus had a work to perform in this campaign. These agencies supplied or created information concerning labor officials and their work, furnished strike-breakers and other union destroying accessories.—*American Federationist, August, 1913*.

In our country there is not any legend nor is there any tradition by which the employers of labor have any interest in the welfare of the workers, as such, except as they are workers and wealth producers. In other countries which have been in existence a thousand and more years, and which have emerged from a system of slavery, serfdom, peonage, and the ownership of workers, there has been some continuous interest which the owner of the slave or the baron of the serf has had in the well-being of his workers; and although countries have broken through the shell of that condition, yet that old feeling is manifest in the conduct of employers in Europe and in other countries to-day. In the United States we have just burst into a nation with conglomerate elements, no responsibility, no care for the workers or for their welfare, and in no country on the face of the globe is there such a relentless disregard of the human race and of the workers of the country, as that which exists among the employers of our nation. There is more regard for the horse owned by man, more regard for the mule, more regard for any animal, for the loss of an animal would have to be replaced by purchase. It is costly. Human life in our country has been so totally disregarded in relations of employer and employee that some power, some factor, which shall mitigate such a condition of affairs, must step in.

We are, in the United States, not less than two decades behind many of the European countries in the protection of the workers. And to what, without want of recognition and appreciation of the service rendered by public-spirited men, to what is attributable the protection which has come to the workers except the agitation and the organization of the workers who have created the public sentiment and demand for the enactment of these laws? Without the associations of labor, without their activity before the Legislatures and before Congress they would be still working their twelve or more hours a day, and there would be no protection to life and limb and health in their work.—*From abstract of testimony before House Lobby Investigation Committee, Washington, D. C., December, 1913.*

It should be clearly understood that an employer who employs numbers of workers in his establishments places them under an organization where they individually have no control over environment and are unable to furnish for themselves even the most necessary things such as water, toilet provisions, and things of like nature. Any person who is in any degree responsible for the physical well-being of human beings can not with good conscience disregard the obligation. If he has intelligent imagination and foresight he will refuse to poison the bodies and lungs of his workers, or to permit them to render their product unfit for use or consumption, to ruin their eyesight or mutilate their bodies. He will do these things to satisfy his own sense of decency and justice, anything less would do violence to his conscience and cause him discomfort. Such deeds are not favors but only a decent respect for humanity.

The spurious kind of welfare work, intended only to rob the workers of independence of action and of just compensation, has met with deserved discredit and disrepute. Justice, not charity however disguised, is the right of all the workers. Let welfare work become what it should be—conscience work.—*American Federationist, December, 1913.*

These new unions advocated by capitalists are much like the soliloquizing mule which had neither pride of ancestry nor hope of posterity. They are made-to-order institutions, patterned after capitalistic concepts of usefulness.

The Westinghouse Company of Pittsburg foisted upon its employees a denatured union of the C. W. Post type. They called it the Employees' Congenial Union. It was intended that the "Congenial's" discussions should be carefully expurgated and its activities chastely restricted to "proper spheres." But when the employees came together, like all the rest of the human species they naturally discussed things in which they were most interested—matters affecting their conditions of employment and the so-called efficiency or speeding-up system.

But such naturalness was contrary to the rules of the Westinghouse game. The workmen who took part in such discussions were reported by the Westinghouse spies and were promptly discharged. When the "Congenial Union" protested and endeavored to send a delegation to ask the reason for the discharge of the men, they in turn were discharged also. Then, alas, for this experiment, the model "Congenial Union" went on strike in protest.

The employers may make a union after their own ideals but it will not stay made. It will either die for lack of roots and nourishment or it will adapt itself to conditions and manifest new characteristics.—*American Federationist, August, 1914.*

Only recently have even the most advanced employers and industrial managers included in production plans either intelligent or humanitarian consideration for those who furnish the indispensable human ability. Industrial organization for production has been concerned with materials, technique, machinery —the material side exclusively. The human side was represented only by the employment agent who filled vacancies reported. The management paid no attention to the employees who might come or leave. The motives that induced them to stay or go were of no interest until employers began to calculate the expense of each new person coming into the plant. . . .

When the economic advantages of avoiding changes in employees became apparent, employers began to investigate how many new employees were engaged during the year and why the old ones left. The reasons were found to be perfectly normal, human, because wage-earners are 100 per cent. human. They have human aspirations and desires for self-betterment. They do not want to stay where they feel humiliated by injustice or by arbitrary authority determining their lives. They not only want fair conditions of work but they also want home life under pleasant surroundings. . . .

Upon what principles must industry be organized to enable each plant to develop coöperation for increased production? This is the problem of personal relationships between managements and workers. Workers are not an impersonal factor in production as the term "labor" is usually interpreted—workers are human beings whose characteristics, impulses, ambitions, are exactly like those of all other human beings.

Coöperation for production depends fundamentally upon good-will. Good-will cannot be forced—it must be earned. Coöperation of workers can be earned only by those employers who determine with workers the terms and conditions under which production is carried on. The day's work is just as big a thing in the life of the wage earner as it is in the life of the employer. As a free man, he feels the same right to a voice in deciding conditions and determining them. The only way in which workers in industry may express and defend their rights and interests is through organization and responsible representatives. This method insures a feeling of justice and constructive consideration of industrial problems. Organization leads to progress. Through orderly organization we open the way to consideration of difficulties and reduce the possibilities for industrial disruption.

In addition to providing for negotiations between managements and organizations of workers for the determination of those things which constitute industrial agreement, managements have a still further responsibility if they are to secure coöperation for increased production. Industrial health, safety and morale are vital As these problems are primarily scientific, the management must look to specialists for information and suggestions. In order to protect themselves against propaganda, individual fads and commercialism, employers should ask the government to supply them with uncolored data, advice and practical service in making their industries safe and healthful, and in dealing with technical employment problems.

Workers whose physical creative power is conserved as something valuable not only from the production but the humanitarian standpoint, whose capabilities are studied in order to give them fullest opportunity for service, whose creative instincts are stimulated, whose valuable contributions are recognized, are workers whose production quantitatively and qualitatively far exceeds that of workers under autocratic control of industry, without adequate managerial consideration for all factors that affect production.—*From address before convention of Associated Advertising Clubs of the World, New Orleans, La., September 22, 1919.*

III

ECONOMICS AND ETHICS OF HIGH WAGES

I trust no one misapprehends my position so far as to believe that I favor a governmental enactment of a "living wage" for wage-earners in private employ, for, as a matter of fact, I recognize the danger of such a proposition. The minimum would become the maximum, from which we would soon find it necessary to depart.

In laying the basis of, or giving a definition for, this discussion I submitted the following: "A minimum wage—a living wage which, when expended in the most economical manner, shall be sufficient to maintain an average-sized family in a manner consistent with whatever the contemporary local civilization recognizes as indispensable to physical and mental health, or as required by the rational self-respect of human beings."

The statement that machinery primarily changes the conditions of workers is just the reverse order of cause and effect. With each improvement in the condition of the workmen, better wages, better conditions and more leisure, is created a greater demand, and necessitates improved and more rapid machinery to meet this demand. Where wages never rise above the point of a mere existence, improved machinery would be ever unnecessary.—*American Federationist, April, 1898. (From article in reply to Edward Atkinson, on minimum living wage.)*

It is one of the cases where a new machine [the Mergenthaler typesetting machine], revolutionizing a whole trade, did not involve a wholesale disaster, even for a time; and it is due to the fact that the International Typographical Union has grown to be an organized factor, and recognized by those employing printers as a factor to be considered. The membership of the entire organization throughout the country had taken an intelligent view of the situation and, guided by wise counsel in their executive officers, did not antagonize the introduction of the machine, but insisted that the men who had spent their lives learning the trade, and who were employed at the trade, should have the first opportunity to operate the machine. The organization also stipulated that there should be a minimum wage for the compositor on the machine, and the fact that wages were not reduced is the best evidence of the power of the organization of the International Typographical Union. . . . With the introduction of the Mergenthaler machine in the newspaper work, the newspapers were very much enlarged, and it also increased to a considerable extent the number of newspaper publications. It was the wise action of the organized printers that saved the trade from destruction, so far as printers' conditions were concerned.—*From testimony before Industrial Commission, Washington, D. C., April 18, 1899.*

I am opposed to overtime work except in a case of absolute necessity—for the safety of life and the preservation of property from destruction. Overtime is nothing more than the lengthening of the day's work. It becomes habitual, and when it becomes the habit of the employers the rule is that the wages paid for overtime, including those for the day's work, do not exceed the wages which have been paid for the regular day's work; that is, after a while it happens that overtime—overwork—becomes the rule and is no longer overwork. Overwork, unless in the emergency I have stated, is unjust to the men. When there are men unemployed, to employ more men fewer hours is better. Overtime shortens the seasons of employment; overtime makes the workman slovenly, deadens his senses, makes him careless of himself and fellows.

I would say the sliding wage scale has been in operation in a number of trades where organizations are carrying it on, but they have learned to insist that there must be a point at which they can not slide down any farther. The organizations, when they were in their infancy and adopted this sliding scale, found that it was always sliding one way, and they adopted as an addendum to it, or as a part of it, a minimum standard wage, and with that minimum standard wage established, the sliding scale is not disadvantageous. On the contrary, it is advantageous to all concerned, who operate for a specific period, usually one year, when the representatives of the workers and the employers meet and determine as to the sliding scale they shall operate under for the following year.

The living wage I regard as one of the important contentions of labor—the contention that a wage shall be paid to the laborer sufficient to maintain him and those dependent upon him in comparative comfort commensurate with his economic and social surroundings.—*From testimony before Industrial Commission, Washington, D. C., April 18, 1899.*

[Q. Where you have time work is not the first-class workman placed on a level with the inferior workman?] A. No; except that in the case of the individual workman there is a minimum wage determined, not the maximum. The superior and better qualified workman may and does, I think, without exception, receive a higher wage than the minimum scale. In the printing trade the union minimum scale is, say, $18 a week. You will find that there are quite a number of printers who get higher than the wage scale because of the excellence, the perfection of their work—compositors who are known as clean compositors, those who set their type without error or with few errors. We know, too, of proof readers who, after proof has reached them, when it has passed their supervision, scrutiny, and correction, there is absolutely no typographical or grammatical error overlooked by them, and they get very much higher salaries than the average proof reader or the ordinary readers. So it is among the iron molders; so it is among the hatters; so it is among the furniture workers—all industries where there is day labor in any branch. For instance, the bricklayers have a minimum scale, I think, of $4. There are quite a number of bricklayers who get $4.50 and $5 a day. The hodcarriers' wages are, say, $2.25 a day. There is not very much change. I think that the minimum is paid all around. The minimum is practically the maximum, because there is perhaps little difference in the excellence of the work they perform. But where there can be ordinary work and where there can be excellence of work there is quite a contrast between the minimum scale and the higher scale.—*From testimony before Industrial Commission, Washington, D. C., April 18, 1899.*

It [the store-order system] is a species of tyranny and wrong. The fact that under the store-order system the workman can not buy at the same advantage as any other citizen is in itself a sufficient condemnation of it. It restricts his right to buy where he pleases, so far as that is concerned. There is not a case that I know of, or which has come under my observation in many years, where the people could not buy the things they needed from 10 to 20 and in some cases 50 per cent. less in other stores than they were required to pay in the company's stores. The store-order system is in a measure a system of peonage, where a workman does not receive wages for his labor but something in kind. A workman has a right to be paid his wages in the lawful money of the country, of which he can dispose to the best advantage, as he pleases. Under the store-order system the employers deduct from the wages the amount that the workers may be indebted to the store. This has led, first, to overcharging; secondly, to compulsion of purchase at the place, whether they desire it or not, and has encouraged the custom of overcharging not only in the price of the article but frequently items are added which the workmen or their families have never had. I had occasion to go to Norwich, Conn., within the past few days, and there, in Taftville, Conn., a village four miles from the city limits, they have the store-order system, too, and the company houses, and weeks and weeks and months and a year have passed where the workmen have not received a dollar in wages. They are practically bound to the soil. They can not move; can not quit. Under the system they are deprived of the right of American citizens, to move where they please. The strike there now is as much due to that as it is to an increase of wages—the strike of the textile workers there.

Two years ago I had occasion to go through the mining district of Pennsylvania, and there I saw store orders, or rather there I saw checks made out by the company for balances of two weeks' wages, 5 cents and 8 cents, which showed the balance was owed to the company store. And it was just in one of these stores, belonging to a company in Pennsylvania, that I heard it stated that the company could not conduct its mine operations unless it had this company store. I contend that if a man desires to conduct a grocery store, or other store for the sale of merchandise, that is his privilege, and if he can make money out of it, that is his lawful privilege, but I deny him the moral right to conduct a coal mine in order to make a grocery store pay. It involves very grave wrongs. If laws such as were passed in Pennsylvania—but unfortunately declared invalid—requiring corporations and employers to pay their wages to employees in the lawful money of the United States, were passed and enforced, it would contribute very largely to improving the conditions—moral, material, and social conditions—of the people. And while I have not very great hopes that the lawmaking body of the United States will do that in a very short time, I have very great confidence that the miners' organization will very shortly insist that the mine owners must quit their operations of the one or the other.—*From testimony before Industrial Commission, Washington, D. C., April 18, 1899.*

Wages, as has very often been truthfully said, will find their level, not absolute, but relative; and the higher paid workers will be compelled to come down to the lower paid workers, if the lower paid workers are not raised relatively higher; so they will reach relatively the level of the higher wages of the better paid wage-earners. It is the constant effort of organized labor to bring about a greater equality of wages paid, not as a maximum, but as a minimum wage. I know that organized labor is charged with making the effort to have men all of one grade; that we want no more wages paid to the highest skilled and deftest worker than we insist upon for the sluggard and the shirker of his duty. That, I want to say, is as far from truth as anything can be. What we insist upon is that when a man or woman is employed as a wage-earner, a minimum wage shall be established, a living wage, a life-line, a line below which society must recognize it is unsafe, aye, even dangerous to ask a man or a woman to work, and that living wage must be the first consideration in the cost price of any product.

To say that an industry does not admit, or will not allow, the payment of a living wage is a libel upon the human race. If this table is of any value to man, if a coat is of use to man, it is worth while the paying of a living wage in its production. . . .

Employers nibble in this attempt to undermine each other. They nibble at it in a reduction of wages here, and an attempt

ECONOMICS AND ETHICS OF HIGH WAGES

to reduce them there, the same, for instance, as we saw about a year ago with the Arkwright Club of Massachusetts. We saw the New England manufacturers reduce wages in the cotton, the textile industry, "in order to meet the southern industries"; and immediately after that, we found the textile manufacturers in the South reducing wages "to meet the cut in the East"; and the result was that this nibbling process had gone on at both ends, much as in the fable of the two mice who had stolen a piece of cheese and fell to quarreling as to its division, but who finally determined to leave it to the first who should come along. A large, beautiful Sir Thomas cat made his appearance upon the scene; and, on being appealed to, cheerfully made an improvised scale, and breaking the cheese in two unequal parts, the larger on the scale overbalanced the smaller, and immediately he proceeded to nibble and nibble at the cheese until the large piece became the smaller; and as the scales shifted, he nibbled at the other piece, and repeated this process until there was no cheese left; and, when the mice protested there were no mice left!

If this process of nibbling at wages here and there, as here in New England last year and a month later in the South, whether it be in any one city or town or in different States, it matters not; if this nibbling process goes on unchecked, it simply means the brutalizing, the "Chinesizing," of the American people. The difficulty is, how can charity be applied and yet prove no injury to the progress and development of that idea of the payment of the highest possible wage that an industry will afford? For, after all, that is the main question.—*From address before the Monday Evening Club, Boston, March 20, 1899.*

Mr. Hubbard says that if he were an employee he would "never mention wages," but would focus right on his work and do it. He would never harass an employer, but would give him peace, and let his work tell its own story. He says that the man who makes a strike to have his wages raised from fifteen to eighteen dollars a week may get the raise, and then his wages will stay there. Had he kept quiet and just been intent on making himself a five-thousand-dollar man he "MIGHT have gravitated straight to a five-thousand-dollar desk."

Ye gods! What reasoning, and what a wonderful exhibition of want of information!

In each plant employing, say, one thousand workmen, there are not more than five occupying "a five-thousand-dollar desk," and according to Mr. Hubbard's reasoning the remaining nine hundred and ninety-five should surrender their opportunity of a raise in their wages from fifteen to eighteen dollars a week upon the thread of hope that the occupants of the five-thousand-dollar positions may die so the workman "MIGHT gravitate straight to a five-thousand-dollar desk."

If the workers were to surrender their effort to secure a material improvement in their condition, the employers of labor would do the striking for them in the form of forcing lower wages, longer hours, and worse conditions.

It is not difficult to say glibly, as does Mr. Hubbard, that if the workmen's positions do not give them the opportunity to grow, and they "know of a better place, why go to the better place." The fact of the matter is that despite our present industrial revival there are now thousands of workmen vainly seeking employment and the opportunity of sustaining themselves and those dependent upon them; while the unity of effort among the employed workers is designed that the places and positions they occupy shall be bettered.

There is no surer cause for deterioration in the condition of the workers than their lack of interest in their own welfare and the welfare of others. To use an apt illustration, we quote Mr. Hubbard against himself when he elsewhere says:

"Depend upon it; the best antiseptic for decay is an active interest in human affairs." This is as true in industry as in all other fields of human activity.—*American Federationist, April, 1902.*

If the raising of wages should result simply in raising the price of the article produced, and the increased wages must be expended in the increased cost of living, then it is idle and purely a waste of time and effort to endeavor to increase wages.

Following logically Mr. Darrow's fallacious proposition it would make little, in fact, no difference at all, whether wages are increased or whether they are reduced. If the cost of a finished product is raised by an increase in wages, it necessarily follows that it will lessen with each reduction of wages.

Good marble cutters in Athens, Greece—men capable of carving images out of stone—receive twenty-five cents per day, working twelve hours. Ordinary laborers receive eighteen cents per day. Apprentices in skilled trades work twelve hours and receive nine cents per day. The food of the working people consists in the main of black bread, and olives as a substitute for butter. Except on great holidays, meat in the workmen's families is unknown. Railroad train crossings in Spain are flagged by women, who receive two cents per day for their work. To a greater or lesser degree these conditions exist in many countries until we reach China, where wages are the lowest of all.

Does Mr. Darrow really believe that the conditions resulting from low wages are a matter of utter indifference and of no consequence to the working people and to the people in general?

He leaves wholly out of consideration the facts that only in countries where wages are high is it possible to introduce machinery, and that, as wages are raised, new and better machinery with the highest developed propelling forces are introduced and applied.

New tools are brought into existence, division and subdivision and specialization of trades and industries follow, making production far greater and at a lesser cost than ever before, despite—yes, because of—the increase in wages. A traveler recently stated:

> Up along the Nile I found the natives lifting water up in buckets from point to point for at least 75 feet. The American windmill could do the work of hundreds of these people, but it would be as much as a man's life was worth to even suggest it, for by the bucket is the only way thousands of these people live.

In other words, the people there regard the American windmill as a machine to displace their labor, and its introduction would be opposed.

Traveling South some few years ago we observed river dredging by hand, that is, by buckets fixed to long handles. Inquiries as to why improved or automatic dredging machines were not introduced were answered by the statement that it would take away the labor of the black forty-cent-a-day dredger.

Such are the facts in all cases, in all industries, in all countries.

Low wages mean primitive methods of production.

With each recurring advance in wages, improvements in machinery and motive power are introduced, tending always to lessen the cost of production.

It is a fact easily demonstrable that a given finished product is produced at a relatively lesser cost and sold at a lower price in high-wage countries than in a country in which low or the lowest wages obtain.—*American Federationist, July, 1903.*

"Is there any limit to the demands of labor as to wages and hours?" asks John C. Havemeyer in his list of foolish questions addressed to the unions of Yonkers, N. Y. Many other employers echo this utterly immaterial question.

There may be, in a scientific sense, a limit to the upward tendency of wages and the downward tendency of hours of labor; but who can authoritatively tell us when that limit is reached?

Is there a limit to the employer's profits? Is not the rule, "charge all the traffic will bear"? Where is the law of nature ordaining that employers shall have all the comforts and luxuries and the workmen the bare necessaries, and not always even that? What is, "too much"?—*American Federationist, August, 1903.*

It is the height of economic unwisdom to curtail the consuming power of the masses as a means to industrial revival or prosperity. No industry, no country, has ever become great, or ever can become great, founded upon the poverty of its workers. . . . Surely, it is not rational to suggest, for the relief of an over-stocked or glutted market, that the workers shall curtail their power of consumption and then work longer hours to increase production. I submit that the policy of the labor movement is wiser and has in it the means to the sooner restore industrial activity and bring about its revival. We urge as a way out that wages be maintained, even, if necessary, to resist reductions; that as a substitute for discharges of workmen, the work to be performed be divided, thus not only helping to bear each others' burdens, but more quickly to restore activity in industry, trade and commerce.—*From report to A. F. of L. convention, Boston, Mass., November, 1903.*

The old theory that the selling price of an article shall determine the wages paid to the workmen is hollow, shallow, and unnatural. The order must be reversed and the first consideration in the selling price of an article must be a fair wage to labor. Wages must dominate prices, not prices dominate wages. It is a libel upon the human family to assert that in the production of any article for the use and benefit of man a living wage can not be paid. . . .

If an industrial reaction shall set in, would not a curtailment of the consuming power of the masses still further intensify the industrial depression? What determines more potentially the consuming power of the workers than the wages they receive in return for labor performed? . . .

We have advised and shall continue to advise our fellow-workmen to resist reductions in wages by every lawful means within their power, for as we have said before, "It is better to resist and lose than not to resist at all."

Let workmen complacently accept reductions in their wages and it will be an invitation to repeat the reduction at will, intensifying the depression and provoking an industrial crisis; forcing down the workers in the economic and social scale and bringing on fearful poverty, misery, and degradation. Resistance on the part of labor to reduction of wages will check this to a great degree and at least demonstrate to the ignorant and short-sighted employers that such a course is exceedingly expensive to them, and will prevent its repetition.—*American Federationist, January, 1904.*

Our opponents say let this matter alone, and the law of supply and demand will regulate it, because the law of supply and demand is immutable. One of them went so far as to say that it is an almighty law. In primitive society and under ordinary conditions of life the law of supply and demand operates; but is it true, as our opponents say, that the law of supply and demand is immutable and that any one who undertakes to interfere with its operation will injure and destroy themselves? What are the associations of employers doing? What are the trusts doing when they limit production; when they close down their plants for a given period? What is that but an interference with the "immutable" operation of the law of supply and demand? The mines close down by the direction of a few men and production ceases for a given period. They say, in the language of the directors, that it is in order to give the market an opportunity to recover itself. What is that but an interference with the law of supply and demand?

It is all very well to interfere with the law of supply and demand when it is done by the capitalists of the country, but it is an entirely different story when the workmen endeavor to have something done which shall mitigate the most cruel features of the law of supply and demand if its manipulations are left to the juggling of the employers. Do our opponents permit the natural operation of the law of supply and demand to be invoked when they scour the poorest countries of the earth and bring hordes of men into the United States to glut the "labor market"? When we had the representatives of the employers before the Congressional committees having under consideration the bill to exclude the Chinese, they wanted the hordes of Chinese coolies to come into the United States in order that they might be thrown into the balance against the workingmen of our country. But when these hordes come here, those who would have them come throw their hands into the air and declare that the almighty and immutable law of supply and demand stands in the way of any legislation having for its purpose the improvement of the condition of labor.

It is true that there is now more agreement than formerly between the employers and the employed, between employers and organized labor, as to the conditions of employment and the hours of labor. I submit to you that if the employers refuse to concede that which we regard as fair conditions in the last analysis that we have not only the legal but the moral right to strike in our effort to enforce them.—*From testimony before Senate Committee on Education and Labor, 1904.*

It is better to resist the inauguration of a period of industrial stagnation and thereby prevent it than to blindly accept it and then try to devise a means to emerge from it. By organized labor's attitude we have maintained a better parity between production and consumption. . . .

The unprecedented and firm stand taken by the representatives of the hosts of labor at the Boston convention in declaring that wage reductions would be resisted, and the very general adoption of that policy by our fellow workers, saved the day, and beyond peradventure of a doubt prevented an industrial crisis with all its attendant suffering, poverty, and misery. . . .

In my report to the San Francisco convention last year attention was called to the advantages resulting from our previous year's declaration of policy, and it was indicated that we were then not yet "out of the woods"; that the advice and watchword should go forth from that convention to the toilers of our country to resist by every honorable and lawful means at their command, any and every attempt to reduce wages. Firmly and boldly and wisely the San Francisco convention reiterated and emphasized the declaration of organized labor's policy and polity, and it affords me the keenest gratification to record the fact that at no time in the history of our country have the people been more generally employed at gainful occupations and in the production of wealth or have been larger consumers of their products than at this hour and this day.—*From annual report to A. F. of L. convention, Pittsburg, Pa., November, 1905.*

To-day labor is very generally employed. From the authentic reports received at our office the state of unemployment would indicate that whereas for the year 1905 the unemployed was about three per cent, yet from the indications for the present year it will be about two and three-quarters per cent. Of course, so long as there is one wage-earner unemployed through no fault of his own, so long is there a great wrong from which he suffers, and just so long will it be the mission of the trade union movement to right it.

In this world of ours, and especially in our own country, with the wonderful fertility and extent of our land, the magnificent ingenuity of our people, and particularly the tremendous energy and industry of our workers, there should not be any workers who are workless.

Some have taken unction to their souls and loudly proclaimed that they are the cause for the better general conditions of employment of the working people of our country. Without discussing the hypothesis upon which they base these claims, we assert and emphatically re-affirm that whatever improvement in a material, moral, social, and political way has come to the toiling masses of America, is due to their own efforts in their more thorough organization, their higher intelligence and their positive determination to aid and stand by each other in the contention and struggles for the common uplift.

It was but a few years ago when the working people of our country were confronted with a condition similar to that which was previously repeatedly presented to the toilers in similar situations. Had we acquiesced or consented to the policy presented to us by the representatives of the captains of industry, we would have experienced all the poverty, misery and suffering incident to lack of employment, and a constantly decreasing opportunity for employment resultant from reductions in wages, one following close upon the other.

It is due to the firm and unequivocal declaration of America's organized workers and their positive repetition since, that wage reductions will be resisted to the uttermost, that we have averted the usual industrial crisis and emerged from it with greater industrial and commercial activity than ever before.

In several countries the people are confronted with the great problem of an immense number of unemployed workers. In some form or other they are endeavoring to ascertain the cause and to find a means to assuage it. Often in the history of our own country have our people been confronted with the same problem.

If we adhere firmly to the policy, establish and maintain it as a fixed principle in the industrial affairs of America, that at any and all hazards we will resist any attempt at wage reductions, we shall establish not only a new economic principle, but a new philosophy by which industrial panics and crises will be obliterated, and we shall set an example for the whole world to follow.
—*From annual report to A. F. of L. convention, Minneapolis, Minn., November, 1906.*

Not alone in our conventions, but in the gatherings of labor generally, "No reductions in wages" has been made the slogan and watchword. That policy has had its beneficent influence, not only upon labor but upon all industry. It has been heard and heeded; at no time has it had greater justification and demonstration of its effectiveness than during recent months. . . . It is due to the determined and clean-cut policy of labor of our country that our princes of finance, despite their machinations, could not influence employers of labor to hazard an attempt at wage reductions. If all labor will unfalteringly adhere to the determination to resist any and all reductions in wages, we shall not only avoid the misery, poverty and calamity of the past, but we shall teach financiers, employers and economists in general a new philosophy of life and industry.—*From report to A. F. of L. convention, Norfolk, Va., November, 1907.*

A glance at the part which wages play in keeping money in circulation will prove instructive.

The merchant, no matter of what class, depends largely on the volume of purchases made by wage workers every week for food, clothing, household goods and even many things not classed as absolute necessities. The more freely such purchases are made, the greater the volume of money kept in circulation. The amount of furniture, for instance, which is purchased all over the country in a month is the regulator of how much furniture the factories will produce. The same argument applies to all other commodities necessary for civilized existence.

It must be remembered that while the individual purchases of the wealthy are often striking in amount, yet the great volume of trade in everything that pertains to living comes from the masses of the people—those on wages or salary.

Cut wages and you instantly curtail the purchasing power of the worker. He buys less, therefore he puts less money into circulation and he utilizes less of the products of factory, farm and shop.

A general cut in wages for the workers means factories piled up with products they cannot sell and farmers with enough to feed the country and those who need the food unable to buy it.

Transportation suffers also when the demand for products fall off. Let the wage workers' power of consumption be lessened by a cut in wages and the retail merchant first feels the loss in the lessening of daily sales but the whole vicious circle of ill effects may be traced back to the fountain head of production!

Some have complained that the wage worker has lived too well and spent too freely in the past few years.

Not so, every dollar spent in better clothing, better food, better furniture, higher class amusements, better education for his children—every dollar has been a vital element in the marked prosperity of the past few years.

No more effective way of bringing on a season of real industrial depression could be devised than to cut wages because there is a flurry in finance and there seems need of retrenchment somewhere.—*From (New York) "Journal of Commerce" article, December 27, 1907.*

The entire history of industry demonstrates clearly beyond question that every effort in the past to reduce wages, every reduction of wages made to relieve a like situation, has simply accentuated and made the condition worse. You can not reduce wages without reducing the consuming power of the people, and every time you reduce their consuming power, you make your situation worse. It is the largest possible consumption of things produced which makes the largest possible prosperity and I may say this, without further attempt at serious argument—I may say this, that the *employers of labor who make or believe they can make an attempt to force wages down are not going to have the easy sailing they had years ago,* for the American workmen have come to the conclusion that if for any reason—and I shall not attempt to assign one to-night—the financial situation is as it is, it is due to no fault of theirs; that whoever is to blame, it is in the hands of the financiers or the captains of industry and the representatives in Congress, if you please, if you care to blame them; but I repeat, it is not due to any fault of the working people. They have made up their minds that they are not going to be the chief sufferers either by reason of an artificially-made panic or by the blunders of those who have the affairs of finance and industry under their direction.—*American Federationist, February, 1908.*

In the days when political economy was known as the dismal science, certain theorists asserting the "iron law of wages" declared that law as inevitable and immutable as the law of gravitation. These followers of Malthus held that diminishing returns from agriculture in connection with the strong tendency of the human race toward over-population, make impossible permanent improvement of the working people.

The wages-fund theory is equally dismal and unwholesome. It is based upon the supposition that the employer sets aside a fixed portion of his capital with which to pay wages—this is the wages-fund; that the amount of capital and the wages-fund available for use at any one time are predetermined and fixed; that wages paid individuals are the quotient found by dividing the wages-fund by the number of wage-earners. The only way to affect wages, according to this theory, is to change either the wages-fund or the number of wage-earners, for, since the wages-fund is not elastic, any attempt of individual workers or groups of workers to increase their own wages would diminish the relative shares of all the others.

The theory is wrong in assuming that wages are paid out of capital—wage payments are advanced out of capital but are ultimately paid out of product. That is to say, wages are the discounted product of labor. Capital, from which temporary advances are made, is no more inelastic than any other element of production—there are certain indefinite limits set by credit, loans, etc., but these are subject to various modifying influences. Neither the wages advanced to workmen nor the product out of which these are ultimately paid is rigid or predetermined. An increase in the number of workers does not invariably decrease wages—this result may be prevented by variables, which we shall mention in connection with the theory of supply and demand.

The wages-fund theory has been invoked for most pernicious and repressive purposes. Incidentally it has tended to exalt the function of the capitalist as the appointed custodian of the sacred exchequer from which issues the wages-fund. It was maintained that the capitalist must be undisturbed and unhampered in his operations, because he was considered the pivotal element in production. Adherents of the wages-fund school regard the efforts of the workers to better their condition through organization and collective demands as a menace to the foundations of economic stability, and an obstacle in the way of progress. Although the wages-fund fallacy has nearly vanished from economic theory yet its by-product, popular and ignorant discrediting of the trade union movement, still operates in practical affairs.

Another theory that has been heralded as the explanation of all economic problems is "demand and supply." But "demand and supply" deals with glittering generalities and describes what is rather than explains why it is what it is. It can be glibly asserted of any market price that it represents the equilibrium point between supply and demand without in any way touching the underlying value problems or revealing the forces that have affected either side of the equation. In considering consumption goods, or products on the market, price determining may be described according to the supply and demand formula, with some degree of satisfaction. But in connection with production problems, the formula affords chances for most misleading deductions.

Those who observe price-lists know that even where a vastly increased supply is counterbalanced by a vastly increased demand, prices may be reduced greatly; for example, the great metropolitan newspapers which formerly sold for 5 cents or more, are now almost uniformly 1 cent. Again increasing demand may supply sufficient incentive to secure such greatly improved methods of production that prices steadily fall; this is the case with rubber coats, which formerly cost a small fortune, but now are considered necessities by many. The demand resulted in lessening the cost of production, the increased supply followed. The supply and demand theory may furnish interesting but elusive descriptive matter, but it explains nothing.

Increases in the number of workers do not lead to lower wages—increased productivity, improved processes and machinery, cheaper operating power, improved managerial methods, increased demand, and innumerable other modifying variables may tend to maintain the wage-level, or to raise it. But, perhaps, the most potent factor of all in raising wage-levels is the combined and determined efforts of the workers themselves. This force operating on the distributive side of industry, has been most persistently ignored by many theorists, although its influence has been felt by the capitalists themselves and has been invoked and called blessed by the wage-earners.

Without introducing any other new factor into the situation, if the employees of an industry paying extremely low wages are organized, wages may by collective action be repeatedly raised. Innumerable permutations and adjustments make this increase possible. That a limit is set to this increase by the marginal productivity of the laborer is generally and historically accurate. The worker who can make one shoe a day may feel perfectly sure that this productive limit will effectually bar him from receiving as wages the value of two shoes, but he may not feel at all sure it will guarantee wages commensurate with the value of the productive labor he put into the one shoe he did produce. Added to productive efficiency must be effectiveness in making wage demands. But to say that each employer knows the productivity per workman, not to mention the marginal productivity in the industry, is an absurdly preposterous claim. Wages are for the most part paid on the trial and balance principle, fixing them as low as the workmen will stand and not according to any rational, well-formulated theory. That is to say, the distributive share allotted to the wage-earners is the result of human activity, either of the employers or the employees, and not the normal or inevitable result of any natural law. . . .

Professor Simon N. Patten, in his *Reconstruction of Economic Theory*, repudiates the theory that wages are controlled by any natural law. He considers wages a complex resultant of many forces, one of which is collective bargaining. "The reasoning of the wage-fund theorists," he said, "was an upper class view of those who wished to pose as humanitarians without being so." After stating his theory of distribution, he concludes:

"Such statements differ from those of the wage-fund theorists. They differ not less in the action called for than in the theory itself. The one view demands activity of the workers in securing their rights; the other gives them an income fixed by natural law. It seems simpler and less troublesome to have the laborers penned within bounds and to have their income handed out to them by fixed economic laws. In reality, however, the difficulties are thereby increased. The laborers will act in any case, and if industrial relief is denied them, whether by nature or man, they will resort to political action to enforce their demands. The choice is really between a political socialism that would absorb all profits, and such direct action on the part of laborers as will insure them a share in the social surplus. In the one case, they act unitedly and are interested in the overthrow of existing institutions. In the other case, they act as an industrial group, and force such changes in prices as will permit of increased wages."

In the past whenever any financial crisis was threatening or pending, whether intentionally caused by some prince of finance alone or in collusion with associates and forced by most questionable methods, or whether produced by the incompetency of the so-called captains of industry, it was customary to throw the burden of it all upon the shoulders of the workers by making it appear that continuance of production was only possible if wages were reduced. It was against this practice that during the financial panic of 1907 the American Federation of Labor declared unqualified resistance to all wage reductions. In that year portentous of panic, organized labor called a halt to the usual wage-cuts which always result in perversely intensifying the financial stringency. The unorganized also determinedly refused to accept wage reductions. This policy had a steadying effect; confidence was restored; normal conditions were reëstablished.— *American Federationist, July, 1913.*

The American Federation of Labor is not in favor of fixing, by legal enactment, certain minimum wages. The attempts of the government to establish wages at which workmen may work, according to the teachings of history, will result in a long era of industrial slavery. There was a time in English history when the government and the courts in quarter sessions established wages. During periods when there was a dearth of workmen and employers offered higher wages, both the workmen and employers were brought into court and punished by imprisonment and physical mutilation because the one asked, received, or demanded, and the other was willing to offer, or did pay, higher wages.

There is now a current movement to increase wages by a proposal to determine a minimum wage by political authorities. It is a maxim in law that once a court is given jurisdiction over an individual it has the power, the field, and authority to exercise that jurisdiction. "I fear the Greeks even when they bear gifts." An attempt to entrap the American workmen into a species of slavery, under guise of an offer of this character is resented by the men and women of the American trade union movement.

When the question of fixing, by legal enactment, minimum wages for women was before the Executive Council of the American Federation of Labor for investigation and discussion, and subsequently before the convention of the American Federation of Labor, there was a great diversion of views. I am betraying no confidence when I say that. The official decision of the convention was that the subject was worthy of further discussion and consideration. In my judgment the proposal to establish by law a minimum wage for women, though well meant, is a curb upon the rights, the natural development, and the opportunity for development of the women employed in the industries of our country.

If the legislature should once fix a minimum wage it would have the opportunity to use the machinery of the state to enforce work at that rate whether the workers desired to render services or not. I am very suspicious of the activities of governmental agencies. I apprehend that once the state is allowed to fix a minimum rate, the state would also take the right to compel men or women to work at that rate. I have some apprehension that if the legislature were allowed to establish a maximum workday it might also compel workmen to work up to the maximum allowed. I ought to say, however, that I am in favor of the legal enactment fixing the minimum hours of labor for all workmen in direct government employment and for those who work for contractors substituted for governmental authority.—*From testimony before U. S. Commission on Industrial Relations, New York City, May 21-23, 1914.*

Minimum wage legislation has made a powerful appeal to the hearts of the people. It *seems* the most expeditious way to insure a more just wage for workers. In the *American Federationist* for May was related the movement of organized labor in Porto Rico to approve such legislation and our effort to convince them of the fallacy of the underlying principle. I said in substance that if such a declaration for the establishment of a minimum wage for all workers in private employment were enacted, the government of the island might find it convenient to enforce compulsory service to labor at the wage set by law. Such a development would reëstablish the old conditions of serfdom, peonage, or slavery, and every effort to increase wages the working people might make would have to be based upon political agitation in order to secure the change. Indeed the proposition was going back to the old, rather than making for the new. I stated that a minimum wage for governmental employees was justified as in that case the government was the employer, but workers in private employment must depend upon the intelligence, the energy, and the solidarity of the organization of wage-workers. . . .

This species of effort to better human conditions does more credit to our hearts than to our heads. It secures immediate relief, perhaps, but in such a way as to hinder future initiative. Whatever is purchased at the expense of liberty of action and personal rights is purchased at a price too dear for any free people to afford. Freedom of personal contract is the one narrow distinction between the free worker and the unfree. It is for the workers then to guard their freedom as something more precious than life itself—for it is that which makes life worth the living. Be not deceived by any specious sympathy and guileful interest in your welfare, but like men and women work out your own problems and determine your own lives. Benefits, improvements gained by the power of collective action may be slower, but they do not menace future welfare—they do not transfer to others control over future activity, policies, or methods. Self-help leads to independence, reliance, and true welfare.—*American Federationist, June, 1914.*

The attempt by any process, directly or indirectly, to curtail the earning power of the working people will, I am sure, be not only resented, but create much more discontent than the cause for complaint as you indicated it to exist. After all, wages, or more clearly expressing it—higher wages or better wages—are an aspiration for a better life. Nothing could be more hurtful, not only in the present situation in which our country finds itself but for all time to come, than to attempt by direct or indirect means to place an obstacle to the fullest development of the highest aspiration of man. No doubt the tendency toward higher wages may have some discomforting aspects to some; but that it makes for a better manhood for the large mass cannot be successfully disputed.—*From letter to Major August Belmont, July 6, 1918.*

It is said that requests for increases in wages necessitate increases in prices, which increase cost of living and in return result in more wage demands—a vicious circle that leads to no progress. It should be remembered that wages constitute only one of the factors in production costs and that high-wage labor invariably leads to labor saving machinery and improved production processes. High wages do not inevitably lead to the vicious circle. On the contrary, they have invariably resulted in constructive changes, beneficial to workers and resulting in increased production. This is vividly brought out by the contrasts in production in low-wage countries such as China and

ECONOMICS AND ETHICS OF HIGH WAGES

production in high-wage countries such as ours.—*From address before convention of Associated Advertising Clubs of the World, New Orleans, La., September 22, 1919.*

Seasonal work is the curse of American industry. It demoralizes both the employer and the employee. The employer gets in the habit of shutting down the moment that sufficient work is not afforded and the employee is continually harassed by a feeling of uncertainty and is easily led away into the delusion that by soldiering on his job he can prolong it. Here is a point in which the interests of the employer and the employee are not in conflict and where their best brains can well be pooled to take advice with production engineers for the planning of the work in such a way as to avoid slack seasons. . . .

It will develop that both profits and wages are too low because of the excessive waste of seasonal business. If capital and labor will only coöperate to war upon waste they will both find it far more profitable than warring upon one another. As an employer (and this is, of course, not so easy as it sounds, although I am convinced that it is not impossible) I should plan my production on a schedule, make my markets and prices accordingly, and then I should be in a position to bargain with my men on a twelve months' wage basis and abandon the chaotic and uneconomic notion of making all of my profits in six months and paying a wage based on similar principles. This would make a very great difference in the prices that I should charge and to attain this end I should consult with the union officers in order to gain that coöperative knowledge which is essential to good business, always taking as a fixed matter a minimum standard of living for those that I employed.—*From interview with Samuel Crowther on "What I Should Do If I Were an Employer," in "System Magazine," April, 1920.*

MEMBERSHIP
AMERICAN FEDERATION OF LABOR

1881	50,000
1884	100,000
1887	150,000
1889	200,000
1892	250,000
1899	300,000
1900	550,000
1901	750,000
1902	1,000,000
1903	1,450,000
1904	1,650,000
1906	1,450,000
1908	1,550,000
1909	1,450,000
1910	1,550,000
1911	1,750,000
1912	1,800,000
1913	1,950,000
1914	2,000,000
1915	1,950,000
1916	2,050,000
1917	2,350,000
1918	2,700,000
1919	3,250,000
Dec. 1919	4,050,000

IV

THE SHORTER WORKING DAY

The general reduction of the hours of labor to eight per day would reach further than any other reformatory measure; it would be of more lasting benefit; it would create a greater spirit in the workingman; it would make him a better citizen, a better father, a better husband, a better man in general. The "voting cattle," so-called, those whose votes are purchased on election day, are drawn from that class of our people whose life is one continuous round of toil. They cannot be drawn from workingmen who work only eight hours. A man who works but eight hours a day possesses more independence both economically and politically. It is the man who works like his machine and never knows when to stop, until in his case perpetual motion is almost reached—*he* is the man whose vote you can buy. The man who works longest is the first to be thrown out on the side-walk, because his recreation is generally drink.—*From testimony before United States Senate Committee upon the Relations Between Labor and Capital (Henry W. Blair, chairman), August 16, 1883.*

I must now refer to one of the most important facts with which the labor movement has to grapple. The displacement of labor by machinery in the past few years has exceeded that of any like period in our history. The United States Commissioner of Labor in his report on "Industrial Depression" says: "One man with the McKay machine can handle 300 pairs of shoes per day, while, without the machine he could handle but five pairs in the same time."

In the broom industry "each machine displaces three men."

Carpet industry—"In spinning alone it would take by the old methods from seventy-five to one hundred times the number of operatives now employed to turn out the same amount of work."

Hats—The displacement has been "in the proportion of nine to one."

Cotton industry—"It is quite generally agreed that there has been a displacement, taking all processes of cotton manufacture into consideration, in the proportion of three to one."

Manufacture of flour—"Three-fourths of the manual labor has been displaced."

Furniture—"From one-half to three-fourths are now only required to do the same work."

Metals—"Manual labor decreases thirty-three and one-third per cent."

Musical instruments—"One boy does the work of twenty-five men."

Coal mining—"One hundred miners, getting out two hundred tons of coal per day. Two machines with fourteen men mine forty tons per day."

Paper—"A machine now run by four men and six girls will do the work formerly done by one hundred persons."

Railroad supplies—"There has been a displacement of fifty per cent of the labor formerly required."

Woolens—"Weaving, one machine equals six persons; in spinning, one machine equals twenty persons."

Wall paper—"The best evidence puts the displacement in the proportion of one hundred to one."

These quotations are taken from the report of 1886, pp. 85, 86 and 87, closing with July, 1885. It can be readily understood that since that time the displacement has been going on with undiminished intensity. In this same report the Commissioner states that on July 1, 1885, there were no less than 998,839 working people out of employment. Surely the indications are that this vast army of unemployed has not since decreased.

Is it not time that something should be done to reclaim from misery the many thousands of good and true men whose only fault is that they have stomachs to fill, with ready and willing hands to supply their wants, but continually receiving the stereotyped reply in answer to their appeals for work, "No job open"?

Much can be done by the trade unions to relieve the distress caused by the displacement of labor by machinery. Within the past few years the trades unions have sought and in many instances secured a reduction in the hours of labor; for a brief period there has been a stagnation in this direction.

I appeal to the trades unions of the country to go on in this

THE SHORTER WORKING DAY

work. The answer to all opponents to the reduction of the hours of labor could well be given in these words: "That so long as there is one man who seeks employment and cannot obtain it, the hours of labor are too long."—*From annual report to A. F. of L. convention, Baltimore, Md., December, 1887.*

It is true, as many say, that the eight-hour movement of 1886 was not entirely successful; it is also true that no movement that has for its purpose the improvement of the conditions of a whole people ever could succeed in its first, aye, even in its second attempt. It is always a hard struggle to achieve any improvement, but the benefits which we gained in 1886 and since then by reason of the eight-hour movement are sufficient to encourage us to make the venture again. We should not lose sight of the fact that as a result of the movement of 1886 there have been a number of trades that reduced their hours of labor from ten and twelve to eight; others again from twelve and fourteen to ten and nine, and many thousands of workingmen who before that time worked from fourteen to eighteen hours a day have had the hours of their labor reduced to twelve. It has been estimated that more than eight million hours of labor have been spared the toiler; in other words, employment has been found for thousands who would otherwise be in want of it.

There is no question as to the justice of our movement, and there can be no doubt as to success if we are but earnest, sincere and energetic in organization and in its agitation. If we exhibit a proper spirit in directing our movement to the achievement of this object, we shall have on our side all the thoughtful men in the country; we shall have the professional classes; we shall have all those on our side whose interests are not at the moment materially injured, and of those who are injured surely there are but very few, if any. Let Forward! then be our watchword. In that spirit and with that object in view, I recommend that some day be set apart at this convention, not later than 1890, when the working people of the entire country shall be called upon to simultaneously demand the enforcement of eight hours as a day's work. Certainly in this, the latter part of the nineteenth century, with all the implements of machinery, science and knowledge contributing towards the production of wealth, I maintain that we have arrived at that stage in life when **eight hours is more** than sufficient to produce all the necessaries and the luxuries that a people can reasonably want, and if that does not suffice, there is no good reason why machinery should not further be applied to produce that which may still be wanting.—*From annual report to A. F. of L. convention, St. Louis, Mo., December, 1888.*

In the whole history of the labor movement there has not been any question upon which the thoughts of the civilized world have been so thoroughly centered as upon the eight-hour movement inaugurated by the American Federation of Labor at its last convention.

When we met last year at St. Louis, the combined forces and influences of the employing and speculative classes so thoroughly held the master hand over labor, they had become so overbearing, had so thoroughly awed the working people into submission, that every meeting night of labor organizations was but the repetition of the various notices of reduction in wages, the imposition of obnoxious rules, the presentation of iron-clad obligations to sign away our right to organize for self-protection, propositions to increase the hours of labor—in a word, labor seemed to have no right, economic or political, that capital was bound to respect.

It was at this time that our proclamation to the world was made, to call on the toilers of the country to the movement to enforce the eight-hour work-day, May 1st, 1890.

From that moment a change took place. Hope was instilled into the hearts and minds of the workers to supplant despair. The rallying cry of eight hours was sounded. The working people again stood erect and staunch in their manhood. The tide had changed.

I trust that the charge may not be made that we take too optimistic a view of the situation, or that the condition of labor is "satisfactory" to us. On the contrary, the very fervency of our advocacy of the movement to reduce the hours of labor is the best evidence we can give that we are at war with wrong, and that our best efforts will be devoted to the eradication of every injustice and evil from which labor suffers.—*From annual report to A. F. of L. convention, Boston, Mass., December, 1889.*

Since August of this year we have been in the greatest industrial depression this country has ever experienced. It is no exaggeration to say that more than three millions of our fellow toilers throughout the country are without employment and have been so since the time named. This lamentable industrial condition is attributed by many to various causes, and it seems to me that the accurate statement of them here is both requisite and appropriate, so that we may be better enabled to so frame our legislation that it may tend to a proper solution of the problem dependent upon the wage-workers for solution.

From the time industry began to emerge from the panic of 1873-79, there began the introduction of vastly improved machinery, tools and methods of production. The inventions in electricity, the general application of this force as well as steam to industry was indeed "displacing labor faster than new industries could be founded." Production, production, production, faster, greater, was the impulse, the thought and motive of the capitalist class. That in the end the great body of workers comprise those who must of necessity consume the production was given no consideration whatever by our "Captains of Industry." As a result, the great storehouses are glutted with the very articles required by the people, without their ability—or rather their opportunity to obtain—consume—them. Does it require more than ordinary observation to discern that from conditions so abnormal and abominable industrial stagnation must ensue? We, the representatives of the organized toiling masses of our country, offered the only reasonable, practical and tangible solution to meet the changed conditions of industry. . . .

It is unnecessary to repeat the lamentable incident which frustrated the eight-hour movement of 1886. But in 1890, true to its mission, the American Federation of Labor resolved to engage in the movement to gradually enforce the eight-hour work day in which we were partially successful. Had we been met by less antagonism of the capitalist class and by those who should have been our friends it is safe to say that the panic of 1893 would have been averted, deferred or certainly less intense.

The only method by which a practical, just and safe equilibrium can be maintained in the industrial world for the fast and ever increasing introduction of machinery, is a commensurate reduction of the hours of labor. I am very sure that if the employers were to substitute a division of the work required, among *all* their workers, instead of the discharge of a number, we would much sooner emerge from the present industrial and commercial stagnation.—*From annual report to A. F. of L. convention, Chicago, Ill., December, 1893.*

Differ though we may upon all else, we agree that what will really advance the material, hence the moral and social wellbeing of labor, must beneficially reflect and act upon the whole world of civilization. We cannot successfully improve the foundation of a structure without correspondingly permanently perfecting the structure itself. The simile holds good when applied to the structure of society the foundation and support of which is the great body of labor, the producers of wealth. Let us see then what effect the reductions of the hours of labor have had upon the interests of labor, and judging the past by the present, it is safe to venture the prediction that the same causes will produce the same results in the future.

In every industry where the hours of labor have been reduced, through the efforts of organized labor, it has been followed with these results:

Wages have been increased; periods or seasons of employment have been lengthened; the number of unemployed has been reduced; the consuming power of the laborer has increased; the leisure resulting from the lesser hours of manual labor has opened up a vista of opportunities which have made the laborer not only a worker but more of a man, with all that that ennobling term implies.

It has made him more temperate in all things and given him a clearer conception of his rights and duties as a worker, a father, a citizen and a man. It has made him more independent, more enlightened, broader in his views and in his sympathies. He has become a better safeguard to his country's honor and its interests, a stancher defender of his home and fireside. He struggles more intensely and more wisely against every form of wrong and injustice and to attain the highest conception of human rights. Are these claims merely the result of fancy or too great an optimism, or are they the consequences of the movement to reduce the hours of labor?

Do wages increase when hours of labor are shortened? I venture the assertion that in no industry in the whole world has there been the slightest deviation from the affirmative to this claim. We may view any industry we please, wherever it may be located, and the results will be found to be the same. Not only this, but it is easily discernible, and may be taken as a general rule, that wherever the working day is longest wages are lowest, and wherever and in whichever industry the daily hours of labor are least, wages are highest.

Compare any two or more countries on the face of the globe; compare any two States in the United States; compare any two cities in any one or more States; compare any two industries in any one city; yes, compare any two establishments of a similar industry in any one city and there is no departure from this rule that the longer the working day the lower the wages, and *vice versa*.

We will go even further in illustration of this invariable rule and cite a fact which every one can easily ascertain and observe for himself:

Take any one establishment where a large number of workers are employed, and it will soon be learned that those workers whose hours of labor in that establishment are the longest receive the lowest wages paid to any employees therein; while those who enter the works daily the latest in the morning, and depart earliest in the evening, are in receipt of the highest wages.

In the study of this apparent economic paradox, we shall see, too, that this rule of which we have spoken does not even vary when the skilled and unskilled workers are compared. That is, all other things being equal.

When skilled workers in any one industry work longer hours daily than do the unskilled workers in another industry, or calling, the same rule will apply. An instance will demonstrate this.

Factory wood workers work from ten to twelve hours a day; wages from $1.25 to $1.75 per day. Machinists usually work ten hours a day; wages about $2.00 to $2.50 per day. Hod carriers work usually nine and, in some instances, eight hours a day; wages range from $2.25 to $2.75 per day. Were the machinists, wood workers and others to devote more of their skill to the plain as well as the scientific consideration of their interests, and secure a reduction in their hours of labor to eight per day, is there any doubt that it would be followed by increased wages?

Suppose the workers would argue somewhat as follows: "The greatest article of value known to man is time. Heretofore we sold you ten hours of our time each day, for which you paid us $2.00. When we demurred to this low price you answered that there was a great glut of that article—time (labor)—in the market. Now since time (labor) is the only article that we possess and have to sell and must sell, and since there is such a glut of it in the market, we propose to economize and to offer you only eight hours daily of our time (labor), reserving the means (vitality, strength) to sell you the same quantity of time (labor) to-day, to-morrow and the days yet remaining to us. This will relieve the glut in the market, and, according to the law of "supply and demand," the immutability of which you have so often and so unctuously spoken, the price of the article we have to sell, time (labor), will rise.

Perhaps many of the workers do not argue in this fashion, but their movement to reduce the hours of labor is in line with this reasoning. Where is there the business man, the thinking business man, who is in business for other reasons than "his health," who will say the laborers nay? Is business conducted on other, or more equitable, principles? At least the laborers have on their side all that is just and humane in their claim. They see the genius of ages centered in the wealth producing and wealth distributing methods; they see the unemployed going a-hungered and those depending upon them wither like tender buds before a late blast or frost in spring; they see themselves that they soon may be compelled to change places with those whom society regards as the sub-merged—the unemployed; their children suffer and wane and die; they know that they themselves are unnecessarily required to work burdensome, wearisome and enervatingly long hours; that they and theirs are consequently deprived of the opportunities, which leisure alone affords to lead a better, a higher, a nobler life.

But entirely apart from the reasoning along the lines presented by the above monologue, it can be demonstrated that a reduction in the hours of labor is of the greatest interest and advantage to the wage earners as well as the whole people.

There must be some other cause or incentive which really

THE SHORTER WORKING DAY

forces the workers to demand higher wages for less hours of labor than the mere fact that a better opportunity for demanding it has come or will come.

The fact is, that the workers who have secured a reduction in their working hours can no longer afford to work at such a low rate of wages as was paid them under the old régime of long hours. They have time and leisure on their hands with which they must do something, and do what they may. New tastes are acquired, new desires have been created, with them new expenses are incurred. It may be that the increased leisure brings forth a desire, a taste, a demand for a book, a paper, a magazine, either of which creates a further demand; perhaps, yes, generally for an additional room in the worker's home. An additional room requires additional furnishings, a carpet upon the floor, a picture upon the wall, a musical instrument. Leisure forces the worker's attention to the clothing of the wife and the children, it compels the worker to be in the streets at the time when people are best dressed, he and his must be clad near an approach to the average or be regarded as social inferiors.

Leisure instills the desire to travel, to see other parts. Leisure cultivates tastes for art, music, the concert, operas, the theater. But the new opportunities devoted to or directed in any channel are no longer luxuries. The luxuries of the past have become the necessities of to-day, and all mankind agrees that in order that the workers may be counted upon to continue their labor, their necessities of life must be assured them. It follows, therefore, that to make the luxuries of to-day the necessities of life for the morrow—to continually raise the standard of life of the workers —is in the highest degree sound economy; moral, social, and material progress in the interests of the workers is progress in the interests of all.

Of course, it would be idle to attempt to ignore the charge which is often hurled against the workers' movements to reduce the hours of labor, that the increased leisure would be spent in the saloons in drink. To this charge we can point to the fact that there is even to-day a lesser production and consumption per capita of the liquors the poor usually drink than ever before since statistics have been ascertained, while on the other hand the liquors which the means of the rich only can afford to supply have increased largely per capita and in the aggregate. There is, however, other and better evidence to disprove the charge that the increased leisure of the workers results in drunkenness and debauchery. Workmen as soon as they organize seek meeting rooms in the buildings in which liquor is not sold. The rendezvous of labor, when unorganized, is usually the saloon; when organized, it is transferred to the meeting room, the club room, or library. Before the era of trade union activity, the saloons were the employment agencies. The trade unions in every large center now conduct free labor bureaus, free from saloon influences. Many, particularly unskilled, workmen have had to bear the sacrifices of prolonged strikes to force a change in the places to receive their wages on "pay day," from the saloon to the "job." Countless instances are in evidence that in the old era men had to loiter in and around the saloons to obtain employment, and the "best fellows," who would spend the most time and money to get into the good graces of the saloon keepers, were the ones who obtained employment soonest.

One need but observe the workers whose hours of labor are comparatively low as compared with others whose hours of labor are longer and the contrast is at once noticeable and striking. The short hour worker's complexion is clearer, his eyes are brighter, his carriage and head more erect. These indications are necessarily and invariably absent from the long hour and hard drinking workman. Then again look through the police statistics and notice the comparative scantiness of the number of arrests for drunkenness and disorderly conduct of cases coming from the workmen of those trades where the short hour day prevails.

Those who have carefully observed the changes which have come to the workingman from a reduction in the daily working hours have marked most gratifyingly the fact that they have become most temperate in the liquor as well as in all other habits.[1] Well has it been said that the men who have the spirit

[1] (1) The manager of the extensive paper mills of Prince Paskievitch, of Dobrusch, says that he has been the manager for twenty years, and adds: "The nature of the business requires that the work be carried on day and night. Up to May, 1894, the length of the shifts was 12 hours. Eighteen months ago I determined to try and reduce the hours of those working by the day to 9, and of those employed on shifts to 8. Instead of increased drinking by the workmen, the

THE SHORTER WORKING DAY 91

ground and crushed out of them by their too long hours of toil seek to regain that spirit in the cups at night and at every other conceivable opportunity.

Among thinking men there is no dispute that there is but one way to permanently improve the conditions of the people, that is by improving their habits and customs. We submit to the candid mind that there is no possible way to improve the habits and customs of men whose hours of labor are so long that their opportunities of life are circumscribed by eating so that they may work, sleeping so that they may work, scarcely dreaming or hoping for anything but work. They live to work instead of working to live. What reform, social, moral, political or economic, was ever achieved by the effort of long hour workmen? Which of them ever secured the eradication of a great wrong, stood for, or were identified with, a struggle for a great principle? If the progress of the world depended upon the long hour workers, our civilization would halt, reaction would set in, slavery or serfdom would be the lot of the workers, barbarism and savagery would be the order of the day. Yes, thrice yes, the movement to reduce daily hours of labor to eight, its agitation, inception and enforcement is in the interest of the workers of our country and of the whole world.—*From "The Eight-Hour Workday," American Federationist, April, 1897.*

result has been that the only drink-shop in the place has had to give up business, its place being taken by a tea-shop, where only moderate quantities of spirits can be obtained. "St. Monday" (Blue Monday, S. G.) is almost a thing of the past. The older people, as a rule, employ their leisure time in tilling their plot of land. . . . The younger ones have taken to reading. An orchestral and vocal union has been established, of which 36 factory operatives are members. Between 400 and 500 operatives regularly attend lectures. . . . Such things were impossible under the old 12 hour system; for *there is only one recreation for exhausted workers, and that is spirit-drinking, which quickly stimulates their energies.*"

(2). "It is a flippant libel upon the laboring class which for more than half a century has been constantly repeated but never sustained, viz., that the reduction of the hours of labor tend to lower wages, raise prices, increase idleness, dissipation, and drunkenness. . . . The elimination of poverty, ignorance, pauperism, intemperance, crime, and their accompanying evils, moves parallel with and proportionate to the increase of the social opportunities of the laboring class." Prof. George Gunton's "Economic and Social Importance of the Eight-Hour Movement," page 20.

With the division or subdivision of labor occasioned by the introduction of new tools and machinery the production of wealth or the necessaries and luxuries of life is carried on with greater velocity and speed than ever before. It tends to the cheapening of the selling price; it tends to the cheapening of the cost of production; and the movement on the part of labor for less hours of daily toil increases the demands, wants, and desires of the great body of consumers and gives an additional impetus to production again, and each in turn causes a still greater cheapening in the methods of production and gives an opportunity to the shorter-hour workers to gratify more desires and wants and be greater consumers of the wealth produced; so that there is not by any means a lessening of production. It does not mean the annihilation of the industry. It is true that under the present economic conditions during the process of the introduction and the period immediately after the introduction of new machinery and the specialization of different branches of industry it disarranges that industry, and as a consequence large numbers are thrown out of employment. It rearranges itself in the course of time, but unless the workers avail themselves of the opportunity to get still less hours of labor and increase their consuming power numbers of men are rendered what is popularly known as useless and superfluous, and the lack of a sufficient power of consumption on the part of the people, or rather the lack of opportunity for the widening and broadening of their consuming power, is the fact which contracts seasons of employment and throws workers out of employment. The productivity of labor is so great that unless the hours of labor are reduced those who are employed as producers have little leisure; then again, as consumers, if they do not increase their consuming power of necessity plants close down because labor with machinery has produced so much and the people have not consumed the production commensurately with the increased amount produced.

[Q. Would you say that new machinery, bringing in more rapid processes of production, has lightened the toil of the operatives?] A. No. The organizations of labor have lightened the toil of the workingman, if the toil has been lightened. As a matter of fact, the velocity with which machinery is now run calls forth the expenditure of nearly all the physical and mental force which the wage-earner can give to industry. In substantiation of my negative answer to your question, I would call attention to the fact that after the introduction of machinery, machinery propelled by the motive power of steam, the hours of labor of the working people were from sunup to sundown, and the machinery, which was costly, was not of advantage to the possessor unless it could be operated for a longer period than from sunup to sundown, and it was in that case, as perhaps in all, that necessity being the mother of invention, that which was absent was forthcoming; that was, artificial light to take the place of the rays of the sun after it had set for the day, and with the introduction of artificial light, gas, came the lengthening of the hours of labor of the working people both of the United States and continental Europe. Wherever machinery was introduced the object was to have the machinery operated as long as possible, and with the aid of gas the opportunity came. The organizations of the working people were very fragmentary, and few and weak. The hours of labor were lengthened until lives were destroyed by the thousands; and then came the introduction of woman and child labor. There was no restrictive legislation for them; and then came the efforts of the organizations of labor that called forth a yearning and cry of the whole human family against the slaughter of the innocents in the factories of Great Britain particularly, and subsequently in the United States. . . . It was the efforts of the trade unions of Great Britain, first in their protest, second, in their strikes, and third in their appeals to the public conscience which called forth the factory legislation which limited the hours of labor of women and children in certain industries.—*From testimony before U. S. Industrial Commission, Washington, D. C., April 18, 1899.*

My experience is that it is more difficult to persuade an employer to reduce the hours of labor of his employees, say from 12 to 11, than it is to persuade the employer to reduce the hours of labor of employees from 9 to 8; for as a rule the employers have had the experience after they have the 8-hour day—know what it means. It has never been attended by any other than beneficial results. There is not a reputable business man, there is not a reputable employer of labor, who has given a fair chance for the system of shorter work day but who has invariably become convinced that it is economical as well as socially sound. One of the greatest difficulties in our present movement is to get over the transition period, from the 10- to the 8-hour day, for as a rule it is claimed that the 9-hour day is not satisfactory. There is not any geometric proportion in the division of the day—the division of the time of the day. When 12 hours was the rule, of course if there were two shifts machinery could be operated in two shifts. When 10 hours, there were two shifts, and operators worked dividing up 4 hours; one-third or a portion of the workmen employed for half a day or the machinery would lie idle for repairs, cleaning, etc., for the 4 hours. With the 9-hour day there is a greater period of idleness for the machine, but when the 8-hour day is established, it is not only in its proportion—it seems to be the logical division of the day as well as the economical one. You will find, say, in one establishment the hours of labor are 8, and in another establishment in the same industry the hours are 9; my contention is, and I think it can be easily demonstrated, that the employer who operates his establishment under the 8-hour day does not suffer by reason of the competition of the employer who works his employees 9 or more hours; not even in the much-vaunted disadvantage which the New England textile manufacturers claim to suffer by reason of longer hours of labor in the southern States.—*From testimony before U. S. Industrial Commission, Washington, D. C., April 18, 1899.*

One contended in one breath that it would mean a loss of wages to the employees, and in the next breath that the product would cost more. Of course they cannot reconcile these two conflicting statements; still they were both urged in opposition to the bill. For instance, Mr. Cramp said he could not compete with the foreign shipbuilders if the eight-hour day was fully inaugurated, yet he admitted that the French shipbuilders were anxious to secure the contract from the Russian Government for the building of some warships; that the Frenchmen were largely the holders of Russian bonds, and the influence of the bondholders was thrown in favor of the French shipbuilders; but in spite of this fact and in spite of the further facts that the French workmen work 11 and 12 hours a day and at lower wages than do the American workmen, while the American journeymen in the shipbuilding trade work 9 or 10, the Cramp company secured the contract, built the ship at a lesser cost than the offer of the French shipbuilders and in just one-half the time. In other words, the French builders wanted five years to build the ship, and, in the language of Mr. Cramp, they built them in 30 months, 2½ years. We contend that reduction in hours of labor does not diminish production; that is, all things being equal. It might not increase production, but all things never remain equal when a reduction of hours of labor is established, for the hours of physical labor that are saved will become hours of opportunities for thought, for improvement, and the millions of hours that were formerly given to manual labor are the millions of golden opportunities for new thought, new inventions, and the cultivation of new tastes which become desires, and finally become necessities of life, and these give the impetus and opportunity for the new machine, for the new tool, that makes production ever greater.—*From testimony before U. S. Industrial Commission, 1900, on the Eight-Hour Day.*

Mr. Moseley called attention to what he believed to be the danger of American employers consenting to a reduction in the hours of labor unless it was universal. In that I take issue absolutely with Mr. Moseley and those who take sides with him. Are we to wait in the United States, and with England with us, until Germany and France and Italy and Spain and Austria and Russia and several other continental European countries shall establish the eight-hour working day before we introduce it in the United States? We say to you gentlemen, "We thank you for your suggestion; we thank you for your good intentions, but we cannot follow your advice."

Incidental to that I want to take cognizance of a remark made by my friend Mr. Gunton last evening in connection with that same subject, when he said that he had known me for many years, rather favorably; that he had always agreed with me and that he finds himself at odds with me on the eight-hour bill which has passed the House of Representatives of the United States and is now before the Senate Committee on Education and Labor. He said he was opposed to that bill because it would result, if enacted, in establishing the eight-hour day "in spots." . . . The fact is that there never yet in the whole world was a great industrial reform inaugurated universally. It always has been inaugurated in spots. . . .

Supposing we were to follow the advice, as workingmen, and join with the employers of labor in the United States in saying that we will not make any effort to introduce the eight-hour work-day in the United States until it becomes universal. Well, perhaps Mr. Rockefeller might send a delegation of trade unionists of the United States to Great Britain, and then we will learn and teach in turn. Then the workingmen of the United Kingdom and the workingmen of the United States having agreed that they are up to date, will send a delegation overseered by Mr. Moseley and Mr. Rockefeller to Germany, and then we will undertake to inaugurate a campaign of education until we have secured the assent of the German manufacturers and the German workingmen. And then we will still continue and jointly, the three perhaps with some successor of Herr Krupp, or some other gentleman of that character, send over a delegation to France, and so on and so on. And in the meantime little Japan will develop into a great industrial country and then we will have to go to Japan and then we will have to wait until China is prepared for the universal eight-hour day.

I say to you, Mr. Moseley and gentlemen, that we won't wait; we won't wait. We know what a shorter workday means; there is not any man upon this floor or anywhere who dares dispute the proposition that a shorter workday means better men, better workmen; more productive workmen; more intelligent workmen; better citizens, more humane men.—*From address before The National Civic Federation, New York City. (American Federationist, February, 1903.)*

Gentlemen, I do not know why they should be opposed to it, for it cannot be, as they allege, and as others have alleged, that it would destroy industries and ruin them financially. They say as follows: "The cost of manufacture cannot be advanced without the loss of these foreign markets, which in turn might deprive them" (meaning the workmen) "of employment."

Now mark you this. We were met by our opponents years ago when we advocated the eight-hour rule, with the statement that "we are building up, and we want to build up our foreign markets. Do not hamper us with eight-hour laws." Now, that

THE SHORTER WORKING DAY

they have built up their foreign markets they say: "We have built up our foreign markets now; we have got them built up; do not reduce the hours of labor for fear we will lose the foreign markets."

But the hours of labor of our workmen have been reduced within the past 20 years. Many industries have gone upon the nine-hour basis, and a large number upon the eight-hour basis. Have our foreign markets been reduced or hurt? Wages have increased. Have we failed in building up our foreign markets? Let us see. . . .

As a matter of fact the United States is now the largest exporting country on the face of the globe, and Great Britain is the second. This fact goes to show that only in those countries where the hours of labor are least and where wages are highest is it possible for employers of labor to successfully compete in the markets of the world. . . .

A gentleman forcibly stated some time ago a fact which I think may bear repetition. It was that he favored an eight-hour workday because it was a human advantage as well as a great industrial and social advantage; that if you want to get all the work you could out of a man immediately, the best thing would be perhaps to work him for 24 hours, and in two days you would have him "all in," and all out of him that you could get out of him; but if you want to work a man for five or six years, work him about 16 hours a day; if you want to work him for 10 years, work him about 11 hours a day; if you want to work him for about 15 years, work him 10 hours a day or nine hours a day. But when you want the very best that can be gotten out of a man, during his whole lifetime, work him eight hours.

I have not the statistics with me now, but I might say to you, gentlemen, that in several of our craft organizations they have proved that the lives of the members of these crafts have been prolonged from five to eight years by reason of the fact of a reduction in the hours of labor. Men have grown in stature by an inch or two by reason of reduction in their hours of labor.—*American Federationist, May, 1904. (From testimony before House Committee on Labor.)*

Interesting facts are being constantly demonstrated relative to the economic advantage resulting from the movement to reduce the hours of labor to eight per day. It is clearly shown that there has been neither diminution in the quantity produced, nor has the quality of work deteriorated by reason of the shorter workday.

A Berlin (Germany) publication, the *Hilfee,* has recently had a symposium of articles contributed by persons qualified to discuss the question from the standpoint of the employer.

It is shown that in 1894 the working time of about forty-three thousand men employed in the English government works was reduced to 48 hours per week, the war department contributing nearly 20,000 men, specially employed by it at Woolwich, the shorter work time aggregating five and three-quarters hours weekly. After more than ten years of this experiment the official report is now made. It says:

When the 48 hour week was commenced the war department figured that the time necessary for stopping and starting machinery at breakfast would be saved, because under the new regulations work would begin after breakfast. Saving of light and fuel was also expected. It was furthermore supposed that the later start of work would induce more regularity and a greater capacity for work on account of improved bodily condition. The department did not, therefore, foresee an increased manufacturing cost. This confidence has now been fully realized. The production has not diminished, and the wages of the piece workers, on the other hand, have not suffered notable reduction, in spite of the fact that the prices remained the same. Workmen employed at time wages received an increase to equal the earnings of the 10-hour day. It was not necessary to raise the number of men working on time. Similar results were obtained in the English marine administration.

Some time ago the French government enacted a law, which goes into operation January 2, 1906, by which the nine-hour day limit for men working under ground is prescribed. The time is counted from the descent of the last man into the shift until the arrival of the first one upon the surface. On and after January 2, 1908, the time will be eight and one-half hours, and after January 2, 1910, eight hours will constitute a day's work. This rule will be absolute. Exceptions will be allowed only after a public investigation has been had to demonstrate its necessity.

In connection herewith it is interesting to note that the contractors employing workmen and performing work for the federal government of the United States are governed by the eight-hour law. By reason of the peculiar interpretation given it by several attorney-generals, this law does not extend to the private shipyards.

However, the building of the two great battleships, the "Connecticut" and the "Louisiana," bear out labor's contention, despite the protest of a number of manufacturers who claimed that the eight-hour day would endanger industry, is uneconomical, and would raise the cost of production. The "Connecticut" was built by the United States federal government at its navy yard at Brooklyn, N. Y., its sister battleship, the "Louisiana," being built by private contractors at their shipyards at Newport News, Va.

The construction of these two ships has demonstrated the wisdom and economy and advantage of the eight-hour day. Upon the privately built ship, the "Louisiana," the workday was 10 hours; on the "Connecticut," built in the Government navy yard, the hour limit was eight. The official report shows that after 528 days, 54.5 per cent. of the hull of the "Louisiana" work was accomplished, while the "Connecticut" showed 53.59 per cent. after 570 days. The material wrought in the "Louisiana" shops weighed 12,216,154 pounds, and the aggregate working time amounted to 2,413,888 hours. The corresponding figures for the "Connecticut" work were 11,391,040 and 1,808,240. During the 10-hour day 50,608 pounds were consequently wrought in one day, and almost just as much, or 50,396 pounds, under the eight-hour limit.

The above facts, absolutely demonstrated beyond question, are another commentary upon the "wise" action of the last House Committee on Labor in propounding its unanswerable questions to the Department of Commerce and Labor.

Time and circumstances will only more clearly show how logical, economic, and advantageous is the demand of organized labor for the general establishment and enforcement of the eight-hour workday among all the toilers of our country.—*American Federationist, November, 1905.*

Why an eight-hour day? Why not a four-hour day? Why—the frivolous query was once put to a representative of labor appearing before a congressional committee—why work at all?

The reply, in soberness and earnestness, is that, whatever may be the future workday when man's command of the forces of nature shall have reached its limit and the instruments of production been carried toward perfection, it is the consensus of opinion, first, that to-day's production in industry is amply sufficient to yield in wages what will permit our wage-workers to support their families at the American standard of living, and, secondly, that eight hours are as many as a man of average strength and health can work and keep up his physical and mental forces, doing justice to his work, and retain his powers during the full possible working period of a lifetime. . . .

The testimony as to what the wage-workers who enjoy the eight-hour day have done with the two hours now their own which once were given to the employer is to be seen in a number of callings in many parts of the country. One effect is beyond doubt. Their new-found time they have employed in such a way as to decrease the death rate, and hence obviously the lost time through illness, in their occupations. Every trade union which pays a death benefit shows from its books a decrease in payments per thousand members since it has had the eight-hour day. In this fact alone, the body of the argument for an eight-hour workday, on the score of health, is carried to the point of conviction. Men who are living longer than their predecessors at the same calling are obviously living better in all the implications of the word. They and their families are housed better, dressed better, fed better, educated better—in all respects, as a whole, are happier. This truth is to be seen in so many industries and communities, it is a truth that so appeals to common sense and ordinary observation, as well as to the conviction developed in us with experience that man tends to elevate himself with opportunity, that to attempt to prove it by statistics and recapitulations of the inquiry were to misapply man's discriminating faculty.

In proposing an eight-hour day the first question to be settled is economic. It is whether the total output will warrant the possible lessening of effective toil. In other words, can society sustain itself and progress on eight hours' work? To this query the industrial wage-workers reply: There has been no diminution of output by reason of the reduction of hours of labor from ten to eight; in not a few occupations the output has not varied from the results of ten hours, the number of human workers remaining the same in proportion. Workers with the aid of new machinery within the period of the present generation have in nearly all occupations vastly increased product. Besides, the cessation of the two hours' work in his vocation has given the worker opportunity to add to his product in his avocations. His leisure hours, it may be said without paradox, have given him the time, opportunity and pleasure of caring for his house, his garden, his side ventures. The eight-hour day has given more, not less, of material things to the world. A whole continent, as is the case with Australia, may have the eight-hour day, and mankind be the richer.—*From "The Eight-Hour Day on Government Work," American Federationist, December, 1910.*

An eight-hour day established by law is enforced by governmental agents. The workers' welfare is taken from under their immediate control, and if not well administered, control can be regained only by prolonged effort and indirect methods. It has been demonstrated that governmental officers perform their duties in a spirit which general opinion demands. Enforcement of labor legislation depends upon the effective force of organized opinion among the workers, which in turn depends upon economic organization. Now, it has been demonstrated that when the achievement of economic ends is entrusted to governmental agents, economic organization is weakened. So proceeds the vicious circle that saps the strength and vitality of the only dependable protection for the toilers.

Some trades have established the eight-hour day by legislation. The miners of Missouri did, and their organization has dwindled away and the spirit of progress has departed with it. The miners of Colorado assert that there is an eight-hour law on the statute books of Colorado—but there was no eight-hour day in the mines. Economic action forced that law upon the attention of the state authorities. Civil war compelled the American people to realize that legislative enactment does not automatically establish the reality.—*American Federationist, January, 1915.*

The socialists and other advocates of securing the eight-hour day by law declare it the "short cut."[1] But is that term ac-

[1] See Vol. I, LABOR AND THE COMMON WELFARE; chapter on "Organized Labor's Challenge to Socialism, the I. W. W., and Bolshevism."

curate? Securement of legislation is a practical problem, not a theoretical one. Lawmakers have regard for those who have power—economic power is what gives John D. Rockefeller political power—organization secures for wage-earners economic power that makes them a political force. For placing labor laws on the statute books and for their enforcement economic organization is necessary.

But the mere passage of a law secures no benefits or protection to wage-earners or any other group of citizens. Laws are enforced by administrative agents and then policies and interpretations determine whether laws afford the desired protection or relief. All interested parties bring their power to bear upon these administrative agents to secure enforcement or non-enforcement of laws. Only through their economic organization can wage-earners obtain power and wield that influence for the appointment of desirable administrative officials or the fulfillment of the duties of these agents.

Redress for the violation of an eight-hour law lies in the courts. The wage-earners in their organized capacity would have to protect their interests and rights in the courts and would have to get the judiciary to understand the labor side of the cases.

To secure the eight-hour day by such a "short cut" it would be necessary for the wage-earners to control the legislators, the administrative agents and the judiciary. At no time would they retain in their own hands control over conditions under which they spend the best hours of their lives.

The stipulation of industrial relations by law does not result in industrial freedom—it only restates all industrial problems in terms of political issues. It substitutes a political boss for an industrial employer. What would it profit the wage-earners working for the Rockefeller interests to exchange Rockefeller for a Root or a Taft?

Industrial freedom can be achieved only when workers participate in determining their own hours, wages and conditions of work. This is an industrial problem that must be worked out in the industrial field. It becomes a political problem only when the government is connected with the industry or where the industry is especially hazardous.

There is no "short cut" to industrial freedom. Industrial freedom can not be bestowed on workers. They must achieve their own freedom and enjoy it as the reward of a good fight to establish their rights.

It has been affirmed that the initiative, referendum and recall put the people in control of the government. Verily did not all these exist in Colorado, together with an eight-hour law for the miners, and yet is not the memory and the present consequences of the Colorado miners' strike a disgrace to our American nation? Until the miners of Colorado are organized in their trade union they can not maintain their rights! That they will so organize through trade union effort is as sure as the rising and setting of the sun.

The socialist pamphlet falsely states that the United Mine Workers of America have built up one of the strongest unions in the world by urging men to struggle for an eight-hour workday both through agreements with their employers and *through legislation.* The facts contradict this statement. When the miners began their efforts to organize, the American Federation of Labor put itself back of that movement. Where the miners have built up strong economic organizations they have the eight-hour day which was secured and is enforced by the economic organization. For years the miners were unorganized and suffered reduction after reduction in wages, alternating the work in a week of days of long hours with others of no work at all. Miserable, impoverished and serf-like! It was a tremendous task to make the miners conscious of their own miserable condition, but it was done, and when the 1897 strike was inaugurated, the spark of renewed life of regenerated people was manifest among the miners, and as a result of that great victorious strike, the eight-hour day was achieved, established and maintained by the coal miners in the bituminous regions. The spirit of the men and the movement found its counterpart among the coal miners of the anthracite regions, and after the great strikes the nine-hour day among other achievements was established. At this moment a great campaign is being conducted for the thorough organization of the anthracite miners to secure the eight-hour day. The eight-hour day for the miners was, therefore, not secured through legislation, but by the misunderstood and misrepresented trade union movement. The miners of Colorado attempted to secure the eight-hour workday by law but the eight-hour day was one of the *demands* of the Colorado miners in their recent strike. The official journal of the mine workers plainly states in its editorial columns that the United Mine Workers of America owe their successes to economic organization.

Where the miners have built up strong organizations and have depended upon those organizations for securing industrial betterment they have made progress and have secured greatly improved conditions. A most significant incident is connected with the recent strike of the miners in eastern Ohio. They have recently secured through their trade union an agreement for the "mine-run" basis of payment, a condition which they had vainly endeavored to secure through legislation. After many years, they had secured the enactment of a law providing for the run-of-mine payment. It was opposition to this law that caused the mine operators to close down their mines before the law went into effect, and to use every influence to secure the repeal of the law by the state legislature. Through their economic power the miners persisted in their demands and secured recognition of this claim even while the state legislature was repealing the law that made the provision.

So far as statutory enactment is concerned, the miners of Illinois have no better conditions of work than the miners of Colorado, but any one who has any knowledge at all of the mining conditions in Illinois and mining conditions in Colorado knows that the conditions under which the miners of Colorado are forced to work are incomparably worse than the conditions under which the miners of Illinois work. The miners of Illinois are solidly organized. The miners of Colorado are struggling to organize.—*From pamphlet, "The Workers and the Eight-hour Workday," 1915.*

Trade unions have been derided as materialistic and lacking in idealism because they concentrate their forces upon securing higher wages, a shorter workday and better conditions of work. Very recently their position has been justified and endorsed by a man recognized as a world authority on human health—Major-General William C. Gorgas. General Gorgas has demonstrated his ability as a practical scientist by transforming the deadly Panama Canal Zone into a healthful community.

General Gorgas recognizes that community healthfulness must

THE SHORTER WORKING DAY

be accompanied by individual healthfulness. A condition necessary to health of mind and body is wages adequate to buy sufficient nourishing food, adequate clothing and to provide proper surroundings. In a recent interview this practical scientist said:

"Add to the laboring man's wage from $1.25 to $2.50 a day, and you will lengthen the average American's thread of life by thirteen years at least."

It is a matter of common information that wages vary inversely with daily hours of work—decreasing the length of the workday is invariably accompanied by wage increases and increased productive ability.

Low wages have vicious effects upon national vigor and power —poorly paid workers usually deteriorate in physical and mental ability and in power to produce. Low wages increase the numbers of the unemployable. No nation can retain its power when the masses of its citizenship are existing upon inadequate wages.

The importance of the rank and file of the nation General Gorgas recognizes:

"The rich are overeating. The poor are undereating. Both are contributing to short lives.

"But where overeating shortens the life of one person in one hundred, undereating shortens that of ninety-nine. If we are to lengthen the average life, we must pay attention to the poor man."

This splendid enunciation of the fundamental principles of true statesmanship confirms the justice and the value of the purposes which trade unions attain. Whether or not high wages is a materialistic ideal depends upon the uses to which the wages are put, but they are the necessary means for attaining even the most exalted purposes. It is necessary to sustain life in order to do things in this world—the better the life the greater energy there is to do things.

The report which Geo. W. Perkins, president of the Cigarmakers' International Union, made to the Baltimore convention of the cigarmakers in 1912, contains illustrations of the principles General Gorgas has declared. In 1886 the cigarmakers secured the eight-hour day. Since then they increased wages more than 50 per cent.

In 1888 the average length of life of members of the Cigarmakers' International Union was thirty-one years; in 1890 the average had been increased to thirty-seven years; in 1900 to forty-three years; in 1910 to forty-nine years and in 1911 to fifty years. The organization which decreased daily hours of work and increased wages had thus increased the average lives of cigarmakers by eighteen years in a period of twenty-three years.

These principles are further confirmed by the life statistics of the wives of cigarmakers. In 1890 the average life of the wives of union members was thirty-eight years; in 1900, forty-six years; in 1910, fifty years; in 1911, forty-eight years. The average increase during this period of twenty-one years is ten years.

What the cigarmakers' union has accomplished has been duplicated by nearly all other trade unions; the latter have not taken occasion to so accurately set forth their achievements.—*From pamphlet, "The Workers and the Eight-hour Workday," 1915.*

The mere enactment of eight-hour legislation would not decrease one iota the necessity for economic organization and the economic struggle. Indeed, instead of helping, it only adds another obstacle to the achievement of a real, general eight-hour day. Instead of employees dealing directly with their employers, it would be necessary for the organizations to use their influence upon lawmakers to secure the enactment of an eight-hour law in all private industries and occupations, and then continue to use their influence even more remote and indirect upon the administrative agents whose duty it would be to enforce the law, and again, whatever influence they might have still more remote and indirect, in securing an understanding and a favorable interpretation of the eight-hour law by the judiciary. Who knows but that by judicial interpretation and enforcement an eight-hour law would work to the undoing of labor's fight of ages for freedom?—*American Federationist, March, 1916.*

The workers recognizing the futility and injury in the lowering of standards to lengthen working hours will resist all efforts in that direction. Their position is justified by experience wherever the eight-hour day has been tried.

This is the declaration of the Ford Motor Company:

THE SHORTER WORKING DAY

"A certain group of men working nine hours under the old system assembled 750 radiators. The same group working eight hours under the new plan assembled 1,300 radiators. A group of men working nine hours under the old plan turned out 38 fenders. Under the new, working eight hours, the same men turned out 50 fenders. A group of 65 men working nine hours under the old system turned out 800 gas tanks. Under the new, working eight hours, the 65 men turned out 1,200. Hours were reduced, wages increased and cost went down."

The McElwain Company (whose experience is fully recorded elsewhere in this issue) reached this conclusion:

"To sum up, our whole experience tends to justify the shorter-hours movement. We are absolutely convinced that it is right for the community as a whole, because we feel sure it would increase the *net* productivity of society. We *believe* it is right for the individual factory unit because we have come to realize that even in an individual plant the real problem is to get the maximum amount of work done by a given thousand people, not in a day, in a week, or in a year, but in a lifetime."

The contentions of the workers are based upon facts. They refuse to be swept from their position by war hysteria.

Eight hours in peace or in war is our slogan to conserve human life and insure greatest output.—*American Federationist, June, 1917.*

V

THE UNION SHOP AND THE "OPEN" SHOP

Agreements for the closed shop, says the court, are void because they tend to create a monopoly; because they discriminate against workmen who are not members of unions.

Think of the absurdity of this argument!

Does not any contract with A exclude B, C, D, and all the rest? Let the reader mentally question himself somewhat as follows:

"If I have work to do am I bound to give it to a dozen men instead of to one man?"

"If I am a real estate owner and build a whole row of houses must I employ as many architects and contractors as there are houses in the row?"

"If I am an owner of a mill and need raw material for the production of cotton cloth must I buy my cotton of a number of parties?"

"Does any law prohibit my making a contract with one planter for all the raw cotton I need?"

What difference is there between buying raw material or tools and machinery and employing labor?

Is the employer obliged to make individual contracts with workmen?

Is it the business of any one whether he employs union men or non-union men?

If it is not, and he chooses to make a contract with a union, has anybody the right to object? . . .

A manufacturer may buy all his raw material, all his machinery, from one company. No one is idiotic enough to tell him that he must patronize a dozen different companies. Why may he not buy all his labor of one union? He may close his shop to all manufacturers of raw material except one; he may not, if he be "American," close his shop to all workmen but those who are members of a given union which offers to supply him with labor. . . .

And why should not the union man work with and beside the non-union man? That, frankly, is none of the employer's business. Labor is under no obligation to justify its likes and dislikes to him. We were constantly told that supply and demand regulated the employment of labor, and that the market was free and should remain so. This being the case (we grant it for the argument's sake), the workman may say to the employer that he will not work for him except on certain terms, which terms may include an agreement on the employer's part to engage no men obnoxious to him.

These propositions cannot be denied. No one has been hardy enough to contend that union men may be *compelled* to work with non-union men, or that the former may, by law or judicial process, be prohibited from striking against the employment of the latter. In view of these facts, what life or meaning is there left in the "open shop" proposition? . . .

As was pointed out in the open letter issued by the Executive Council of the American Federation of Labor, we do not deny the right of the non-union man to work where, when, and for whomsoever he pleases. We simply insist upon the same right of all union men to refuse to associate with them in factory or in the club, and we insist upon our right to tell employers that they must have either union shops or non-union shops. They will not bully us into working under objectionable conditions by affecting to believe in any straw or impossible "principle." If they want our labor, they must make it pleasant for us to work for them. . . .

Since every man has the right to sell his labor as he sees fit, he has the right *not to sell it* to the employer who wants an "open shop."

Every man has the right to say: "I will not work for you unless you make a contract with the union to which I belong, and agree to employ none but members of that union." To say that he may not say this is equivalent to saying that he must sell his labor, not as *he* sees fit, but as the employer sees fit. . . .

Even if all the courts in the country should decide that the union shop contract is illegal, an impossible supposition, the union shop would not disappear. The only result would be that no such contract would be made; the condition would be enforced without written contract.

You can not, the courts of the whole United States can not, force American citizens to work for employers they do not trust or like, or associate with workmen they do not like or respect.

Men can not be imprisoned for refusing to work under certain conditions and the injunction can not be employed in such a case. . . .

So much for this, for the open shop nonsense is general. As to our friends, the clothiers, fair newspapers have pointed out that even those who do not like the union shop prefer it to the sweat shop. We quote the following from the *Boston Transcript*, a conservative and dignified newspaper:

> Some years ago, when the shops were "free and open," the employment of an American in the clothing shop was the exception. The garment maker took advantage of unrestricted immigration, and filled the sweat shops with the cheap labor of distressed European refugees until the conditions became so appalling that society stepped in and laws were enacted to improve the sanitary condition of the shops and limit the hours of labor of women and children. The manufacturer who had brutalized the clothing operatives by taking advantage of the supply of labor in the market was compelled to halt by the exercise of a vigorous humane public sentiment, not by their own disposition.
>
> Now it is all very well to talk about the "old American system" and win a little applause for seeming patriotism, but it is not within reasonable comprehension that a return to the primitive conditions of clothing manufacture in this country is possible. The sweat shop is distinctly un-American, and anything which tends to bring it back must be resisted by an enlightened public sentiment. Indeed, if we are to return to a distinctly American system we must go back of the sweat shop to the time when the wool was cut from the back of the sheep, carded, and spun and the clothing made at home. . . .

The unions, through the "closed" shop, abolished the sweat shop and secured for the garment workers the right of contract, an "American" right, and decent conditions.

We could call attention to a symposium in the July number of the *Monthly Review* of the Civic Federation on the question of the "closed" shop. Eight lawyers discussed the Adams opinion and only one of them, a corporation and trust attorney of Chicago, upheld the view that a union shop contract is void and contrary to public policy. Some of these articles used lan-

THE UNION SHOP AND THE "OPEN" SHOP

guage nearly as strong as that which we, a lay critic, used in our editorial last month. Let us give a few extracts:

Mr. John Frankenheimer, of New York, says: "There can be nothing illegal in the efforts of unionists to make the shop in which they work a union shop, that is, to agree with the employer as a condition of rendering services to him that he will employ only members of the union. The employer is at liberty to refuse to limit employment to unionists, but if he does this the unionist must be at liberty to cease to work for him, that is, to strike."

Mr. John B. Parsons, of New York, writes: "They (workingmen) may strike without notice and under circumstances which are most favorable to the accomplishment of their wishes, even if most injurious to their employers, always provided that they do not resort to criminal means or to anything which is in the nature of intimidation or violence, and equally do I understand that in the absence of statutory legislation to the contrary it is the right of employers to employ or not to employ whom they choose, and to make with their workmen any agreements which are for mutual interests, etc."

Mr. William V. Rooker, of Indianapolis, says: "It is to be supposed that if some paper manufacturer were to agree that for a certain price for a certain quality he would for a certain time furnish the Chicago *Tribune* all its white paper, that contract, according to Judge Adams, would create a monopoly and be void. . . . Judge Adams seems to be suffering from judicial strabismus to the extent that he can not see that the employers' constitutional right to contract would be destroyed rather than conserved by such a rule."

Mr. Jackson H. Ralston, of Washington, D. C., writes: "The learned court ignores the fact that labor is property, so to speak, in the hands of the laborer quite as much as a right to do business is property in the hands of the head of a mercantile establishment. . . . Suppose they (organized workmen) unitedly determine not to labor in association with negroes or under a red-haired foreman or with men of another nationality, why may they not do so? In so doing they simply dispose of their own property rights as deemed meet by them."

Mr. Louis D. Brandeis, of Boston, writes: "It does not interfere with an employer's right of contract to induce him to enter into a certain contract. Every contract which any person enters into interferes in some way with his future freedom of contract of other action. That is the very purpose of entering into a contract. The "right of contract" is the right to restrict one's freedom of action. No sufficient reason suggests itself why he (an employer) should not be permitted to agree in advance for a limited time or until further notice to employ only union men."—*From pamphlet, "Open Shop Editorials," reprinted from American Federationist, 1903 and 1904.*

The non-union man accepts all we win for him, but he contributes nothing of time or money or thought to the struggle. We invite him to come into our ranks and help himself. We admit his legal right to stay out, but we deny his moral right to withhold his assistance in such a fight for bare justice. . . .

The strikebreaker is simply the man who undersells prices and breaks the market. We ask him not to break the standard rate of wages which it has taken so many years to establish. We ask him to join us. We are doing everything for him. He is doing nothing for us or for himself. We are fighting for a minimum wage, for a living wage.—*American Federationist, February, 1903.*

Recently the opponents of organized labor started an agitation for what they euphoniously designate as the "open shop;" and several employers, otherwise fair, having been persuaded that the proposition on the surface appears to be ethical, have advocated it. On the other hand, our movement stands for the union shop, not, as our opponents designate it, the closed shop; for, as a matter of fact, a union shop is not a closed shop. Any wage-earner, a member of an organization in any part of the country, can enter the union shop. And any wage-earner, competent to fill any position in the union shop, is not only eligible to ·enter to work therein, but the organizations have their hundreds of missionaries at work, in and out of season, urging and pleading with them to enter the wide-open doors of the union. This so-called open shop is the disintegrating factor that leads to the non-union shop; in other words, the shop which is closed to the union man, no matter from whence he hails or what his skill and competency.

The so-called open shop influences wages and the standard of life to the downward course, for it is based upon the sycophancy of the most docile, and the most immediate needs of those in direst distress, of the poorest situated among the workmen.

Agreements or joint bargains of organized labor with employers depend for their success upon the good will of the union and the employers toward each other. Neither should be subject to the irresponsibility or lack of intelligence of the non-unionist, or his failure to act in concert with, and bear the equal responsibility of, the unionist. Hence, the so-called open shop makes agreements and joint bargains with employers impracticable, if not impossible. The union can not be responsible for non-unionists whose conduct often renders the terms of the agreement ineffective and nugatory.

Inasmuch as the most conspicuous antagonists of organized labor are sponsors for what they term the open shop, upon the pretense of the liberty of the individual, the thought forces itself upon us to ask:

"When, in history, have the opponents of any movement for the uplifting of the masses constituted themselves the advocates and defenders of the liberty and freedom of the people?"—*From annual report to A. F. of L. convention, Boston, Mass., November, 1903.*

The union shop *rests* on the freedom of contract, or individual liberty. There is no greater element of "monopoly" in it than in any other contract for services or materials. If you give work to A, you can not give the same work to B. Has B any grievance? Would it not be ridiculous for him to object to the contract in the name of equality? . . . There is no blow at idealism in the union shop. There would be if the unions were close corporations, monopolies, aristocracies. But are they not working day and night to extend their influence to convert new men, to organize all their fellows?—*American Federationist, October, 1904.*

Even taking the charge as it is intended, that the unions deny to workmen the right of employment. I have denied it; I deny it now, and stoutly state that it is not true. But suppose for a moment that it were true; what do we find our employers and our business men doing when their interests are involved?

Take a newspaper publishing house; the proprietor enters into a contract with the machinery manufacturer to furnish him with machines; he enters into an agreement with the paper company of the paper trust to furnish him with all the paper he needs; certainly every other machinery manufacturer is excluded from furnishing that newspaper company with any machinery, and has as much right to complain of being excluded of the opportunity to furnish machines as has the non-union man to complain that he is denied the right of employment in a union shop.

The master builders, when they undertake the erection of a building, contract for the furnishing of iron, and steel, and brick, and mortar, and lumber, and other material; the contracts are given to certain establishments; all others are excluded from furnishing this material.

It is the contract relations between the newspaper publisher on the one hand and the men who are to furnish them with materials on the other; and what is true of those industries which I have named is true in the largest measure of every industry in the country; and, while all this is admitted to be perfectly correct, particularly when the newspaper publisher, when the master builder, when the iron manufacturer, when the clothing manufacturer, when the sheet and iron manufacturers, give out their contracts, yet it is denied to labor, to the workingman and the workingwoman, the right to jointly come together and determine that they will effect a joint bargain for the sale of their labor, and endeavor to secure the best business conditions for the sale of the only thing they possess in this world—their power to labor.—*American Federationist, April, 1905. (From address at Rochester, N. Y.)*

We sometimes still hear the demagogic claim put forth by organized labor's opponents that the union shop, with its agreement with employers, is improper and unjust. Our opponents pretend that they stand for the liberty and the rights of workmen. That, as a rule, "open shop" declarations were accompanied or immediately followed by wage reductions or the imposition of poorer conditions upon employees, is a fact patent to all who have given the subject thought and investigation.

Is it not a novel position for the worst antagonists to labor's

THE UNION SHOP AND THE "OPEN" SHOP

interests to assume that they are the advocates and defenders of the rights and the liberties of workmen? The mere statement of such a position demonstrates its hypocrisy and absurdity.

Organized labor's insistence upon and work for, not the "closed shop," as our opponents term it, but the union shop, in agreement with employers, mutually entered into for the advantage of both and the maintenance of industrial peace with equity and justice for both, is to the economic, social and moral advancement of all our people.

The union shop, in agreement with employers, is the application of the principle that those who enjoy the benefits and advantages resulting from an agreement shall also equally bear the moral and financial responsibilities involved.

In my reports to previous conventions and in editorials in our official magazine, I have often dealt with this subject definitely and fully. Our Federation has approached this question intelligently and manfully. There should be no recession from our logical and just position. It should be reiterated and emphasized. At the same time we should direct our effort still further and better to organize our fellow wage-earners; to instill in them the principles of duty well done—the principles of fraternity, solidarity, and justice—to make our organizations of still greater benefit to them than is even now the case, and that by reason of greater advantages the unions will be more deserving of their good-will, respect, and confidence. Thus will the still lingering opposition to the union shop be eliminated from the field of industrial controversy.—*From annual report to A. F. of L. convention, Pittsburg, Pa., November, 1905.*

It is true beyond doubt that there is a change of feeling among a large number of employers. This is shown by the employers' association in Seattle and many other cities throughout the country who have tired of the Van Cleave slogan of the so-called "open shop" and are now in agreement with organized labor; who find by experience that the most competent, intelligent, and self-respecting workers are in the ranks of the much misunderstood labor organizations of our country. The Typothetæ (employing printers' association) recently adopted a resolution departing from the so-called "open shop" policy, giving their members power and authority to enter into trade agreements with the printing trades unions, and to establish the eight-hour day.

The collective bargain, the trade agreement, is coming to be recognized as the proper method by intelligent, far-seeing employers. They realize that these are an intellectual and economic advantage in adjusting the relations and labor conditions with employees.

In the recent negotiations between the representatives of the United Mine Workers of America and the coal operators in the anthracite regions, the agreement reached, while not recognizing the union in specific terms yet agreed that the representatives of the organization should represent all the men before the companies and arbitration boards in any grievance which they might have. It was agreed that ordinary business between the unions and their members may be transacted upon the companies' grounds and in the mines, and that men discharged for activity in the cause of unionism may appeal, have the case reviewed, with a view to reinstatement.

The modification of the Buck's Stove and Range injunction against the American Federation of Labor by the District of Columbia Court of Appeals, and the recent Minnesota decision of Justice Elliott, all tend to show the broadening of the public conception of the rights of the wage-earners to organize, to protect and promote their rights and their interests, and to secure for themselves and their fellows the very best possible conditions under which they render so valuable a service to society.—*American Federationist, June, 1909.*

One of the great compromises of the protocol [agreement between cloakmakers' union and manufacturers' association, New York, Sept. 2, 1910] was the "preferential" union shop—each member of the manufacturers' association to maintain a shop where union standards as to working conditions, hours of labor, rates of wages were to prevail. In hiring workers, as between two of equal skill, union members were to be preferred. This agreement was based on the theory that the union is an agency working for the uplift and betterment of all its members; that cooperation between the union and the organized manufacturers is necessary to the interests of all concerned in the industry. As the protocol stated, "the manufacturers declare their belief in

THE UNION SHOP AND THE "OPEN" SHOP

the union and that all who desire its benefits should share its burdens," and for this reason they granted preference to those who belonged to the union.

This was indeed a tremendous step in advance of the old times when the employers declared themselves unalterably in favor of the "open shop." The preferential union shop in practice has resulted in the establishment of the union shop. Boards to carry out the purposes of the protocol were provided for in its terms. A joint board of sanitary control, composed of seven members, was created to establish standards which unions and manufacturers obligated themselves to maintain.—*American Federationist, March, 1913.*

VI

CHILD LABOR AND WOMEN IN INDUSTRY

And now I would call your attention to the fact that the annual reports of the various Bureaus of Labor Statistics show a large and abnormal increase in the employment of women and children in many industries. It becomes our duty to endeavor to modify the evils resulting from such employment. We know to our regret that too often are wives, sisters and children brought into the factories and workshops only to reduce the wages and displace the labor of men—the heads of families. First and foremost, we should bend our energies to the organization of laboring women in trade unions, and secure education for the children. The children must be protected alike from the ignorant greed of their parents as well as the rapacious avarice of their employers.

The demand for "equal pay for equal work regardless of sex" is only a *demand* made by trade unions but often enforced at the cost of hardships and sacrifices entailed by bitter and prolonged strikes. It is one thing to mouth a sentiment and another to make sacrifices for its achievement.—*From annual report to A. F. of L. convention, Baltimore, Md., December, 1887.*

Within the last twelve months many workingwomen of our country in several industries have been emancipated from false sentiment in the labor movement and organized upon the practical basis of trade unions, and in each of the instances referred to a material improvement in their economic and social conditions has been the result. I again recommend that special attention be paid by our friends and fellow-toilers to aid and encourage, with all the means at our command, the organization of trade unions among women and girls, so that they may learn the stern fact, that if they desire to achieve any improvement in their condition, it must be through their own self-assertion in the trade union.

So far as the labor of children is concerned, it is the same sad story; the exploitation of the tender and young, drawn into the factory, into the shop, into the mill, into the mine and the stores by the drag-net of modern capitalism, frequently to supplant the labor of their parents; robbed in their infancy of the means of an education, dwarfed both in mind and body, what may we expect of the future manhood and womanhood of America? Apart from all material considerations, humanity and patriotism cry aloud against this great wrong of our time. I am conscious of the fact that the general Government under present conditions can do very little towards bringing about a change in this deplorable state of affairs; but I urge upon you, as I do upon all the working people of our country, to do all that lies in your power in the various States to see that a law shall be passed, absolutely prohibiting the employment of any child in any occupation until it shall have arrived at least at the age of fourteen years. I repeat what I said one year ago, "children must be protected from the ignorant greed of their parents, as well as from the rapacious avarice of their employers."—*From annual report of A. F. of L. convention, St. Louis, Mo., December, 1888.*

Of all the ills that mankind suffers from, the unjust and cruel tendencies of modern methods of wealth-producing, the one that seems to me to rise to horrible proportions is that of child labor.

Our centers of industry with their mills, factories and workshops, are teeming with young and innocent children, bending their weary forms with long hours of daily drudgery, with pinched and wan cheeks, and emaciated frames, dwarfed both physically and mentally, and frequently driven to premature decay and death. The innocent smile of youthful happiness is soon transformed into wrinkles and other evidences of early decay. The life's blood of the youth of our land is too frequently sapped at the foundation.

The hope of a perpetuity of free institutions is endangered when the rising generation is robbed of the opportunity to enjoy the healthful recreations of the play grounds or the mental improvements of the school house,

The children of the workers have none to raise a voice in their defense other than the organized wage-workers, and I appeal to you to take such action as will protect them from the contemptible avarice of unscrupulous corporations and employers.—*From annual report to A. F. of L. convention, Detroit, Mich., December, 1890.*

One of the consequences of modern industry has been the forcing of women and girls into the factories and workshops, not that the result may inure to their benefit, but to the injury of the male workers.

Hood's "Song of the Shirt" has just as much cause to be sung to-day as it had when written, and when it thrilled all humanity and cast a blush upon the cheeks of the people. Now, however, we trace the cause of the wrongs inflicted upon the women workers, and find that it is due to a lack of that one factor, by which it is at all possible to raise them from the sloughs of poverty, despair and helplessness, namely—organization.

The lack of organization among our sisters of labor is the main cause of their misery, and the unfair discrimination in the wages paid and consideration given to them.

I commend to your consideration the absolute necessity of taking special action looking to a systematic agitation for the organization of the women wage-workers. To give a clearer insight to the delegates to this convention, invitations have been extended to two women (who have given this question particular study) to read a brief paper each before this convention.—*From annual report to A. F. of L. convention, Birmingham, Ala., December, 1891.*

Of the many injustices and wrongs growing out of our modern industrial system, none is so grievous or so inexcusable as that of the employment of young and innocent children who should be in the schoolroom, the playground or the home; developing their physical, mental, and moral well-being. Surely, in our day, with the wonderful productive forces of steam and electricity, and the highest developed machinery found anywhere on the globe, there is not even a semblance of an excuse to exploit the labor of children of tender years for profit and private gain to the detriment of the manhood and womanhood of our day, and the future of those who are now too often dwarfed through the rapacity of conscienceless employers.

From the earliest period our modern trade unions have always been in the forefront to demand the protection and safety of the children, insisting that inasmuch as they are liable to the cupidity of the profit-mongers as well as the ignorance of some parents, they should be regarded as the wards of the state; that it, with its power, should step in and see to it that its future citizens, men and women alike, should not become mental or physical deformities or derelicts in the body politic.

Conforming to this purpose, the American Federation of Labor at the last convention, issued instructions that further and strenuous efforts be made to secure the enactments of laws in those States of the Union which have none for the prohibition or restriction of the labor of children. Pursuant to this instruction the coöperation of the organized workers and sympathizers with our movement in the southern States was sought and obtained. Bills were introduced in the legislatures in Georgia, North and South Carolina, Alabama and Tennessee. Despite our strenuous efforts, we were unsuccessful in securing the passage of these laws in the four first-named states.

The committee has reported favorably on the child labor bill in Alabama. With strenuous efforts we hope that it will be enacted into law. It would be an advantage and honor to the people of Alabama which we hope will soon be followed by similar humane, safe, and economically sound laws upon the statutes of every State in the Union.

In South Carolina the mill owners induced the legislature to defeat the bill by a promise to inaugurate the 66-hours-a-week rule, providing no law on the subject was passed. When, by indirection, it is thus made manifest that children are required to work more than 11 hours per day, and the employers, fearing the enactment of a 10-hour a day law, prevent the enactment of a 10-hour limit, it is not difficult to determine how necessary it is that our work shall be prosecuted with earnestness and vigor until we shall have secured the passage of just and humane laws, and that the present well-being and future safety of children shall not be subject to the whims or the tender mercies of those who have no conception of their duties to the human family and whose only divinity is the almighty dollar, or a per cent. in dividends.

In Tennessee, through the coöperation of all labor's forces and with the aid of sympathizers with our cause, we were enabled to secure the passage of a law prohibiting the labor of children under fourteen years of age, and restricting the labor of minors above that age to ten hours per day.

In those states in which laws upon the subject are not on the statute books, and whose legislatures are in session, efforts on these lines have been renewed and are now being vigorously prosecuted. In the interests of the children as well as of all our people, now and for the future, the American Federation of Labor will persevere until success has finally and fully crowned our efforts.—*From annual report to A. F. of L. convention, Scranton, Pa., December, 1901.*

It is not my purpose, either now or at any other time, to discuss the race problem; but it may not be amiss to call attention to an event in connection therewith, and to draw from it the lesson it teaches. Several of the southern States have practically disfranchised the negro by prescribing an educational qualification and test. The fact is that a large part of the negroes of the South are making every effort to secure an education for their children. On the other hand, the children employed in the mills are white. They are being physically and mentally dwarfed; they have not the time, opportunity, or physical ability to attain an education of the most elementary character; and unless the relief we demand shall be accorded by the legislatures of the southern States, the people thereof may find themselves in the position of having missed their mark, for the disfranchised will be the immense number of the white men of the future. Child labor is a menace to our civilization, involving as it does the deterioration of our race.—*From annual report to A. F. of L. convention, New Orleans, La., November, 1902.*

Nor do I wish to be understood to be opposed to the full and free opportunity of woman to work whenever and wherever necessity requires. It has been the policy of my associates and myself to throw open wide the doors of our organizations and invite the working girls and working women to membership for their and our common protection. It is in the unions of labor that the full rights of the working women are proclaimed and asserted, defended and contended for; and many a contest has been waged by union men to secure for women equal wages and conditions for equal work performed.

It is not for any real preference for their labor that the unscrupulous employer gives work to girls and boys and women, but because of his guilty knowledge that he can easily compel them to work longer hours and at a lower wage than men. It is the so-called competition of the unorganized, defenseless woman worker, the girl and the wife, that often tends to reduce the wages of the father and husband, so that frequently in after years, particularly in factory towns, the combined wages of the husband and wife, the father and daughter, have been reduced to the standard of the wages earned by the father or husband in the beginning.

I contend that the wife or mother, attending to the duties of the home, makes the greatest contribution to the support of the family. The honor, glory, and happiness that come from a beloved wife and the holiness of motherhood are a contribution to the support and future welfare of the family that our common humanity does not yet fully appreciate. . . .

There is no reason why all the opportunities for the development of the best that woman can do should be denied her, either in the home or elsewhere. I entertain no doubt but that from the constant better opportunity resultant from the larger earning power of the husband the wife will, apart from performing her natural household duties, perform that work which is most pleasurable for her, contributing to the beautifying of her home and surroundings.

In our time, and at least in our country, generally speaking, there is no necessity for the wife contributing to the support of the family by working—that is, working as here understood, by wage labor. In our country, rich and fertile as any in the world, producing wealth in such prodigious proportions, the wife as a wage-earner is a disadvantage economically considered, and socially is unnecessary.—*American Federationist, January, 1906.*

It has been within my recollection when the Hon. Elbridge T. Gerry, of New York, for many years active in the movement for the protection of children, came before the conventions of the American Federation of Labor, and said that the hope and the mainstay for the inauguration, the enactment, and the enforcement of child labor laws rests in the last degree upon the organizations of labor.—*From address before National Child Labor Committee, Washington, D. C. (American Federationist, March, 1906.)*

The humane work inaugurated and conducted by the labor movement to eliminate child labor in the industrial and commercial affairs of our country has borne good fruit and is destined to bring still better results.

In the early history of labor's efforts to obtain this end, we were met by the bitterest and most relentless antagonism. Our motives were aspersed and our efforts ridiculed just as are now the demands which organized labor makes upon society in its claims for the present and for the immediate future.

To-day there is not an institution in our country, political, commercial, financial or religious, but which is committed in some way to the abolition of child labor. Better than all, it is now the universal judgment of all our people that the facts as to the existence of child labor shall be investigated and ascertained and such legislation enacted as shall take the children from the factory, the work-shop, the mill, the mine and the store or anywhere they are employed for profit, and give to them the opportunities and advantages of the home, the school and the playground, that they may imbibe the sunshine and the light to grow into the physical and mental manhood and womanhood of the future.

Several organizations have been formed to coöperate with the labor movement and the awakened public conscience in pressing home upon the law-making bodies the necessity for the abolition of child labor. A number of legislatures have given this subject their favorable consideration and action.

Congress has discussed the evil of child labor with a view to the enactment of a federal law dealing with the question generally. As to the advisability of that method of eradicating the evil, there is a divided opinion. Some contend that the States can more effectually, and under our form of government should more properly, exercise that authority. In any event, the discussion in Congress clearly indicates the general trend of advanced thought upon the question. At least, Congress could enact a law upon the subject covering the Territories and the District of Columbia.

The last Congress directed the Commissioner of Labor to make a comprehensive sociological investigation of the labor of women and children in the United States, and the matter is now receiving attention and action at the hands of the Commissioner and his assistants.

A few months ago a conference was held in Washington, where representatives of a number of organizations met and discussed the question of child labor. Acting under the authority given by the Pittsburg convention, I appointed a committee consisting of James Duncan, John Mitchell, D. A. Hayes, John Golden, B. A. Larger, Daniel Harris, and Herman Robinson to participate therein.

The conference decided to coöperate with the Commissioner of Labor in the investigation, and, if necessary, to ascertain all the facts obtainable with a view to such coöperative action as shall at an early date free our country and our people from the stigma of exploiting young children for profit. There is not one question more important to the solution of which we should continue to give our unqualified attention than to the elimination of child labor from our industrial and commercial system.—*From annual report to A. F. of L. convention, Norfolk, Va., November, 1907.*

The most precious heritage of a nation is its children. This truth is scarcely yet fully realized. One of the greatest dangers to the health and patriotic life of a country has been the exploitation of our helpless children. Children are the wards of the nation, the responsibility of which can not and must not be shifted. The century past was noted for many remarkable discoveries, but none was greater than that of the great economic and social power of women. Our present century will be noted for much greater and more significant advance, the importance of the discovery of child nurture, the value of childhood. The science of raising and training children has only just begun to appeal to the great mass of the people as a serious proposition. When the young heads, hearts, and minds are trained in an intelligent, scientific, and humane course, the era of the industrial slaughter of the innocents will have been obliterated, and they will in their innocence be preserved, cultivated, and developed to their fullest mental, moral and social welfare.

Due to the patient and persistent efforts of the men and women in the great army of organized labor, the dawn of the emancipation of children from the workshop, in all its forms, where their tender bodies are stunted to satisfy rapacity, is now clearly discernible.

In 42 states and the District of Columbia laws now obtain to control and protect children in some form or other, particularly in reference to their employment. The tendency of legislation on this subject is to effectiveness.

In connection therewith it is necessary that your attention, and through you the attention of the great rank and file of the workers and the people generally, be called to the need not only of improved laws upon the subject of children, but that every effort be made so that as near as possible greater uniformity in the laws of the States may be obtained. In the past it was the policy of our opponents to play the backwardness of one State against another, and under the plea of hindrance to economic and industrial progress, the road to success was made doubly difficult. What now is required is to raise the level of the poorest laws in the most backward States to the standard of the best laws in the most progressive States. Let the efforts of all be directed to follow this suggestive plan systematically, and the evil of child labor will be more readily and effectively eradicated from our entire industrial and commercial life.—*From annual report to A. F. of L. convention, Toronto, Can., December, 1909.*

Some other influential portions of society have at last, after our repeated warnings, continual struggles, and gratifying successes, been convinced that we are right in asking protection for the child. They are taking a leaf from our book of endeavor and aspiration and are now rendering us valuable aid in behalf of better child labor laws. This is as it should be, and as it should have been years ago. If it had been so, our newly discovered auxiliaries could more consistently claim credit they are now appropriating without stint. This is another evidence of the truism, "Nothing succeeds like success."

The period has now arrived when the average member of a legislature is proud if he can make a good record on "child labor legislation," and while this inclination prevails it will be well to press home in every State legislature the most complete and efficient measures in the interest of the children.—*From annual report to A. F. of L. convention, St. Louis, Mo., November, 1910.*

Those who deal in or buy the finished products should be made to know and feel the responsibility of the evils of child labor, that any one who in any way encourages the practice that robs helpless little children shall do so in full consciousness of his terrible responsibility. Every buyer and dealer should know when his "bargain" is purchased at the cost of worn, torn childish fingers; of cramped, withered little muscles that ought to be free and easy in play; of bleared, stained child eyes; lungs that are compressed for want of fresh air.
These "bargains" are the price of weary, dreary childhood, aching little hearts that must bear the burdens of life before they have known anything else. Are children so cheap that the "bargains" are of greater value? Or may the little children be turned out to play and be given a chance to live?—*American Federationist, January, 1914.*

The industrial world is no place for those who can not protect themselves. Women must learn to take their work seriously and to solve their own problems. Though their individual connection with employment may be temporary yet the employment of women is not temporary. Women must learn that work problems are concerned with life problems of tremendous importance to other women and the race. They must feel individual responsibility as members of society.—*From article prepared for use in New York State suffrage campaign, September, 1914.*

Because the Cleveland school board had refused requests for higher wages, because no other methods remained, the Cleveland grade teachers organized a union. A union secures results in proportion to the power it can wield. Therefore the teachers considered affiliation to the American Federation of Labor.
The school board declared that no "union teachers" could teach in Cleveland schools. The teachers secured an injunction from Judge Neff forbidding the execution of this declaration.

Nevertheless Superintendent Frederick refused to reappoint teachers who were union leaders. On Sept. 9 Judge Neff cited the superintendent to appear before him for contempt and later found him guilty. . . .

Discussing the right of teachers to organize, the court held:

"The anti-union resolution of the board was vicious in its principle as well as subversive of constitutional liberty. If the board can validly discriminate against labor unions, then it may discriminate because of race, or color, or nationality, or creed, or for any other arbitrary reason. There is no necessary conflict between affiliation with the A. F. of L. and the vocation of a teacher. The testimony submitted in the case shows that all the alarm of strikes and boycotts that seems to have disturbed the board is utterly unfounded, for the reason that strikes among public employees are not tolerated by the Federation. It is un-American and grossly unjust to legislate in any way against those who toil.

"The greatest good to the greatest number can be achieved only by the rule of the common people. The submerged tenth, that is, those whose lives from day to day are merely a continual struggle with poverty, take no part in public affairs. Those at the other end of the social scale, the topmost tenth, the very rich, are too much absorbed in the mad race after money, or in pleasure or dissipation, to take any part in public affairs. So the other 80 per cent, or the middle class, people who work, who labor in some department of life, rule this country. We have a government of the common people, by the common people, and for the common people.

"From all this it results that the board's anti-union resolution is void. The board had no right to pass it. And yet no sooner was this resolution passed than the superintendent and his assistants made haste to enforce it to the letter; but the injunction in the original case was granted and that prevented the slaughter of the innocents that was planned—the dismissal of the hundreds of teachers who voted for the union."

Teachers throughout the country are reaching the conviction that they must help themselves if they wish better things and that better things are directly dependent upon purchasing power. Read the recent report giving the salaries paid the teachers of the United States, published by the United States Bureau of Education. It is full of convincing proof that something must be done.

Teachers have been prevented from adopting practical methods because of false standards and so-called sentimental motives. They have been told that teachers receive a higher pay than mere wages. They have tried to keep the atmosphere and traditions of a "profession" lest they lose caste with "influential" citizens.

What has it profited them? Their real friends are the masses of the people, the people whose children constitute at least 90 per cent. of those attending public schools.—*American Federationist, December, 1914.*

Every plan for national conservation and development must be based upon appreciation of the significance and the importance of the child—the child of the poor man as well as the child of the wealthy. There is wrapped up in every child born into the world an infinite potentiality. Into what a child may develop no one can say, but we all know well that the development is conditioned upon assuring to that child the protection and conditions that make for healthful physical development and opportunities for developing its mental powers. The whole physical structure is a delicate mechanism reflecting every influence that comes into the life and environment of the child, and all of these influences, whether material or spiritual, are reflected directly in personality and life.

There is a very direct connection between the nourishment of the body, adequate clothing, pleasant surroundings and untrammeled mental and physical development of the powers of the individual. Unless its life is to be perverted or dwarfed in some degree each child must be assured from the beginning a chance to live and grow and opportunities for development. Each child has an important significance in the life of the whole nation, for national development is conditioned by individual development. There is no greater crime and no more fundamental mistake that a nation can make than to neglect its children. . . .

Child labor is a wicked practice—one totally abhorrent to all ideals of intelligence and devoid of heart understanding. There is nothing in later life that can ever compensate a neglected or abused child for the losses which were a part of its childhood. As the human body, the human mind, and the human personality develop they remain fundamentally unchanged. There is a time to grow and a time to develop which never returns. The fundamental problems which confront our nation are those of child labor and education.—*American Federationist, February, 1916.*

Women are now accepted as workers in practically all trades and callings. It is recognized that they must have some relationship with commerce and industry. This is not a new condition—women of all ages have worked. The new element is that where women are now gainfully employed, they must receive just wages as compensation.

Women's work has been hampered and shadowed by old ideals that never had a meaning except for a select few. According to those ideals, women were to be sheltered from the conflicts and the hardships of the work-a-day world, they were to be protected and supported by husbands, fathers, or other male relatives; they were regarded by the state as wards. The few who benefited by this policy purchased special consideration at the price of rights and opportunities.

The effect of this attitude toward women has been most pernicious in the economic world. Because every one assumed that women were not to work out their own problems, they were left without protection, exploited, made the victims of all manner of abuse and injustice.

The industrial and commercial struggle has very little opportunity for ideals of chivalry. Women have been learning that they must organize and make their own fight for economic rights, justice and freedom. Fellow-men workers will coöperate with them and will help them, but they can not make the fight for them without their own assistance. . . .

There is no difference in the industrial problems and difficulties which confront women from those which confront men. The fundamental principles which underlie all efforts of women to establish their rights and industrial justice are those which underlie efforts of men. Men and women united can work out a general plan for the economic welfare of all, and together they can enforce their demands and ideals. Divided in their efforts, or working along separate plans, there must be some degree of conflict and wasted activity.

That there are general principles of human welfare which are common to the industrial problems of both men and women has been demonstrated with appalling forcefulness by conditions that are developing in Europe. This demonstrates that if women do not organize and coöperate with men along common lines, both will be used to counteract the efforts of each other and to undermine the standards that have been established.—*American Federationist, March, 1916.*

There has always been a barrier that has separated the teachers from other wage-earners and, in fact, has prevented the teachers from seeing their own problems clearly and from engaging in a practical solution of their problems. This barrier has been the erection of a caste, setting the teachers apart simply as a sort of "professional group" and yet leaving them without the means of self-protection, relying entirely upon "benevolent paternalism." ... However, a change has been coming. Teachers have come to realize that material welfare, wages, the protection of their physical and mental energy, the insurement of time for their own development and recreation are fundamental and are necessary to the performance of the better, higher service. They have come to realize that their fundamental problem is economic and must be worked out by the economic organizations. There is a nation-wide movement toward organization of teachers in teachers' unions. ... Organization of teachers is encouraging not only because of its influence upon the democracy of the country but for the dynamic influence it will have upon education and the spirit of public schools.—*American Federationist, June, 1916.*

May I be permitted a personal reference? My school years ended at the age of ten when I became a factory boy—never have I lost that sense of deep injustice at society that denied me opportunities for child life and study. Whatever I have learned since has been under adverse conditions and because of my insatiable desire to know. It is my earnest desire that others may be protected against similar injustice.—*From address before the National Educational Association, New York City, July 7, 1916.*

Despite the warnings of foreign experience the development of women's work is rapidly progressing in this country as befits individual convenience of the employers and industries. There is no constructive thought that is guiding the development in furtherance of human protection and welfare. On the other hand agencies and well-meaning individuals are hastening plans that would bring a greater number of women into gainful employment and would prepare the way for constantly increasing numbers through registration. The peculiarity of this registration method is that it is confined to women instead of covering in a comprehensive way the general field of employment of both men and women. Much of this feverish anxiety to get women into industry is the result of war hysteria and an emotional desire to experience real conditions of war. . . .

In the United States there are in existence now many women committees who deal in some way with women's work during war. It is urgently suggested that one of the first activities of these committees ought to be to determine clearly what trades and callings are adapted to women and which they ought not to enter except in direct emergency, if at all. When this has been done we will be in a position to advise women as to their welfare, and at the same time ensure the best development of industry and thereby secure the greatest production with the least interference or fluctuation in output.—*American Federationist, September, 1917.*

As it is necessary for women of the United States to come into industry in increasing numbers, they must organize. Their organization is essential for the maintenance of standards not only for women but for men. Organization is necessary to develop and make effective industrial morality, or the just meaning of standards, and the responsibility of one worker to his fellow-workers in maintenance of common welfare. These results will come through the affiliation of women workers to existing trade unions wherever that is practical, and unswerving insistence upon equal pay for equal work. These matters are of vital concern not only to the women workers themselves, but to the men who remain in the trades or may come back to them after the war. They are necessary in order that there should be an advanced, not a backward, movement in the standards and conditions of life and work.—*American Federationist, July, 1918.*

VII

UNEMPLOYMENT, INSURANCE AND COMPENSATION

The hundreds of thousands of our fellows, who, through the ever-increasing inventions and improvements in the modern methods of production, are rendered "superfluous" because (through no fault of their own) they are thrown out of employment; who are fast degenerating into an impoverished idle class; who are a constant menace to the employment, wages and conditions of the employed workers, and a danger to our civilization and progress, have few to say a kind word to them, and none to give practical aid to rescue them from their awful and inhuman condition except the organized working people.

We must endeavor to save the unemployed from the fearful consequences of modern greed and avarice, we must find employment for our wretched brothers and sisters by reducing the hours of our labor or we will be overwhelmed and destroyed. If a humane feeling for our kind does not prompt us to do so, our intelligence and self-interest should compel us.—*From annual report to A. F. of L. convention, Boston, Mass., December, 1889.*

Joseph H. Choate, the great corporation lawyer, recently said that the suffering, severe as it is among the vast number of unemployed workers, would be intensified beyond description were it not that the poor, who have little, most humanely share that little with their fellow-sufferers.—*American Federationist, March, 1894.*

There are a number of trade organizations which have provisions regarding the number of apprentices. It is not very extensive, and, in many cases, unenforceable. The organizations that have the laws on the subject seek strenuously to enforce them for this purpose: They realize that the employers are endeavoring to bring a number of young boys into the trade, not to teach them the trade, not even to teach them the branch as perfectly as they should, but simply that they shall become slipshod workmen, doing a very indifferent part of the work, and then employ perhaps one workman to do the finishing-up of what these young lads cannot do. The whole effort being not for the employment of the boys, but for the purpose of supplanting men and cutting wages, so that frequently the boys are employed and the men are walking the streets. The boy is perhaps supporting the father. . . . I want to assure you, as a result of my experience, that the action of the employers, as a rule, in insisting on having boys in their factories is not prompted by philanthropy or patriotism. . . . Man, by his physical condition, is the natural breadwinner of the family, and it is his duty to work; and not only is it his duty, but he has the right to work; the right to the opportunity to work. When that right is denied him society does him and his an injustice. May I add this thought: Perhaps there are none who so viciously attack the trade unions in their attempt to make some regulations regarding the apprenticeship as our friends of the legal fraternity; yet, as a matter of fact, that which they call the period of student life is nothing more nor less than the serving of an apprenticeship, and the diploma is the certificate that they have served their apprenticeship; that they are now journeymen lawyers, entitled to practice their trade, work at their trade; and the man who can not show that certificate of having served a lawyer's apprenticeship is not permitted to work in any law shop. . . . They have their scale of prices, too. They have their system of ethics. Any one who would accept a case below the minimum scale, or any one who would violate the ethics of the profession and of the bar association—which may be well termed the trade union of lawyers— would be regarded as a shyster.—*From testimony before Industrial Commission, Washington, D. C., April 18, 1899.*

There are now agreements between organizations of labor and employers as to wages, hours of labor, and other conditions. Some of the agreements contain a clause that the employer, when needing labor, shall apply to the secretary or manager of the labor bureau of the union for such help as he may require. On the other hand, there are agreements of unions with employers that contain no such provision at all, the simple stipulation being the employment of members of that union, obtained as he may choose. I would like to add that that is one of the principal reasons that has impelled many unions to adopt the principle of requiring the employer to secure his help from the secretary of the labor bureau of the union, or the manager, because with the system previously in effect the employer would get his help from some employment agency with which the men out of work would enter into an agreement to give its private agent a bonus to get employment; or the employment agency may have been in a liquor saloon, or liquor store, and the men who spent the most money with the liquor store were the men who were recommended to the employer. It was to avoid these evils that several unions have adopted the system of requiring the employer to apply to the union for help, and the cases I have in mind are particularly the bakers, the barbers, and the brewers. There the system was that the saloon keeper was the employing agent, and generally he got a large bonus for recommending a man to employment, and the more frequent the changes the greater the number of bonuses that came to him, and, of course, with total disregard whether the men were competent or otherwise, the only consideration being his bonus and the amount of money that the poor fellows would spend in order to curry favor with the saloon keeper.—*From testimony before Industrial Commission, Washington, D. C., April 18, 1899.*

The old fallacies like "assumption of risk," "contributory negligence," "fellow-servant," responsibility, and recognition by courts of the validity of "waiving rights" in order to obtain employment, are fast becoming obnoxious to right-thinking men, and instead of the wage-earner and his family being compelled to endure all the mental and financial, as well as the physical suffering due to accidents in industry, it is now becoming more acceptable to the minds of those who would conserve the interests of the working forces as the preëminent and most logical of all public questions, that the industry should bear the financial burden of accidents to the human factor, exactly as it does now to the mechanical accidents, or accidents through natural elements.

This view of the subject is becoming so pronounced that the conviction is fast growing that there should be speedily enacted uniform laws by our States for intra-state employments together with a comprehensive federal statute covering all interstate and foreign commerce that will provide for, and guarantee to, those who are injured during employment an automatic compensation for accidents instead of undertaking expensive and wearisome litigation before the courts to recover damages.

This plan has become almost universal in European countries, so much so that the last President felt so keenly on the subject that he practically rebuked Congress because of the inhuman conditions tolerated in the United States and its multiplicity of industries. . . .

In presenting this subject to your thoughtful consideration, it may not be amiss to impress upon all the need of uniformity in the enactment of these laws. It has been the bane of our peculiar form of dual government that State laws differed so widely, in some cases almost outrageously, and then again the most of them differed from, and some in fact almost opposed, federal statutes. It is therefore necessary again to urge that the legislative committees of city central bodies, State federations, etc., act in harmony and with the advice of the American Federation of Labor in the work of securing labor federation of an effective character.—*From report to A. F. of L. convention, Toronto, November, 1909.*

When employers find that it is more expensive to have accidents occur in their establishments than to prevent them, they see to it that precautionary measures are employed in that plant. I say this not because there may be any particular employers who are avaricious or negligent, but the fact is that when by want of uniformity in the laws of our country what is everybody's business becomes no one's business, the employer simply takes his chances. In employers' liability suits, under the established practice in the courts and the rules of law, the employer sets up as his defense the assumption of risk on the part of the worker, or his contributory negligence, or the fact that the accident was due to his fellow-servants, or that he has, as a condition of employment, waived his right to recover. The worker may never have met these fellow-servants who are responsible for the accidents, and yet it is part of his assumed risk. . . . In my opinion, uniform legislation should also cover those subjects of the highest importance—child labor, the regulation of women's labor, the establishment of a normal work day, compulsory school attendance, free schools, free text-books, but even above all these stands compensation for the victims of industry.—*From address before Uniform Legislation Conference of The National Civic Federation, Washington, D. C., January 18, 1910.*

The law may say that a man shall not step upon the train while it is moving; you may say that he shall not get off the train while it is in motion; but the modern train gets into a station upon a given minute and second and must leave within thirty seconds after, and all the changes and inspections and coupling and uncoupling which have to be made cannot be done within the time, and men get into the habit of their work and the performance of their duties; they have done it for years; they do it quicker every year for a period of years. They lose all sense of proportion, of danger, and that which in the beginning would be regarded as absolute carelessness is simply the habit of doing a thing quickly and having it done with. Under the law it may be regarded as carelessness. In industry and commerce it is one of the incidents of quick production and quick distribution and transportation. I heard a question asked and an answer given whether if the principles of compensation were enacted into law it would not have the effect of limiting the power of contract between the employees and employers—common carriers. That is only one of those benefits and advantages which the workmen do not want and which so many of our lawyers want to guarantee to us, and the denial of some of the real rights which are essential to our well-being and our protection.

I shall not attempt to deal with figures. Speaking generally, less than 20 per cent of the amounts in which employers are mulcted in damages reach the pockets of the injured workmen and the families dependent upon the workmen killed. I suppose I am within the limits of truth when I say that of a hundred million dollars recovered for injuries and death, about 50 per cent has gone into litigation and fully 30 per cent of the remainder, or more, has gone into the pockets of attorneys. Apart from the fact that there ought to be compensation for injuries that would not give the injured employee or the family or dependents of the employee killed amounts that would place them in a position of affluence, it is better that they should get something that shall humanely take care of them rather than take the chance of litigation before the courts, for in addition to the possibility of their being nonsuited or defeated in their litigation comes this one thing, and this is an important feature: That as soon as an employee institutes legal proceedings against his employer, the employer feels that it is necessary to defend himself, if not in that particular case and for the effect upon that one particular case, for the influence it will have upon other employees who may be injured. And in addition, if the litigant be defeated, he is not only financially ruined, if he ever had anything to venture in litigation, but he is physically injured and his earning power considerably limited, and he has made of his former employer an enemy, and the man upon whom he might have counted in the future for some sort of employment, for some consideration, has his back turned upon him, and he is glad to rid himself of his opponent in litigation.—*From testimony before Committee on the Judiciary, House of Representatives, February 17, 1910.*

The carelessness of a man in the old-time methods of industry could very well be attributed to him, to his own physical or mental condition; but to-day in modern industry, and in transportation of men and things, the workers must keep up with the swiftest moving machinery, and he who does not falls by the way, whether it be a machine revolving at the rate of 25,000 revolutions a minute, or whether it is a railroad train running sixty miles an hour. The law may say that a man shall not step upon the train or get off while it is in motion; but the modern train gets into a station upon a given minute and second and must leave within 30 seconds after, and all the changes and inspections and coupling and uncoupling which have to be made cannot be done within the time, and men get into the habit of making quick time in the performance of their duties; they have done it for years; they do it quicker every year for a period of years. They lose all sense of proportion of the danger, and that which in the beginning would be regarded as absolute carelessness becomes simply the habit of doing a thing swiftly and having it done with. Under the law the speed may be regarded as

carelessness. In industry and commerce haste is one of the incidents of production and distribution and transportation . . .—
From "The Eight-Hour Workday"; American Federationist, April, 1897.

Thirty-seven States have enacted some form of employers' liability law, very few of which, however, have been interpreted favorably for the workers by the courts. This is to be accounted for largely because the courts have clung tenaciously to certain former precedents, arising out of peculiar judicial reasoning, which have at times been referred to as the "unholy trinity," viz, the "assumption of risk," "contributory negligence," and "fellow-servant" rulings. As if these obstacles were not enough to offset a workman's claim for damages, another method has been devised, which the courts have duly recognized as affording grounds valid and sufficient to prevent an injured employee from obtaining an award for damages. This cunning device has been to induce—manifestly in the last analysis through coercion—an employee when arranging for employment to sign a contract "waiving his rights," or his widow's and orphans', to sue for damages in case of injury or death during employment.

The following States have abrogated the defense of "fellow-servant" responsibility, either for general employments or in particular industries (usually transportation): Arkansas, Colorado, Florida, Georgia, Iowa, Kansas, Minnesota, Missouri, Montana, Nebraska, Nevada, North Carolina, North Dakota, Oklahoma (by constitution), South Dakota, Texas and Wisconsin. The Colorado law is the most notable example. It completely eliminates the defense of the "fellow-servant" rule in all employments, and upon a test case being made (in Vindication Mining Co. vs. Firstbrook, 36 Colo. 498) it was upheld as constitutional. To the credit of organized labor, this humane measure was introduced in the Colorado legislature and pressed to a successful enactment by a trade unionist member of the General Assembly.

In California, Mississippi, Ohio, Oregon, South Carolina, Utah, Virginia, the "fellow-servant" rule is modified without being abrogated.

Several States have enacted legislation modifying the old common law rulings of "assumed risk." Others have modified the rulings of "contributory negligence" to what is more euphemistically termed "comparative negligence," but such tinkering and trifling with measures of such grave import to the workers in industry is but transparent pettifogging. Just, humane, positively affirmative and effective legislation must in honor and duty be enacted by the States and by the United States. All legislation on identical subjects should be uniform among the States, but, pending the time when that desirable end can be reached, it is essential that legislation dealing with the important subject of employers' liability should be uniform among the States, not only uniform in technique, but uniformly good—effective legislation that will forever abolish the antiquated, barbarous, so-called common law defense known as "fellow-servant" rule, "contributory (or comparative) negligence," and "assumption of risk," as well as the waiving of rights. If any reason ever existed for these circumscribed rules, formulated by judges, the time has long since passed when they should be applied.

The modern use of steam power, electricity, compressed air and explosives, often under control of men who fail to understand their nature, and whose routine duties make them so accustomed to danger that they fail to realize it, has made it utterly impossible to protect society against the weakest of all human agencies, viz., the failure or forgetfulness of the human factor. Then also must be considered the dangers to life and limb in the operation of fast-driven intricate machinery as well as the accidents due to the massing together of great numbers of workers in modern industry.

The stubborn resistance of corporations, common carriers, mine owners, and other employers to the most moderate laws for the protection of human beings from injury, and their general reluctance to provide protection through their own volition, ought to convince reasonable and fair-minded legislators that true justice demands an expansion of the law, with more humane interpretation of it on the part of judges, instead of there being, as the court reports in many of the States now so amply record, a studied effort to restrict the law and apply new exceptions to it, to prevent the allowance of damages for the injured and killed workmen in industry.

Seemingly the American public has just awakened to the fact that of all civilized countries of the world, Turkey and the United

States are the only two left that still cling to the old common-law doctrine of liability with respect to industrial accidents. This awakening will force upon the workers of the United States some kind of workmen's compensation legislation, and unless labor takes an active part in the movement its interests in regard to this will not be properly safeguarded.

Industry must bear the financial burden of accidents to the human being, exactly as it does now in case of accidents to machinery or to other property.—*From annual report to A. F. of L. convention, St. Louis, Mo., November, 1910.*

You meet on the street a man you knew years before as one in the crowd in your trade. He is woe-begone. His clothes tell his story at a glance. His sad and care-worn and perhaps pale and thin face confirms the story in detail. He is out of work. He most probably avoids you, though you were always on good terms with him, so far as you had anything to do with him, in the old days. You know he shrinks from your cheerful "How are you, old man?" "How goes it?" or "Where are you now?" He hates to explain. His very appearance is a confession that he has fallen behind-hand; he is averse to adding to it a verbal admission of failure. If you are moved to sympathize with him, however, and take him by the hand and try to pretend you don't see any difference in him, he may give in and talk. He knows very well the pious lie you are acting, but passes it by without mention, feeling you are actuated by a friendly spirit.

He'll tell you what's the matter with him. He was "let out" when "the firm," "the company," or "the boss"—where he worked when you knew him—introduced new machines, or reorganized, or increased the proportion of apprentices, or of younger men or women. For the first time in years he then found himself on the street. Past the age to qualify himself without much trouble for another occupation, handicapped by the lack of the adaptiveness of youth, bunched together with the others of his occupation "laid off" for various reasons, he has since been living 'twixt hope and fear, searching for work. His days of enforced idleness have stretched into weeks, the weeks into months.

What has happened to this man? He may try to think he is the same, as a human being and a workman, that he was when he fell out of his job. He is not. Far from it. He has gone backward and downward every day. He has lost in nerve, for he has seen how he is only one of the many down and out. He has lost in the confidence he had in his knowledge of his trade, for in looking about him he has learned how methods have changed. He has lost in self-respect, for he feels every hour that men may speak of him as not having made good. He has lost flesh and even strength, for he has been economizing on his bodily sustenance. He has suffered every day in his pride; where once it moved him as a man it now merely stirs him to irritability.

When a man in this condition of mind and body finds a job, his difficulties in keeping up with the others on a force are almost insuperable. He balks at any task that is new to him, lacking self-confidence. He fears every day that a new lay-off may be awaiting him. He resents the foreman's eye, or a fellow-worker's show of help, or the silent sizing-up he knows he is getting from the crowd about him. He has the sensation that they are saying he has lost his hold. It is a question in his own mind whether he really ever can "come back" or catch on again.

It is a social truth that the first thing a man in such plight needs is a kind of medicine. If he can be placed in circumstances in which he can be set firmly on his feet again, he may stand upright and do good work the rest of his days. A new suit of clothes, a little feeding up, a helping hand at the right moment at his work, a good-natured bluffing in response to his irritable moods, an acknowledgment by those about him that hard luck is waiting at any and every one's door, the nerve reaction that ensues upon good stiff work, and the reëstablishment of the discipline of routine—with such medicine the worker who quailed in fear lest he might be relegated to the human scrap-heap may become a man again. But if his chance hangs off too long, his fate is to "lay down." He is "gone." Somehow, death often comes opportunely in such cases. The real man having passed away, the poor body remains only to succumb, in its weakness, to one of the hundred forms of illness into which watchful death is ready to lead him.

How many good, honest men every one of us among the elders have seen passing through these sufferings, each a sacrifice to an imperfect civilization! On the other hand, as if to prove that the dead ones were so sacrificed, how many other men, just of about the same general character, we have seen picking themselves up through finding a job in the nick of time, fully recovering their lost ground, and living happily with their families thereafter a good, long lifetime!

Fellow union men, as you have read these lines have you not been reflecting, as have we, upon the fact that when your union was weak, or lacking in out-of-work or other funds, you saw a far greater proportion of men going down and out in the struggle than since your union has become strong? It has become helpful to its temporarily unfortunate members. But tell us, you men among the unorganized, where can *you* look for help in your trade when you lose your job, fall sick, go wandering in search of work, or need insurance of any kind against the misfortunes which the wage-workers of your occupation must face in common?—*American Federationist, April, 1911.*

The usual established American methods for supplying American (or English-speaking) migratory labor to any point in the country where labor is needed at American wages are equal to the performance of their task. These methods are, as we have pointed out, trade union bureaus and comradeship, advertising, and regulated private agencies. Of course, they have to be supplemented by individual hustle, horse-sense, courage, and independence of character. . . . The principal aim and mission of the schemes for immigrant distribution come plainly into view. It is not to supply our country with any needed labor. It is not the building up of any American community. It is not even to assist American labor equally with foreign labor. It is to promote and assist the coming and going steerage passenger regardless of the effect on American labor.

English-speaking labor in the United States can find its way to any job anywhere that will yield a fair living, even if it has to travel in a "box car." The trouble to-day is that, no matter how it travels, it finds on the job a previous arrival—a man speaking a strange tongue, living with a gang of others in a shack, working at a serf's wages, submitting in a slavish spirit to outrages on him as a human being, and in debt to the agencies that have found the job for him and paid his way to it.—*American Federationist, July, 1911.*

My own investigations of the subject of State and national labor exchanges and distribution bureaus in this country have shown me that they are inevitably linked up with the schemes of the steamship combine to bring immigrants to, and distribute them over, the United States. In general the wage-workers seeking situations through State labor exchanges are persons engaged in hotel, restaurant, and domestic service. But whatever other laborers have been moved in gangs by such exchanges have usually been freshly landed from foreign shores. The movement of American wage-workers commonly takes place through trade union labor bureaus, newspaper advertisements, and the information given one another by fellow workmen of the same or kindred trades. It is a serious question how State labor exchanges may be established, immigration being as it is, without their becoming simply one more advantage and benefit to the corporate or private capitalists whose business is to carry labor to markets for it which in many cases are already vastly oversupplied or which may readily be supplied by our own migratory laborers elsewhere idle.—*From annual report to A. F. of L. convention, Atlanta, Georgia, November, 1911.*

Unionism gives rise and emphasis to purely brotherly obligations. Unionism does not stop to pass judgment on "worthiness," or keep written records of misfortunes, or find excuses for withholding the practical sympathy that will relieve pain or assuage grief. Apart from all other causes for fellow union members being "neighborly" are two principal ones. Trade unionists are free to be neighborly, as they brook no interference from their employers in their social relations. They have a broad acquaintanceship among their fellow-workers, and this brings to their minds at once the necessity and the possibility of help in case of need.

A worker is hurt, his family is in need. A member of the same "international" is found, and he asks no other bond of obligation than that he is a union member. The help necessary is rendered without a quibble or cross-examination. A newcomer in a town applies for work; among his fellow-unionists he finds a place.

An "unknown tramp" is reported in a newspaper as having been killed on the railroad. A union card is found in his pocket, and the "local" of his trade buries him, sending a committee of its members to the interment, that he may be buried as a human being, and not like a pauper or a dog.

The examples of union help, in a "neighborly" way, are endless. All over the country, all over the modern industrial world, unions are engaged in systematic, continuous, effective help to the unfortunate, as well as in general uplift work. Time and again have we been told by "social workers"—the representative men and women of various helpful social institutions—that the one fact, surprising because rarely or never chronicled in their college text-books, which they soon learned on taking up their mission, was that the unions are doing more for the amelioration of the masses than all the eleemosynary societies together. True, what is more, much more, emphatically more, is the fact that mutual help in the trade unions strengthens character. It comes as a common right to all. Toward its existence and effectiveness all the members contribute. The object, and the result, is the making, not of paupers, but men, strong men, in body, mind, and spirit.—*American Federationist, June, 1912.*

As the daily press reports show, the unemployed problem is a national problem, hence it can be considered and dealt with satisfactorily only from a national survey of conditions in all lines of industry and all industrial opportunities. Work of this nature can be performed only by an authorized agency of the national government. That division of the government to which this function should logically be assigned is the Department of Labor. A broadening of the scope of the present work of the Bureau of Labor Statistics would throw light upon how to deal with migratory workers. Migratory workers are a consequence of seasonal work. Definite information and help would relieve these workers from the suffering entailed by the short duration of work found in some industrial undertakings which supply the needs of society. . . .

A federal employment bureau should receive the careful consideration of all organized labor in order to secure the establishment of an agency that would prevent to a great extent the demoralization and the suffering that result when numbers seek employment but are unable to find it. Such an institution could not, of course, prevent all unemployment for that naturally results from changes and misfortunes in industry (and often from the ignorance or greed of the captains of industry), but at least it will prevent the workers from being left helpless to bear the brunt of the burden.—*American Federationist, March, 1914.*

Through repetition, partisan, ill-founded, sweeping assertions come to be accepted by socialists as indisputable facts. This is illustrated by Mr. Sinclair in his passage on the glass bottle blowers. He says:

"Take the glass bottle industry, which I studied some six years ago. Bottle blowers were getting $7 or $8 a day and were in clover. I said: 'But suppose some one invents a machine?' They laughed at me. 'Invent a machine to blow bottles? Never!' But a year later it was done, and now one small boy tends a machine which does the work of several skilled men—and the boy gets 50 cents a day."

Now, what are the facts as to the Glass Bottle Blowers' Association? Have the members lost their situations to boys working for 50 cents a day? Has the union been dissolved or even weakened? Nothing of the kind. In 1907, when Mr. Sinclair studied indications and prophesied disaster, the union had 80 votes in the American Federation of Labor convention, representing 8,000 members; in 1913, six years after, it had 100 votes, representing 10,000 members. Wages in the trade were somewhat affected by the machine, yet remain among the highest in the country. This socialist cry of alarm over displacement of man by machine, with want in its wake, has done service for fifty years in every trade imaginable. Twenty years ago it was the printers who were to be displaced, degraded, undone, driven into the ranks of the unskilled. The dreaded machine in their trade had arrived. The result to-day? Sixty thousand members in the International Typographical Union as against 27,000 in 1894; the eight-hour instead of the ten-hour day; wages advanced by 30 per cent. More than thirty years ago, it was the cigarmakers who were to be thrown out of the factories, impoverished, starved. Their union was to be disintegrated and their children were to be forced to earn the family living by slaving at the cigarmaking machines a long day for a few dimes. And the actual result? The union membership increased from 32,000 to 56,000; wages increased; the eight-hour day maintained continuously for a generation, with a complete system of fraternal benefits.—*From "Upton Sinclair's Mental Marksmanship," American Federationist, April, 1914.*

UNEMPLOYMENT, INSURANCE, COMPENSATION

The A. F. of L. favors a system of non-contributing old-age pensions for workers who have reached a certain age to be established by legal enactment and maintained by governmental machinery. The Federation favors a general system of state insurance against sickness, disability, and accidents. It has not endorsed state insurance of unemployment. In regard to the problem of unemployment the Federation proposes to shorten the workday of the employees, that they may share with the unemployed the work that is to be performed, and thereby tend constantly toward the elimination of unemployment. The American workman refuses to regard unemployment as a permanent evil attending the industrial and economic forces of our country. The American workmen propose to share work with those who are unemployed and thereby to help to find work for the unemployed.

The A. F. of L. encourages and stimulates the workmen in their efforts to secure a constantly increasing share in the products of labor, an increasing share in the consumption and use of things produced, thereby giving employment to the unemployed, the only effective way by which that can be done. . . .

The Federation has not declared itself in regard to the establishment of employment bureaus and the loaning of money, without interest, to States and municipalities for the purpose of carrying on public works, but it favors any tangible, rational purpose that would help to meet and solve the question of unemployment. It endeavors to improve the condition of the working people in every field of human activity, to promote and advance their rights and interests.—*From testimony before U. S. Commission on Industrial Relations, New York City, May 21-23, 1914.*

It is false and unwise economy and a lack of statesmanship to retrench public expenditures and improvements when such a course means suffering, misery, hunger. Labor does not advocate extravagant, ill-considered use of public moneys, but insists that public funds shall not be hoarded at such a time as this, but spent in accord with good business sense. As President Wilson said in his last message, "It is not expenditure but **extravagance** we should fear being criticized for."

There is a time to save and a time to spend. **This is the time** to spend—to spend wisely as well as humanely. From all over this land of ours come reports of need. There are great numbers of unemployed, the unknown men and women in the breadlines of our cities. Those people want work, they have hunted desperately for work but work has been denied them. Through no fault of theirs shall others be forced to turn, ashamed, beaten, to ask charity? If we value independent citizenship, we as a nation will denounce policies of false public economy in postponing to some future time work necessary to our country's progress, to our commerce and our safety; work which can just as advantageously be done now, work which if postponed will take from men and women the means of earning a livelihood. It is worse than false economy to waste the manhood and womanhood of our country in order to retrench economically and unwisely in public expenditures for necessary public work.—*From contribution to Philadelphia "Public Ledger," December 19, 1914.*

I may say this in passing, if some time here or elsewhere, the statement may be made which I have heard made in other places that the drinking habit of the working people has been the main cause for industrial accidents, the statement is wholly unwarranted. There is no evidence to sustain the statement that there are more industrial accidents on Monday than there have been on any other day of the week. The New York Workmen's Compensation Commission states, first, that there is but little variation in the number of accidents in industry in the state of New York between those which occur on Monday and those of any other day of the week; and second, this other fact—that inasmuch as the accidents are reported, the hour, the day, and the minute of the accident, so far as it can be correctly reported, data furnished the New York Workmen's Compensation Commission have demonstrated that the largest number of accidents occur after the fourth hour of the morning's work, and after the fourth hour of the afternoon's work. In other words, the bulk of these accidents is not caused by what you call carelessness or negligence, but is indeed the result of overwork and fatigue, when the human mind can no longer have the tense grasp upon itself, nor the human frame the ability to adjust quickly to the every motion of the machine which is driven at the top notch speed.—*From address at Conference on Accident Prevention; Pennsylvania House of Representatives, March 23, 1916.*

There must necessarily be a weakening of independence of spirit and virility when compulsory insurance is provided for so large a number of citizens of the state. Dangers to wage-earners might readily arise under the machinery for the administration of this social insurance that would establish compulsory physical examinations. The purpose of such examinations has been perverted in many places and made to result to the detriment of workers. The discretionary power lodged in the administrative board could readily be used in efforts to coerce organizations of wage-earners, for the administrative body has the power to approve societies and also to withdraw approval at any time.—*American Federationist, April, 1916.*

I am apprehensive that the attempts of government under the guise of compulsory social insurance for the workers in cases of unemployment, sickness and disability will result in every government agent going into the homes and the lives of the workers as a spy. We have enough already of spies and detectives coming into the lives and workshops of the toilers. After centuries of struggle during the past twenty years, we concentrated our efforts in an agitation that has gone through the whole country, to secure from the hands of Congress a larger liberty of action than has ever been accorded to the working people of any country on the face of the globe in the entire history of the world. After years of struggling to secure these things we are not going to let go, we are not going to submit. As I live, upon the honor of a man, and realizing the responsibility of my words, I would rather help in the inauguration of a revolution against compulsory insurance and the regulation than submit. As long as there is one spark of life in me, of my mentality, whatever that may be, of my spirit, I will help in crystallizing the spirit and sentiment of our workers against the attempt to enslave them by the well-meaning siren songs of philosophers, statisticians and politicians. We propose to work out our problems day after day, week after week, and year after year. We are not afraid. We are not running away from the struggle. I do not have to make any professions of faith here that our movement stands for social insurance and government aid, but of a voluntary character and not compulsory . . . in which the rights of the workers secured after ages of struggle shall not be surrendered. Not with my consent or without my protest will I permit the enactment of regulations that will take away one right which the workers have won.

Section 3 of Mr. London's proposition provides that the commission shall prepare and recommend schedules of benefits. It shall prepare and recommend rules and regulations—rules and regulations—rules and regulations. That is the order of society as contemplated in the philosophy of—if I may use that sacred term of our friends—the socialists—regulation of every man's and every woman's every step, the regulation of the government, the regulation of its commissions and its officers.

I am heart-sore, ill and sad when any, the least of my fellows, is hurt in any way. I am so constituted that I scarcely would hurt any one even in self-defense. And sore and saddened as I am by the illness, the killing and maiming of so many of my fellow-workers, I would rather see that go on for years and years, minimized and mitigated by the organized labor movement, than give up one jot of the freedom of the workers to strive and struggle for their own emancipation through their own efforts.

It has been a constant struggle of the workers through the ages, to get the tentacles of government agencies from off the throats of the workers and to break the gyves from off their wrists. Here comes along a movement of men and women, many of them good, whole-souled, true, noble, but many of them led by sophistry as to the causes of the ills and as to the hopes for a better life, and willing to rivet the masses of labor to the juggernaut of government. The A. F. of L. has been attacked and ridiculed as no other organization on the face of the earth, and just by these people—not all, but officially and severally by nearly all of them. But why? Because the American trade union movement, the A. F. of L., refused to yield to any group one inch of the field of activity in the interests of the working people. The advocates of government regulation may fight for it, but they will find a stout contender against them in each human activity. They have been unable to control the American trade union movement, and that is the great sum-total of our offense.

The A. F. of L. and the American trade union movement is

the most effective militant, beneficent labor movement, freer from governmental interference, influence, or control, than any other labor movement in the whole world. It is because we are a labor movement, pure and simple, *per se,* a movement of wage-earners, for wage-earners, by wage-earners, that we incur the flippant, and somtimes the serious attacks and criticisms and subtle antagonism of the socialist movement.

Section 4 of the resolution provides that it shall be the duty of the commission to submit a report and recommendations for the relief of unemployment by the "regularization of industry." In other words, the Government has to regulate industry and, ergo, regulate the work of the toilers. "It shall be the duty of the commission," etc., "to submit a report, plans, and recommendations for undertaking and *establishing industries which are to be maintained by the Government of the United States."* I do not know that it is necessary that I should take any of the time of this committee to discuss this subject. . . . There is scarcely an international—although in saying this, I may be saying it out of sequential order, as I have not arranged my statement or my memorandum in such way that it will necessarily be sequential, depending upon my own experience and understanding to clothe my views with the words best adapted for them—there is scarcely an international union that has not provided some form of insurance against sickness, against invalidity, against unemployment, tool insurance in many of them, traveling benefits, going from place to place in search of employment, railroad fare and enough for meals and lodging, old-age pensions and annuities. I can not give you the figures just now. The assumption that unemployment cannot be completely done away with, is chimerical and unfounded. You have indicated that there are in America a little less than three million organized workers, and if you have in mind the fact of what these three million workers have already accomplished and what they could and will accomplish when we shall have organized six millions or more of the workers in the trade union movement, you will find if you live long enough, and I, if I live long enough, that this problem of unemployment will be solved by the trade unions in America.—*From testimony before Congressional Committee on resolution for a commission on social insurance, April, 1916.*

There are certain species of compulsory social insurance that by their mere statement carry with them the conviction of their self-evident necessity and justice, into which the element of depriving the people of rights cannot enter—such as workmen's compensation and old age pensions. But when compulsory health insurance and compulsory unemployment insurance are proposed, the question arises at once, what are the conditions and regulations to be imposed by the government to regulate the conduct of the supposed beneficiaries. . . .

Recently a gentleman of the highest standing stated to me that during the time he was in Germany, and in position to know, German workmen came to him seeking aid to get out of that country to the United States. They told him that by reason of the taxes which they were compelled to pay into compulsory social insurance schemes they had no money left except for absolute necessities of life, and were unable to secure sufficient funds to come to the United States even in the steerage. He said to me further that in Germany, where compulsory social insurance has been more extensively worked out than in any other country, the workmen of that country, by reason of their property interests in compulsory social insurance, have been compelled to remain in Germany and work under circumstances, wages, hours and conditions of employment which forced them to endure conditions below standards of a living wage.

Is it not discernible that the payments required of workmen for this compulsory social insurance interfere very materially with mobility of labor, and constitute a very effectual barrier to the workers' determining their whole lives?—*From address before Conference on Social Insurance, The National Civic Federation, Washington, D. C., December 8, 1916.*

Social insurance cannot remove or prevent poverty. It does not get at the causes of social injustice. The only agency that does get at the causes of poverty is the organized labor movement. Social insurance in its various phases of sickness insurance, unemployment insurance, death benefits, etc., only provides the means for tiding over an emergency. The labor movement aims at constructive results—higher wages, which mean better living for the worker and those dependent upon him; better homes, better clothing, better food, better opportunities and shorter hours of work, which mean relief from over-fatigue, time for recuperation, workers with better physical development and with sustained producing power. Better physical development is in itself an insurance against illness and a certain degree of unemployment. The short hour workmen with higher wages become better citizens; better able to take care of themselves. . . .

Compulsory social insurance cannot be administered without exercising some control over wage-earners. This is the meat of the whole matter. Industrial freedom exists only when wage-earners have complete control over their labor power. To delegate control over their labor power to an outside agency takes away from the economic power of those wage-earners and creates another agency for power. Whoever has control of this new agency acquires some degree of control over the workers. There is nothing to guarantee control over that agency to the employed. It may also be controlled by employers. In other words, giving the government control over industrial relations creates a fulcrum which means great power for an unknown user.

Compulsory social insurance is in its essence undemocratic. The first step in establishing social insurance is to divide people into two groups—those eligible for benefits and those considered capable to care for themselves. The division is based upon wage-earning capacity. This governmental regulation tends to fix the citizens of the country into classes, and a long established insurance system would tend to make these classes rigid.

There is in our country more voluntary social insurance than in any other country of the world. We have institutions whereby voluntary insurance could be increased. It is true that in many of these institutions there are evils, but the cure for these evils is to make insurance companies organize for mutual benefit and to provide proper regulation and control, and in addition, if those who really have the welfare of wage-earners at heart will turn their activities and their influence toward securing for wage-earners the opportunity to organize, there will be no problems, no suffering and no need that will necessitate the consideration of benevolent assistance of a compulsory character.—*American Federationist, January, 1917.*

The Bureau of War Risk Insurance has the right to order persons to take suitable courses of vocational rehabilitation. During the period of training the government shall continue compensation in accord with provisions established. The Federal Board is given ample discretionary power as to facilities, instructors, courses, assistants that may be necessary to persons taking courses, and also as to placement in industry or gainful occupations.

The proposed legislation has the thorough approval of those who feel the government has no right to require men to risk life in service without giving them every opportunity and facility for maintaining themselves as self-respecting independent members of society.

The question is at once raised if justice to those mutilated by war requires rehabilitation and vocational training, why is it not just as essential to give the same opportunity to those crippled by industry? The war has shown irrefutably the workers in industry are fighting this war in just as real a way as the men on the ships or in the trenches. Our laws should recognize this identity of service.—*American Federationist, June, 1918.*

I should be opposed—I know that my associates would be opposed—to leaving it within the power of the government or its agent or agents to determine what was nonemployment, whether it was justifiable or otherwise, and who would be entitled to the insurance or the benefits that would result from the provisions of the law—that is, insurance against nonemployment.

There was a resolution proposed by a member of the House some two or three years ago covering that feature. The Member of the House was present at the committee hearing, and finally stated that it is true that the government agent would have to depend, or on him would rest the obligation of determining what constituted nonemployment as to entitle an unemployed person to receive the benefits of the insurance. Now, that would mean, where there would be any controversy with the employer, that the man would be unemployed. Who would determine that question? Well, the answer would be, by the government agent: "There is work for you, and so long as you can get work you are not entitled to this government insurance for nonemployment."—*From testimony before Senate Committee on Education and Labor, January 3, 1919.*

I have never met any representative Italian, whether a representative of employers, of business, of working people, whether conservative or absolutely radical, from trade unionists to radical socialists, from the navy to the army, from the private in the ranks to the commanding general, up to the King of Italy, who seemed to care to discuss any other subject but emigration. I am not saying this as a matter of resentment, but they seemed obsessed with this one idea of how they could get rid of their own people to some other country and particularly to the United States. . . . At the Paris International Labor Commission, of which I was a member and over which I presided, the one big thing to which the Italian delegation was committed was emigration! emigration! emigration! . . .

Now you have the proposal that an international office or some agency of an international character shall be established to see to it that the emigrants as they leave their own country and go into a new country shall receive guidance and assistance and protection as they go along. I do not think you have in Europe that sort of guidance for Frenchmen, for Grecians, for Czecho-Slovaks or Britishers, at home, but if they go to another country it is proposed that they there shall be supplied that guardianship and guidance. In other words, in the United States, you may go to any part of the country and nobody cares, but when any one comes here from some other country he must have a guardian to see that he is guided properly and taken care of. Such a course, even if it could be adopted, would simply mean an increase of emigration, at least into the United States.

America has come to the conclusion that it is necessary at least for a time to stop this influx of immigration. We are passing through this transition now from the production of war material to the production of things for civilized peaceful life. During this period of transition there are large numbers of our fellow-workmen who are unemployed. . . . We cannot afford to throw open the doors wide for immigration which is supposed to be reciprocal and universal when we know that it turns but one way. . . . In the American labor movement we look askance upon any project of government payment of benefits for unemployment, and our misgivings upon that score are this: that when the government undertakes the payment of money to those who are unemployed, it places in the power of the government such power over the lives and the work and the freedom of the workers that the American labor movement has protested against it. In some of the questionnaires and documents that I have seen there is included the question of voluntary and involuntary unemployment —involuntary being due to no fault of the workers. But on the other hand voluntary unemployment, men leaving their work either in groups or singly, individually, may be due to unfair and improper and tyrannous treatment accorded to them by the employers or employers' agents. And if workmen are engaged in any movement demanding improved conditions, or against the imposition of rules or conditions under which they conclude they ought not to work, they are held to be engaged in a strike, which of course would not be considered involuntary. The government will determine whether the workmen are justified in that movement, because they are interested whether to pay the money for so-called unemployment insurance.

We know what even the best form of government means. It is always striving for more power and jurisdiction over the masses of the people and particularly over the working people, and we are not willing in America to give added power to the government to regulate and limit and examine into and punish or reward the workers, whether they are good or bad boys, according to the ideas of the legislatures or courts or bureaus in charge.

In so far as the United States is concerned there can be no reciprocal relation in regard to workmen coming from countries which have so-called unemployment insurance, because we have no workmen going to those countries, and who would thereby come under such insurance there. Let me say also, having made some study of the so-called unemployment insurance payments as they have them in some European countries, that these payments would be regarded as a mere pittance in the United States, and therefore would be disregarded. Of course you know that immigration into the United States had grown to one and a quarter millions in the year just before the war, while there have been comparatively small numbers of our people that emigrated from this country to any other, and then mostly on visits. So that it would not be reciprocal; it would be one-sided for the

United States to pay unemployment insurance or benefits to those who came to our country, with the very small number of our own people in other countries entitled to such payments. But the point I chiefly want to emphasize in our opposition to this so-called unemployment insurance is that we do not want to place more power in the hands of the government to investigate into and regulate the lives, the conduct and the freedom of America's workers.—*From address before Committee on Emigration, International Labor Conference, Washington, D. C., November 15, 1919.*

The principal danger is that we may at some time in the future revert to the old conditions of unemployment. The continually increasing cost of living entails the necessity of continually increasing wages, but a surplus in the labor market makes it difficult, if not impossible, for wages to keep pace with living costs. Intermittent employment with low wages is one of the chief causes of poverty with its accompanying misery and its social and personal demoralization. Reasonable farsightedness in readjustment will obviate a labor surplus. We have a right to demand, and we do demand, that such reasonable farsightedness be exercised. The American Federation of Labor expects governments—national, state and local—to adopt every measure necessary to prevent unemployment. During the coming period of reconstruction every wage-earner should be afforded the opportunity of suitable employment and an income and sustenance sufficient to enable him, without the labor of mother and children, to maintain himself and family in health and comfort, and to provide a competence for old age with ample provision for recreation and good citizenship. Governments should:

(a) Prepare and inaugurate plans to build model homes for the wage-earners;

(b) Establish a system of credits whereby the workers may borrow money for a long term of years at a low rate of interest to build their own homes;

(c) Encourage, protect and extend credit to voluntary, non-profitmaking and joint tenancy associations;

(d) Exempt from taxation and grant other subsidies for houses constructed for the occupancy of their owners;

(e) Relieve municipalities from the restrictions preventing them from undertaking proper housing plans;

(f) Encourage and support the erection and maintenance of houses where workers may find lodging and nourishing food during the periods of unemployment.

Much talk has been made about preparing plans for the construction of public buildings, roads and other public works in order to avoid unemployment. All such suggestions are good, in so far as these things are needed, and no farther. There can be no question, however, of the urgent, immediate need of great numbers of wholesome houses at reasonable costs for working people. The environment offered by many of the tenements is unfit to surround the growing children of a free republic. The revolting conditions in many tenement districts, without sufficient light, air or play spaces, tend to produce persons unfit for citizenship. Squalor and almost unlivable conditions are still found in many houses of the workers whose compensation is inadequate, where opportunity to associate with their fellow-workmen for their moral, intellectual and industrial improvement is persistently and successfully denied. Such housing should not be permitted to exist.

The employment of public funds in the provision of homes for workers is a far better investment than large expenditures on ornamental buildings and beautiful boulevards seldom, if ever, seen by the poor. If large expenditures of public money are needed to avoid unemployment, the construction of houses is of far greater public benefit, especially to the poor, promoting health, happiness and good citizenship. Moreover, such investments have the added merit of returning to the public treasury without loss, and even with gain.—*From "Labor Standards After the War"; Annals of the American Academy, December, 1918.*

This vexed question [hiring and firing] I should leave to an employment manager acting in consultation with the union, for in this way the fairest results may be secured. The turnover of labor is one of our most serious industrial problems and it has frequently come to my notice, this time speaking not as an employer but as president of the American Federation of Labor, that employment agencies have contributed to a very considerable degree to abnormal turnovers. In the past it has been not at all infrequent for foremen or superintendents to share in the fees paid to the employment agencies for jobs. It then became to the interest of these officials to have just as many men as possible hired or fired. I remember an incident of this kind with the late Senator Hanna. He owned blast furnaces near Buffalo and one day he telephoned from the Cloak Room of the Senate that his men had gone on strike and would I come over and see him. I knew him very well and I had an inkling of what his trouble was and so I went over, especially since he was not at all a well man and could not easily get around.

I found him fuming—for if a blast furnace ever gets cold no power on earth can start it up again.

"What am I going to do, Sam?" he said. "These fellows have walked right out. They are getting standard wages. What am I going to do? Can you get them back again?"

"I think I know what your trouble is," I answered. "These men have simply revolted. I happen to know that your superintendent gets a bonus from an employment agency on each man that is hired and he has developed a system of firing people and then reëmploying them through the agency so that he and the agency can each get a little money. The men have revolted and don't you think it's about time that they did?"

"Do you mean to tell me that's going on in my place?" he almost yelled. "That's hell. I shall fire every one of them. But is there anything you can do?"

"There is nothing I can do officially," I answered, "because I have no power to command anything, but I shall see if I can get the men back and then we can adjust this employment matter."

I got in touch with the people on the long distance telephone and they returned to work before the furnaces had cooled down. The Senator soon discovered that what I had told him was a fact and it did not take him very long to get rid of the swindling foremen and superintendents. By the next time I talked with him matters had been adjusted and then he complained:

"But why didn't these fellows tell me about this condition? Why did they just walk out and leave me flat? It was so damned undiplomatic."

"I suppose, Senator," I answered, "it is because we do not develop diplomats on 15 cents an hour!"

Which is something that every employer might well bear in mind.—*From interview with Samuel Crowther, on "What I Should Do If I Were an Employer," in "System Magazine," April, 1920.*

VIII

SOME EVERY-DAY PROBLEMS AND CRITICISMS

ORGANIZATION OF THE UNSKILLED

It has been the constant aim of the trade union movement to exercise its power and influence to organize our fellow-workers engaged in unskilled labor. With the invention of new machines and the application of new forces, the division and subdivision of labor, many workers who have been employed at skilled trades find themselves with their occupation gone, which they have devoted long terms of years to acquire. Thus we see the artisan of yesterday the unskilled laborer of to-day.

In providing for the organization of our unskilled workers in federal labor unions, the American Federation of Labor has adopted a splendid haven of protection. Whenever federal labor unions are organized, they are the recruiting grounds for the trade unions, both of the skilled and unskilled workers, and as soon as there is a sufficient number of one calling, whether belonging to skilled or unskilled labor, they are required to form a union of those who follow the same trade or occupation. Thus our federal labor unions are the recruiting stations for the trade union movement. It is a source of gratification to report that within this past year a very large number of federal labor unions have been organized, and from them a much larger number of trade unions, which, in most instances, were of those trades having national organizations, and their organization and transfer have been effected with advantage to the workers themselves, the organizations of the trades, and the general labor movement. It will not be uninteresting for you to know that we have several federal labor unions with a membership in each of more than 2,000, and in which, happily, the differentiation and classification and transfer, as already referred to, are taking place.—*From annual report to A. F. of L. convention, Nashville, Tenn., December, 1897.*

The lot of the migratory laborer in the United States to-day is in some points worse than slavery. The slave was at least sufficiently well nourished to enable him to perform his allotted tasks. He was assured of a shelter and in case of illness of as much care as a thrifty farmer will give to his horse or other domestic animals. But the very large proportion of unskilled or casual workers who at the present time usually find employment only on short jobs or at season work suffer a precarious existence. As they move from place to place, they often go hungry, and while at work their food is usually of a poor quality, ill prepared. Many of them do not earn enough to establish a home or to pay for medical attendance when sick or suffering from accidents. The character of much of the work performed in the United States does not permit of the steady employment of a regular body of men. Railroad extension work, the construction of bridges and highways, much work in lumbering, waterway, canal, and drainage, and in the building trades, which are mostly carried on in the less inclement seasons of the year, are characterized by idleness for months together of tens of thousands of men. In agriculture, large bodies of men are employed during the seasons of plowing, seeding, planting, and harvest, only to be left without steady work the rest of the year. In all, it is difficult to estimate how many men are thus living in the United States to-day, but the number reaches into the millions.

It might be well to establish a Department of the American Federation of Labor in which trade union migratory laborers should be enrolled.

A card in one union must, in case one is formed, permit the holder to transfer his membership to any other union in the Department.

The organization in the whole country, with respect to this class of laborers, would have the same relationship to the American Federation of Labor as that of the international unions through the other departments. Trade union methods in the operation of labor bureaus, in devising systems of relief, insurance, etc., might be established in the case of these laborers.

A well-conducted migratory labor exchange, or office of information, would be of far more help to the migratory laborers' union than any State labor exchange could possibly be. Such a union office could make itself thoroughly acquainted with the character of contractors and other large employers of labor. They could ascertain what any given job was to be, what the food, and what kind of sleeping quarters were to be given the men, with the pay, the hours of labor, time of payment, kind of payment, and all other particulars which the laborer has a right to know, but singly can not obtain.

The American Federation of Labor recognizes the fact that the migratory workers must be organized, and that the labor and expense of so doing must be borne by the organized workers. Its maintenance must be by the members themselves. A patronizing attitude would react and prove the undoing of the entire project to help them to help themselves, and to have them take their position side by side with the others in the ranks of the organized labor movement. Through the exertion of great energy in the labor movement of California ten unions of migratory or casual laborers have been organized in that State within the past year and chartered by the American Federation of Labor. That work must be aided and supplemented by our Federation.—*From annual report to A. F. of L. convention, Atlanta, Ga., November, 1911.*

The fact of the matter is that the large body of unskilled workers of the United States are composed of workmen brought here from Europe, who do not speak our language, and who in many instances have had their suspicions and prejudices aroused by so-called radical socialist "intellectuals"—writers and orators —who thus make more difficult the effort to organize our fellow-workers of more recent entrance to our country. For years the American Federation of Labor has been engaged locally, and more recently, generally, in the effort to organize the casual and the migratory laborers, and that work will go on. Time and opportunity will dissipate the prevailing ignorance and suspicion and prejudices regarding America's bona fide trade union movement, which, under the banner of the American Federation of Labor, will surely extend to every man and woman worker of our broad domain.—*American Federationist, April, 1912.*

Some months ago the American Federation of Labor inaugurated a campaign of education among the steel workers of the United States and Canada, with the purpose of bringing this great number of toilers into the beneficent and protective fold of the trade union movement. The history of the antagonism of the great steel companies toward the organization of their employees is a matter of common knowledge. Their evident purpose being to thwart any attempt made to organize the workers or for them to organize themselves, the plan of employing workmen speaking foreign tongues was adopted. The steel corporations, by the intermingling of the various races, nearly all endowed with pronounced racial characteristics, consider that these differences in temperament will provide an effectual barrier to successful organization. These workmen, many of whom are untutored, born in lands of oppression, surrounded by squalor, inured to hardship, reaching manhood without that full mental development which makes for independence and self-preservation, are lured to America. Upon arrival in this English-speaking country, the light of our civilization but slowly dawns upon them. The rights to which the American citizen is entitled are unknown to them—the struggle for subsistence being the great necessity. With languages not easily understood, and various tongues spoken in a single steel plant, it is not to be wondered that the workers' comprehension of the rights to which they are entitled comes as an exceedingly slow process.

These facts were the first to be considered in our preliminary arrangements for the educational and organizing campaign to be conducted by the American Federation of Labor.—*From annual report to A. F. of L. convention, Rochester, N. Y., November, 1912.*

It has frequently been charged that the American Federation of Labor and its affiliated organizations make no attempt to organize unskilled men in industries; but there are local unions of unskilled men whose membership reaches several thousands, even ten or fifteen thousand in one local union, as in the case of the local union of building laborers in Chicago. One of the leaflets published by the American Federation of Labor issued for over twenty years and distributed in the millions, contains this statement: "To maintain high wages all of the trades and callings must be organized; the lack of organization among the unskilled vitally affects the skilled; general organization of skilled and unskilled can only be accomplished by united action."

Out of the 1,760 organizers, 1,700 of them, voluntary organizers, are doing splendid work all through the country to organize the unskilled as well as the skilled, because the concentration of effort is more necessary for the unskilled than it is for the skilled.

Although the I. W. W. claims to be the champion of the unskilled workers, its total membership (as stated by its own officers), in good standing, amounts to 14,300. There are affiliated to the American Federation of Labor either directly as local unions or indirectly through affiliated organizations, single locals whose membership equals or exceeds that of the entire membership of the I. W. W.; for instance, the Chicago locals of the hodcarriers and building laborers, and of the street-car men.

The American Federation of Labor employs a large number of salaried organizers whose services are directed toward the organization of unskilled laborers. It disburses at least two-thirds of the money derived from per capita tax for the purpose of organizing the unskilled. In addition the affiliated nationals and internationals assist in the organization of the unskilled assistants and laborers of all kinds connected with their trades and callings. The statement that the American Federation of Labor does not organize the unskilled workers of the country is an untruth. It is an unfounded statement made by the opponents of the American Federation of Labor who have repeated it so often that many people are induced to repeat and believe it.—*From testimony before U. S. Commission on Industrial Relations, New York City, May 21-23, 1914.*

You will find that every one of our friends who are opponents of our point of view and our movement, are always saying that we have never given attention to unskilled laborers. Do you know why that is? The fact of the matter is that there are as many if not more unskilled workers organized and in the American Federation of Labor than there are really skilled workers. The fact is, Mr. Chairman, that when workmen and workwomen organize they pass from the common concept of unskilled workers into the ranks of the skilled, because they have manifested some little skill in organizing. What are hodcarriers and common laborers? Skilled workmen? What are laborers in machine shops and in foundries but common laborers? What are street car men and conductors but unskilled workmen? Some have a little more skill than others in the operation of a car or the collection of fares. But they have organized, and as a consequence they decrease their hours of labor and increase their pay. You hardly regard them as among the unskilled.—*From testimony before Congressional Committee on resolution for a commission on social insurance, April, 1916.*

We have been trying for years to organize the men in the packing industries. We have had some little measure of success. For years and years—and principally within these recent years, we have made an effort to organize the workers in the iron and steel industries. And after the expenditure of thousands of dollars, after the expenditure of years of effort, in the iron and steel industries in which there are more than a million and a half men employed, we have only been able to organize about 100,000, and that has been accomplished within this past year. The people have been kept in bondage. They have been permitted to have their own language newspapers which the companies have subsidized and paid for to abuse and attack the American labor movement and its officers and in order that they shall not join the American labor movement but should hate it and keep away from it.—*From address before Pan-American Federation of Labor Convention, New York City, July 9, 1919.*

THE "COLOR LINE" IN LABOR

We had some years ago in the city of New Orleans one of the largest and most general strikes that ever occurred in this country, and the reason of it all was that the working people of New Orleans were becoming fairly well organized. Some of the unions were in existence many years. The draymen, the teamsters—colored men—formed a union and organized labor generally had their agreements with the employers. The colored draymen's union sent a committee to the employers for the purpose of having their agreements signed, and the employers would not talk to the "niggers." Organized labor of New Orleans sent committees to the employers and wanted to have the agreement signed, and they would not sign it—would not enter into any agreement with "niggers." Organized labor of New Orleans went on a strike; every machinist went on a strike; every printer went on a strike; no paper made its appearance; the men working in the gas houses went on a strike and there was no illumination that night; the bakers went on a strike, and all other white workers went on a strike for the purpose of securing recognition to the colored workmen. And I make mention of this as being what appears to me a very interesting episode in the labor movement, and as an answer to those who have always hurled the epithet to us that we will not assist in the organization of the colored workmen. If there is any union of labor that says anything or takes any action regarding the colored man of the South it is not because of his color; it is because he has as an individual or because they have generally in that trade so conducted themselves as to be a continuous convenient whip placed in the hands of the employer to cow the white men and to compel them to accept abject conditions of labor. It is not a question of personal prejudice or color prejudice, and, as I tried to show by that incident of the New Orleans strike, when it comes to a question of the interests of labor, the white men are willing to sacrifice their positions and their future in order to secure a recognition of the rights of the colored workmen.—*From testimony before Industrial Commission, Washington, D. C., April 18, 1899.*

During the past year the question of organization among the colored workers of the South has been brought forward in several instances. Here and there a local has refused to accept members, simply upon the ground of the color of the applicant. In such cases, where there was a sufficient number of colored workers of one trade or calling, the suggestion was made that they be organized in separate unions, and a council composed of representatives of both organizations be formed to determine upon trade questions. This has generally been acquiesced in; and where similar circumstances obtain, its adoption has been recommended.

Another matter on the same line requires the consideration and action of this convention. In some parts of the South, central bodies chartered by the American Federation of Labor have refused to receive and accord seats to delegates from local unions composed of negro workers. To insist upon a delegation from unions of colored workers being accorded representation in a central body would have meant the dissolution of that organization; and thus neither the desired purpose nor any good end would have been accomplished. This matter has been one of considerable correspondence, with the result that the thought has been developed for the formation of central bodies composed of representatives of negro workers' unions exclusively; that they be permitted to work under a certificate of affiliation from the American Federation of Labor; that there should be a general council representing both central bodies upon any matter of importance to labor, locally or generally. Application has been received for charter from such a central body in the city of New Orleans, but the Constitution of the American Federation of Labor provides against the issuance of more than one charter in any one city; hence the matter is referred to you for such action as you may deem necessary.

Realizing the necessity for the unity of the wage-earners of our country, the American Federation of Labor has upon all occasions declared that trade unions should open their portals to all wage-workers, irrespective of creed, color, nationality, sex, or politics. Nothing has transpired in recent years which has called for a change of our declared policy upon this questions on the contrary, every evidence tends to confirm us in this conviction; for, even if it were not a matter of principle, self-preservation would prompt the workers to organize intelligently, and to make common cause. In making the declaration we have, we do not necessarily proclaim that the social barriers existing between the whites and blacks could or should be felled with one stroke of the pen; but when white and black workers are compelled to work side by side under the same adverse circumstances and under equally unfair conditions, it seems an anomaly that we should refuse to accord the right of organization to workers because of a difference in their color. Unless we shall give the negro workers the opportunity to organize, and thus place them where they can protect and defend themselves against the rapacity and cupidity of their employers; unless we continue the policy of endeavoring to make friends of them, there can be no question but that they will not only be forced down in the economic scale and be used against any effort made by us for our economic and social advancement, but race prejudice will be made more bitter, to the injury of all.—*From annual report to A. F. of L. convention, Louisville, Ky., December, 1900.*

For years the American Federation of Labor has declared in favor of, and the necessity for, the organization of all workers, without regard to creed, color, sex, nationality, or politics. In making the declaration for the complete organization of all workers, it does not necessarily proclaim that the social barriers which exist between the whites and blacks could or should be obliterated; but it realizes that when white and black workers are compelled to work side by side, under the same equally unfair and adverse conditions, it would be an anomaly to refuse to accord the right of organization to workers because of a difference in their color.

We have more than 700 volunteer organizers and a number of organizers under salary, among which are several who are devoting their time exclusively to the organization of the colored workers. This certainly should indicate not only our desire and interest, but also the work which is being accomplished. . . .

The real difficulty in the matter is that the colored workers have allowed themselves to be used with too frequent telling effect by their employers as to injure the cause and interests of themselves as well as of the white workers. They have too often allowed themselves to be regarded as "cheap men," and all realize that "cheap men" are an impediment to the attainment of the workers' just rights, and the progress of civilization.

The antipathy that we know some union workers have against the colored man is not because of his color, but because of the fact that generally he is a "cheap man." It is the constant aim of our movement to relieve all workers, white and black, from such an unenviable and unprofitable condition. . . .

If the colored workmen desire to accept the honest invitation of our movement to organize; if those who have influence over the minds of the colored workmen will encourage the earnest, honest effort put forth by our fellow-unionists, we will find larger success attending their efforts, economic bitterness and antagonism between the races reduced, minimized, and obliterated; but, if the colored workers are taught to depend entirely upon the "good will and control" of their employers; that they can be brought from place to place at any time to thwart the struggle of the white workers for material, moral and social improvement; that hostility will increase, and thus counteract the very best efforts of those who are earnestly engaged in the endeavor for the unification of labor, the attainment of social improvement of all the people, and their entire disenthrallment from every vestige of tyranny, wrong, and injustice.—*American Federationist, April, 1901.*

"LIMITATION OF OUTPUT"

The charge that labor unions handicap ability, discourage initiative and put a premium upon mediocrity and incapacity is a gross and wanton falsehood. No man has ever been prevented by unionism from exercising his faculties to the utmost and rising to any position in the social-economic hierarchy. The unions prescribe a minimum, not a maximum, of wages; they insist on a living rate, but where and when have they prohibited an employer from rewarding superior skill and merit?

If the devil's advocates had the slightest regard for fact, the developments of the past few years would seal their lips and put an end to the baseless assaults upon unionism. American labor, it has been conclusively demonstrated, is the cheapest in the world, in spite of the higher wages prevailing here—the cheapest because the most efficient, intelligent, alert, conscientious and productive. American manufacturers have conquered the markets of the world and have defeated their competitors on the latter's own ground. American supremacy as an exporter of manufactured goods is certain and inevitable.—*American Federationist, July, 1901.*

The unions do not limit the output of the individual workmen. There have been attempts at limitation in some exceptional instances, but these have been due to the dishonest policy of employing and secretly bribing "chasers" to set an impossible and fatal pace. Unionists believe in a fair day's work for a fair day's pay. They do not countenance loafing and "going easy," but they object to the pace that kills and disables a workman

SOME EVERY-DAY PROBLEMS AND CRITICISMS 171

after a brief period of labor. They have a moral right to oppose this policy, and it is to the interest of industry and society that they should oppose it. That unions limit output in order to "make work" for more people is a libel and malicious invention of irresponsible and plutocratic foes of organized labor.—*American Federationist, January, 1903.*

Who among the men who have observed the way the working people of our country toil, the industry with which they work; who among the employing class who have observed their own employees and the workers in other industries but have been struck with the great velocity and intensity with which the toilers of our country work. If they doubt it let them watch the men who come from any part of the world to the United States and put them to work in any industry and you will find, as many of them have said to me when working, "Why I have simply become dazed with the rapidity with which my shopmates have worked." Work harder! Work hard! Work harder, my Heavens! it reminds me very much of what a friend of mine one time said and which struck me as very apt, that it seemed to him some men believed they were put on earth not only to work but to be worked, and inasmuch as they were but a very short time on earth, for Heaven's sake work them harder; you don't know when they are going to drop off. The idea of suggesting that American men work harder!

Well, we are going to do our duty, and I want to say to you gentlemen that there are no men in the world who are more impressive in the lesson that they desire to teach their fellow-workers than are the men—mistakenly called the labor leaders—of our country, who try to impress upon the minds of labor and union men the necessity of doing a good, thorough hard day's work. When a man is always pleading and demanding that the working men of our country shall work harder, and knows no other policy, and knows no other relief—well I simply want to enter my emphatic protest. That is all.—*From address before The National Civic Federation, New York City. (American Federationist, February, 1903.)*

I want to enter my emphatic protest against this constant use of the term "restriction of output" as applied to the American workingmen. I don't pretend to say that here and there you won't find some who shirk work. I don't pretend to say that you won't find some here and there who loaf, but there is not in the whole world, civilized or uncivilized, a working people who toil so hard, who give so much of their mental and physical effort in their work, as do the American people.

And it comes with bad grace from our critics and opponents to say to the hardest worked, most industrious and intelligent workers of the world, that they restrict output and shirk work and loaf.

Last year we had the pleasure of having with us at the New York conference a delegation of gentlemen, brought from England over here by Mr. Moseley to investigate the conditions of labor, and while here and after they had returned to their homes they said they had seen no harder-working people in the world than those in America.—*From address before The National Civic Federation, Chicago, Ill., October 16, 1903.*

There was a time when many workmen undertook to restrict output in the belief that the market would be overstocked with products if they worked the limit of their capacity.

That charge is entirely gratuitous and unfounded in our day and for many years past.

Workmen no longer believe that output should be restricted.

Labor has learned the better and more generally advantageous method of reducing the hours of daily labor and of operating the wheels of industry to their fullest capacity.

One can realize that the criticism of restricting output may be made against workmen of some countries, but we submit that it is wholly unjustified when applied to America's toilers, who are generally and truly regarded as the hardest worked and individually and collectively the greatest wealth producers in the world.

Mr. Schwab and others who hold his views should mend their attitude and consider the trade union movement of to-day, not as it obtained in the past.

Organized labor of our time proclaims the self-evident and just doctrine that the day's work should be universally reduced to eight hours; that wealth should be produced to the fullest extent; that the producers should continuously be the larger

SOME EVERY-DAY PROBLEMS AND CRITICISMS 173

sharers in the greater and still greater production of wealth. And what is more, they are determined and will secure it.—*American Federationist, August, 1904.*

While it is true that in a few trades there may be a limit to the output, it might not be amiss to consider also this fact: That if the organizations of labor did not attempt to put some check upon the inordinate desire of the overseer to drive the men of labor, where would the laborer be? The workers, their lives, is a thought not unworthy of consideration. I had a thought in mind before I broached this subject of limiting the output in regard to the subject of these claims. I think it would not be a bad idea sometimes to "put yourself in his place."—*From address before The National Civic Federation, New York City, December 15, 1908.*

Were we to ask Dr. Gladden if he ever heard the same people who complain of union workmen's petty restrictions also rail in virtuous indignation against the petty meannesses of employers' rules against workmen, what could his answer be? Half a day docked for being a few minutes late; a "fine" for spoiling a piece of work afterwards sold at full price; a threat of discharge for an imaginary breach of discipline—do employers dwell on these injustices? On examination, it will often be found that what appear to be arbitrary rulings by unions regarding "give and take" concessions between employer and employee, putting an end to the system wholly, have only been reluctantly adopted by the unions after full and patient discussion in open meeting, painful experience having taught the members that under taskmaster foremen the custom was almost invariably to "take" from the employee continually and liberally, and to "give" him (and especially *her*) but rarely and then grudgingly.—*American Federationist, August, 1911.*

You state that labor unions limit the output. It is easy enough to make that sweeping charge, but upon what can you base such an assertion? Surely not upon the fact that organized labor seeks to reduce the hours of work. But should that be the case allow me to direct your attention to a number of statements of employers who have had actual experience with the eight-hour day, published in a study of the eight-hour day by Mrs. Josephine W. Elston, which was made a Senate document; and also to the recent public statements before the American Association for Labor Legislation by Mr. S. Thruston Ballard, a manufacturer of Louisville, Kentucky, and Secretary of Commerce Redfield, both published in the February issue of the *American Federationist*. It is now an established fact that excessive hours are an extravagance no nation can safely afford. The same is true of excessive work. It certainly is true that trade unions have endeavored to protect the workers from excessively long hours and from over-work. By so doing they have contributed immeasurably to the world's progress and the well-being of all of the toilers.

You say that labor unions "do not try to obtain the best work." It is very easy for the editor to sit apart from the industrial world and to impugn the motives of those who are struggling with the problems of that life and trying to solve them. It is easy enough to make the vague charge that labor unions do not obtain the best work. There are so many ideas of what the "best work" is—but one thing is certain, nowhere in our country can more efficient skilled workmen be found than those that belong to American trade unions. The union is the one institution that stands for ideals that make skilled efficiency possible. It conserves the muscles, nerves, and minds so that they are in a condition to give the best service; it provides for the instruction of the workers; it enables the workers to protect themselves. Labor unions have opposed some so-called "efficiency" schemes, but if the editor of *Harper's Weekly* could know the difference between real efficiency and the terrible devices evolved to drain the last atom of energy from workers who have been reduced to automatic repetition of motions that kill initiative, he would count that opposition as one of the greatest contributions labor unions have made to civilization with respect to which you assume the rôle of expert.
—*From open letter to Norman Hapgood, Editor of Harper's Weekly, March 14, 1914.*

Having fixed upon the minimum amount of work we are to take into account that all men are not equal and there is no suspicion in the union doctrine that all men are equal in ability, and I should therefore arrange to pay my people in proportion

SOME EVERY-DAY PROBLEMS AND CRITICISMS

to the amount of work they did above the standard—not at all in the way of a bonus, not as a gift, and not charitably, but with a mutual recognition of the fact that if prices are calculated upon the man doing ten articles a day, that if he then does twenty articles a day, the employer can well afford to pay the worker who produces 100 per cent more, 100 per cent more wages, because the overhead expense remains just the same. This is a principle recognized by most industrial engineers and it is perfectly fair to all parties. . . .

I am in favor of putting more and not less responsibility upon the workers themselves and upon their union representatives. As an employer I should expect my employees to give me in return for their wages the fair value in work that we had agreed upon just as I should expect a customer to whom I sold on a fair basis to pay his bill, and am confident that such responsibility would find a ready response. If this fair return is not given then I should hold the union strictly responsible, and if the local officers should be derelict in respecting that responsibility then I should go to the higher authority of the American labor movement, for neither the employer nor the union can be permitted to morally go back upon a bargain duly and fairly made, but with the qualification, however, that since the bargain is a human one circumstances that alter the conditions upon which the bargain was premised may so change as to make it inequitable. There are not many buyers and sellers who insist upon their pound of flesh no matter at what cost, and if we consider wage agreements as partaking of this nature then, both sides approaching fairly, there is no good excuse for trouble. If I considered that my labor agreements had become inequitable I should want to have them equitably revised. Nobody can reasonably expect to succeed with a cutthroat policy.—*From interview with Samuel Crowther on "What I Should Do If I Were an Employer," in "System Magazine," April, 1920.*

THE UNION LABEL

The last convention directed that a label be issued for the product of the members of the American Federation of Labor who have no other label of their own. Although the label has not been in great demand, I attribute it to the fact that we have

had very little opportunity to make its issuance generally known.
In connection with the issuance of the label it would be proper to call your attention to the fact that a decision was recently rendered by a Justice of the Supreme Court of the State of Pennsylvania, which, if allowed to stand, would be one of the severest blows which could be inflicted upon the rights of organized labor. It questions our right to issue a label certifying to the character of the product bearing it. In fact, the decision of Judge Williams is, that inasmuch as the wage-workers do not *own* the product, they cannot have a label certifying to the character of the labor employed in its production. A more unjust decision, in the interest of the wealth possessors, and against the wealth producers, has seldom been rendered even in the darkest days of jurisprudence.—*From annual report to A. F. of L. convention, Birmingham, Ala., December, 1891.*

The first label was adopted by the Cigar Makers' International Union in 1880 at its Chicago convention. Since then 37 national and international trade unions have adopted labels, besides the label which the American Federation of Labor issues for such trades and callings of which there is no national union; hence, no label of the particular trade. It is designed—the reading indicates that the label is of a general character. The label is sold to the unions and in some cases given free to the unions, and is in turn given gratuitously to the employers of labor who comply with union conditions and rules. In some cases they are sold to manufacturers at cost or nearly cost price, the simple object being that in the instances where any charge is made at all that the cost—the simple cost—be covered. In several trades organizations there is no charge made at all, the organization paying for the same, the members paying the organization indirectly in the shape of dues. The advantages are, of course, first, better sanitary conditions in the establishment than are usual in the trade. . . .

The union label on the garment is a guarantee that that garment was made in a factory—was not made in the home of the worker; that it was not made by children; that it was the product of adult labor; that it was not made under the sweat-shop system or in a tenement house under sweat-shop system; that the wages paid were comparatively fair to those prevailing in the trade, and the hours of labor were comparatively fair and reasonable.—*From testimony before Industrial Commission, Washington, D. C., April 18, 1899.*

We who have been in the movement for years and have watched its progress, know the splendid influence which the union label has had in encouraging better sanitary, material, and moral conditions among the workers. The union label has not only been the means of organizing large numbers of non-unionists, but better than all, it has stimulated and strengthened unity and fraternity among the organized workers of the different trades and callings. The demand for the union label upon the product of any other trade than that at which the member is employed, is in itself a manifestation as well as a recognition of the solidarity and the identity of the interests of labor.

In demanding the union label, we do not necessarily antagonize the non-unionist or the unfriendly employer, other than by indirection, as we give our patronage and encouragement to those who are associated with us in the effort to benefit the entire working population; in other words, we give our practical support to our associates, and our friendship to our friends. The more faithful, intense, and persistent we shall be in the demand for union labeled goods, the greater will grow the fraternal sentiment, feeling, and interest which shall entwine the hearts of the workers in one grand brotherhood of labor.—*From annual report to A. F. of L. convention, Detroit, Mich., December, 1899.*

There are many good reasons why a local union should not be permitted to issue a union label, one of which is that it is too easily subject to abuse unless restraint or impartial supervision can be exercised by a general officer. Then again, it is liable to be used to the advantage of a single employer, discriminating against another employer who may desire to operate a fair and union establishment. Apart from this, there are other reasons, which are enumerated in the following preambles and resolutions which I drafted, and which received the approval of the Executive Council:

WHEREAS, It is the policy and purpose of the American Federation of Labor to promote the use of and to create a general demand for union label products, and it has indorsed the union label of every bona fide National or International Union of America issuing a label; and,

WHEREAS, We recognize the necessity of avoiding confusion among union workers and sympathizers with organized labor, who desire to give their whole patronage to union labor and union labeled products; and,

WHEREAS, The issuance of labels by local unions creates confusion by reason of the possibility of large numbers of labels being issued; and further, that the issuance of a label of a local union of a trade is calculated to narrow rather than broaden the sympathy and coöperation of the workers in such trades located at different points, and tends further to postpone the time when a National Union will be formed of the trade, and when a comprehensive label for the trade is adopted; therefore,

RESOLVED, That the American Federation of Labor discountenance the use of and will not approve or indorse any union label issued by any local union as such;

RESOLVED, That where local unions desire the use of a union label covering the product of the labor of its members, that the label of the American Federation of Labor be used until such time as a National or International Union of the trade has been formed, when the organization may be in a better position to issue a successful union label of the trade.

—*From annual report to A. F. of L. convention, Scranton, Pa., December, 1901.*

JURISDICTION DISPUTES

Occasionally disputes occur between two unions, either of the same trade or of trades remote from each other. Questions of jurisdiction arise, and particularly the question of the right of one union engaged in a dispute with their employers insisting on calling members of other unions out on strike in support of them, or insisting that they should be ordered to strike by the Executive Council upon pain of having their charters revoked and fraternal recognition denied. More cases of this kind have arisen in the past year than occurred in the aggregate for the past seven years.

The Executive Council has adopted a rule which it regards as fair, as well as safe, and which is here quoted so that the decision of the Federation may be a guide for the future action of our officers, regardless who they be. It is as follows:

"Resolved, That it is the sense of the Executive Council of the American Federation of Labor that contracts made by unions with their employers should be faithfully lived up to by the union so long as it is not violated by the employers; and the occurrence of any trade dispute with such employers by other unions than those having contracts shall not be cause for the violation of agreements by such unions as have regular contracts.

"The Executive Council further decides that when making contracts unions should consult and act in harmony with all unions with interests at stake."—*From annual report to A. F. of L. convention, Chicago, Ill., December, 1893.*

The question of jurisdiction of national unions within the past year has, if anything, become more intensified than at any previous time, in some instances resulting in open hostilities. It is a most difficult problem to determine where one trade ends and another begins, particularly so in our time, when there is an almost constant state of transition in industry.

The invention of a new machine or a new tool, or the discovery of some substitute article, frequently changes and transforms the labor of one craft, or form of labor, to another, and it is easily understood that men and organizations look with jealous care not only for the maintenance of their organizations, but that they also encounter considerable difficulty in conforming themselves and their organizations to the new conditions. It has been my constant aim to endeavor to aid our fellow-unionists in finding a way out of the difficulties by which they are confronted, or to bring about an agreement, even though it be temporary, in the hope that time would aid in solving the problems.

The last convention declared that organizations having disputes of this character should meet by representatives, and endeavor to arrive at an adjustment before cognizance could be taken of the matter by the American Federation of Labor. While quite a number have acquiesced in this suggestion, yet I have found that in many instances the organization which has benefited by any change and has possessed the power has manifested an unwillingness to meet with the organization whose trade has been the loser. Then again, there is a tendency among too many of our affiliated unions to extend their jurisdiction over branches of trade already organized under another head.

Much of the time which could with advantage have been devoted to the organization and furtherance of our movement had to be given to these questions of disputed jurisdiction; for, had they been ignored, they would have resulted in long-continued struggles to the detriment not only of the organizations involved, but our entire movement and our cause.

In these cases an employer inclined to be fair toward organized labor is made an innocent sufferer; or, on the other hand, other employers unfriendly inclined are glad to take advantage of the internecine strife and play one organization against the other to the detriment of both, and from which the employers referred to reap the sole advantage. . . .

If we were now in the midst of an industrial depression wherein the workers would be engaged in a fierce contest to hold their "jobs," there might be some reason or excuse for such an unseemly scramble; but inasmuch as the workers are very generally employed, there is not even good excuse for the strife.—*From annual report to A. F. of L. convention, Scranton, Pa., December, 1901.*

Beyond doubt the greatest problem, the danger, which above all others most threatens not only the success, but the very existence of the American Federation of Labor, is the question of jurisdiction. I may truly record the fact that never for one moment since the formation of our Federation have I entertained a doubt or misgiving as to the growth, success and permanency of the American Federation of Labor, and I would not now be apprehensive of its future were it not forced upon my deliberate judgment, which has developed into a firm conviction, that unless our affiliated national and international unions radically and soon change their course we shall at no distant day be in the midst of an internecine contest unparalleled in any era of the industrial world, aye, not even when workmen of different trades were arrayed against each other behind barricades in the streets over the question of trade against trade. They mutually regarded each with hatred and treated each other as mortal enemies.

Is the great cause of labor to drift into such a dreadful and miserable strife?

Are all the sacrifices made to be ruthlessly thrust into the gutter?

Is organized labor, the only check to rapacious greed and tyranny, the only hope of labor for protection now or liberty for

SOME EVERY-DAY PROBLEMS AND CRITICISMS

the future, to be engulfed in a tidal wave of expansion madness?

No combination of labor's enemies need cause us the apprehension which this fratricidal strife does in the claims made by unions for the extension of their trade jurisdiction.

There is scarcely an affiliated organization which is not engaged in a dispute with another organization (and in some cases with several organizations) upon the question of jurisdiction. It is not an uncommon occurrence for an organization, and several have done so quite recently, to so change their laws and claims to jurisdiction as to cover trades never contemplated by the organization's officers or members; never comprehended by their title; trades of which there is already in existence a national union. And this without a word of advice, counsel, or warning.

Of course it is evident that in some instances there are two or more organizations which should and could, with advantage, be consolidated or amalgamated into one, and efforts by such organizations should certainly be made, assisted or initiated by the American Federation of Labor, but I submit that it is untenable and intolerable for an organization to attempt to ride rough shod over and trample under foot the rights and jurisdiction of a trade the jurisdiction of which is already covered by an existing organization.

This contention for jurisdiction has grown into such proportions and is fought with such intensity as to arouse the most bitter feuds and trade wars. In many instances employers fairly inclined toward organized labor have been made innocently to suffer from causes entirely beyond their control, and other employers, again, have taken advantage of the first inception of the fancy or notion for "expansion" of trade jurisdiction, fanned it into a flame and taking advantage of the excitement and hatred of and war against each other, refused to recognize either organization, pretending to claim it a war among labor organizations with which they do not wish to interfere. On the surface the employers' claim appears tenable, but in their hearts they enjoy the situation by which their pockets are enriched. Nevertheless the employers' contention in regard to this question can not be disputed. But of the organizations the same can not be said. The interests of the wage-earners of the craft, to promote and protect which the organizations were primarily formed, have no moral or lawful right, from a trade union point of view, to be jeopardized by pursuing a policy in an attempt at trade invasion made without the knowledge or consent of the crafts invaded.—*From annual report to A. F. of L. convention, New Orleans, La., November, 1902.*

It may not be amiss to call attention to a feature in jurisdiction controversies which is so close akin to other phases of human life that it is an ill wind that blows no good. None will dispute the fact that with you I deeply deplore the jurisdiction controversies, and particularly when they assume an acute and often bitter antagonistic attitude; but that they have developed a high order of intelligence in discussion among our unionists, keen perception in industrial jurisprudence, is a fact which all observers must admit. That these acquirements and attainments will be of vast advantage in the administration and judgment of industrial affairs, no thinker dare gainsay.

One further comment and suggestion must necessarily be stated, that hurtful in any way in which jurisdiction disputes may prove to the workmen of contending organizations, we should and must do everything within our power to prevent fair-minded employers, desirous of living in agreement with organized labor, from being made the subject and scapegoat of the hostility of either the one or the other of the contending organizations.

It is true that here and there employers have endeavored to play one organization against another, and by pretended friendship refuse to deal with either. By this piece of cupidity they become a detriment not only to organized labor, but to their competitors in trade. But in any event, the fair-minded employer who desires to live in accord with organized labor should not be compelled to suffer the consequences of injury due to jurisdiction disputes between organizations, and so far as the other type of employer is concerned, the opportunity should not be afforded him to take advantage of such a dispute by which he can shirk and place the blame upon any of our unions. It is trade union law and policy that fair employers desirous of living upon terms of amity with organized labor should not be made to suffer from inter-trade union disputes.—*From annual report to A. F. of L. convention, Pittsburg, Pa., November, 1905.*

Our always interesting friend, Mr. Eidlitz, discussed a subject in connection with the trade agreement which the men of labor are constantly trying to adjust. He called it the grab. We call it the jurisdiction disputes. Well, it is lamentable, but it is true. I don't know that there is an agency or force in all society that attempts more honestly and seriously to adjust that problem than do the men in the labor movement and our movement itself. But, just as he described, there are new conditions in industry that constantly arise and new problems arise with them. What are we to do? . . .

How about the employer—even the building trade employer? Is it wholly unthinkable that a contractor in one line of industry will undertake to secure or try to secure a contract in another branch of that same industry? Of course, in so far as Mr. Eidlitz applied it to labor men, it is grab; so far as it applies to a business man, why, it is—it is business acumen.

Jurisdiction disputes arise between property owners; jurisdiction disputes arise between cities and towns; jurisdiction disputes arise between cities and states; jurisdiction disputes arise between states and states; jurisdiction disputes arise between nations and nations, and more wars in which millions of lives have been sacrificed upon the claims of jurisdiction than probably upon any other subject under the canopy of heaven.—*From address before The National Civic Federation, New York City, December 15, 1908.*

Industrial unionism is not a cure for disputes or differences between organizations of workers. That form of organization would only transfer disputed questions to other boundaries and other terms. Jurisdictional disputes develop from necessary changes in organization and differences of opinions as to the best way of meeting the difficulty. They are an inevitable accompaniment of growth and organization. The problem is not to eliminate jurisdictional disputes, for that would eliminate life, but to meet them in the best possible way.

The element essential to the adjustment of these disputes is the spirit of fraternity among the workers, mindful of common interests and desirous of reaching adjustments. The workers must be willing to go along together and to work out practical agreements. This spirit was one of the distinguishing characteristics of the San Francisco convention. Although there were proposals to use compulsion, to revoke charters, to dictate terms of adjustment, yet the true spirit of voluntary organization prevailed and the workers agreed to remain within the American labor movement and to work out their differences with regard for common interests and for the maintenance of the power and effectiveness of the organization.—*American Federationist, January, 1916.*

IX

INDUSTRIAL WARFARE

STRIKES

Strikes ought to be, and in well-organized trade unions they are, the last means which workingmen resort to to protect themselves against the almost never-satisfied greed of the employers. Besides this, the strike is, in many instances, the only remedy within our reach as long as legislation is entirely indifferent to the interests of labor. . . .

The organizations of labor are the conservators of the public peace; for when strikes occur among men who are unorganized, often acting upon illy-considered plans, hastily adopted, acting upon passion, and sometimes not knowing what they have gone on strike for, except possibly some fancied grievance, and hardly knowing by what means they can or may remedy their grievances, each acts upon his own account without the restraint of organization, and feels that he serves the cause of the strike best when he does something that just occurs to him; while the man who belongs to a trade union that is of some years standing is, by the very fact of his membership in the organization and his experience there, taught to abide by the decision of the majority. Therefore, when anything of the kind I have mentioned occurs or is heard of in the organizations that are of long standing, it is condemned in the most strenuous terms and action is taken to prevent the accomplishment of any such purpose, or if it is accomplished to prevent the recurrence of it. The members of our organization are made to understand well that such a mode of warfare in strikes is not tolerated in any well-regulated or well-organized trade union. So high an authority as the Duke of Argyle, in his work, "The Reign of Law," states that "combinations of workingmen for the protection of their labor are recommended alike by reason and experience." When we strike as organized workingmen we generally win, and that is the reason of the trouble that our employers go to when they try to show that strikes are failures, but you will notice that they generally or always point to unorganized workers. That is one reason also why when the employers know that the workingmen are organized and have got a good treasury strikes are very frequently avoided. . . . Arbitration is only possible when the workingmen have, by the power of their organization, demonstrated to the employers that they are the employers' equal.—*From testimony before United States Senate Committee upon the Relations between Labor and Capital (Henry W. Blair, chairman), August 18, 1883.*

For quite a time a great deal has been said in condemnation of strikes by labor or pseudo-labor men, with which, I confess, I have no patience. It is true that no man who has given the question of strikes and the labor movement any thought can look upon strikes with favor; but to be continually condemning them is entirely another thing. To know when to strike, and particularly *when not to strike,* is a science not yet fully understood. To strike upon a falling market, or being insufficiently organized, or if organized, not properly equipped with the ammunition so necessary to a successful strike—funds—is unquestionably the height of ignorance. The story of the strikes that may have failed of their immediate objects yet have prevented reductions in wages and worse conditions, will probably never be entirely told. Mouthing condemnation of strikes, we find by experience, does not abolish or even reduce their number. As a consistent opponent of strikes, though, I do find that those organizations of labor which have best provided themselves with the means to strike have continually less occasion to indulge in them. The most potent factor to prevent or reduce the number of strikes is a well organized trade union with a full treasury ready to strike should the necessity arise.—*From annual report to A. F. of L. convention, St. Louis, Mo., December, 1888.*

Should strikes be condemned by thinking people? Together with those who love their fellow-men and who endeavor to aid in the solution of this great labor question, I believe that strikes should be avoided whenever and wherever possible. I ask myself, however, and I ask you, Will denunciation of strikes prevent them? Should the workers suffer their already scant means to be curtailed? Would you advise them to bear all the taskmaster's oppression, his insults and injustices, without protest? Shall the natural desire for improvement in his social and economic condition be curbed upon the only ground that he is a wealth producer, a worker? I say, No, a thousand times no. Rather would we suffer the pangs of hunger for a time, when we are convinced that our temporary pain will give us at least a little relief from the overbearing tyranny, and a better opportunity to help in the struggle for amelioration in the condition and final emancipation of the toiling masses. Thanks to our trade unions, however, through the accumulation of a good fund in our treasuries, we need not enter into a strike as often as we otherwise would be compelled to, in order to resist oppression or secure improved conditions; nor need we suffer the pangs of hunger when engaged in a strike.

Strikes, as I have said, are but one of the manifestations—aye, only the outward manifestations—of the trade union movement. Inquire from corporations and employers generally. Apply for the information from the Bureau of Labor Statistics or the trade unions, and, with strange accord, answers will come that the greatest work is accomplished, and that matters of wages, hours, rules, and other conditions of labor, are secured without resort to strikes. These concessions, wrested from the employing and capitalistic class every day, are ever going on, unheeded and unheralded, and form the great evolutionary force that builds up and develops a sturdy and a nobler manhood.—*From paper read before American Social Science Congress, September 2, 1891.*

The number of strikes that have been averted by the trades unions can never be correctly recorded. The efforts to reduce wages and increase the working hours successfully checked will be but half written. The concessions gained in the matters of wages, hours of labor, conditions of employment and legislation, are grudgingly acknowledged and frequently unappreciated. As a matter of fact, the greatest victories of the labor movement are those which are achieved, unheralded and unknown to the general public. They are obtained by the unions in conference with employers or their representatives in their offices, and in many cases a condition of settlement being the fact that the victory should not be proclaimed to the world.—*American Federationist, October, 1894.*

In connection with the railroad strike it is necessary to give an account of the stewardship of your Executive Council, more especially since considerable adverse criticism has been indulged in as to the course pursued by us, and particularly the president.

In the early part of the strike the office of the American Federation of Labor was deluged with letters and telegrams giving an account of the movement and keeping us fully advised of the situation. Between the 5th and 8th of July a number of trade unions had resolved to go out in sympathy with the object sought by the strike. On the 9th inst. a telegram was received stating that the trades and labor unions of Chicago had met by representatives on the day previous, and insisted that my duty towards organized labor demanded my presence at Chicago at the earliest possible moment.

It seemed to me that to go there either as an individual or as president of the American Federation of Labor would be most unwise and impracticable, inasmuch as I could not take any tangible official action. It being about the time when an Executive Council meeting would be held at the official headquarters, I placed myself in telegraphic communication with the members of the Council and obtained their consent to call a meeting at Chicago.

It was also deemed opportune to invite the executive officers of a number of national and international trades unions of the country to meet the Executive Council in an advisory capacity. The meeting took place at the Briggs House, Chicago, when the entire subject matter was discussed in all its bearings. Mr. Eugene V. Debs, president of the American Railway Union, was invited to address the Council, and present to us what he in his judgment believed the Executive Council could or should do under the circumstances. He most eloquently depicted the conditions which caused the strike and boycott, and submitted a proposition which he asked your president to lay before the Railway Managers' Association. It is but proper to say that when Mr. Debs made this proposition, every member of the Executive Council and every member of the conference accepted it as a declaration on his part that the strike had failed, since it contained the provision for the strikers to *return to work unconditionally*.

The conference continued to discuss the situation and Mr. Debs' proposition until after one o'clock in the morning, but not desirous of reaching a hasty conclusion an adjournment was taken until 9:30 of the same day. The discussion was renewed and it was then the Council and the conference prepared the statement in which we declared that it would be unwise and disastrous to the interests of labor to extend the strike any further than it had already gone and requested our fellow-unionists of other trades who were out in sympathetic strike to return to work. . . .

I have stated that the action taken in this matter by your Executive Council has been adversely criticised, and I submit to this convention the fact that either the Executive Council acted in a manner becoming the high interests of labor, or we were untrue to the confidence reposed in us.

We have the right to and do insist that this convention shall in emphatic terms either approve or disapprove the course taken by us. I shall certainly accept your verdict as either a vote of confidence or a want of confidence.

We have remained silent under the criticisms and abuse, believing that we owe it to you, the representatives of organized labor of our country, to say whether the course pursued by us was practicable and justifiable or otherwise.—*From annual report to A. F. of L. convention, Denver, Col., December, 1894.*

One of the stereotyped arguments which is urged against the trade unions most often is that strikes are old and effete weapons, that they have lost their power to secure permanent or even temporary advantages. As a matter of fact, there is no one who has devoted thought to our movement but who will endeavor by every means within his power to prevent the inauguration of strikes, or to take such measures as will bring their number down to a minimum. It would not be amiss to say here that I have yet to meet an active trade unionist who does not deplore the necessity of strikes, and who has not, in countless instances, averted them. But to assert that strikes are ineffective is to assert that which has no foundation, in fact.

Your attention is called to the data returned to the office of the

Federation upon a blank forwarded to the affiliated unions for that purpose, and which forms part of your officers' reports. It will be seen, that notwithstanding the year of practical industrial and commercial stagnation, the movement in which the organized workmen were engaged has been mainly fraught with success, and that defeat or loss occurred in but few instances of minor importance and where the workers were poorly organized and illy prepared.

While this data is of first importance in itself, we have a report just issued by the Department of Labor at Washington, which sets forth clearly that in those states or localities, the industries in which the workers were organized, the largest number of successes were secured and concessions granted; wages increased, hours of labor reduced, and other conditions under which labor is performed, much improved. When such tangible and beneficial results have come, in spite of the fact that so small a number are organized compared to the unorganized, it does not require a very great stretch of the imagination to realize that with the organization of vast numbers of workers, we shall not only make further advances, but out of all proportion to the numbers within our ranks. The organization and concentration of the one—capitalists—presupposes the organization and concentration of the other—workers.

In the very nature of our being, we are determined, as we are justly entitled to demand, a larger share in the product of our labor. We want peace, but we shall insist that peace shall be maintained consistent with the increasing needs of our workers and those depending upon them. We organize, and the better we are prepared to enter into strikes, the less occasion will we have to resort to them in order to insure success in securing justice to labor. With organized labor, corporations and unfair employers will soon realize that concession will be less costly than conflict. All being conscious, however, of what is involved, we are now more careful of entering into haphazard strikes than ever before, not because they are ineffective, but because the voice of labor is more distinctly and emphatically heard. . . .

But wholly aside from the indisputable facts which demonstrate that strikes or preparation for strikes are a most potent weapon to secure better conditions for the workers, a cursory view of modern methods by which industry is conducted will convince that now more than ever are strikes most effective. The concentration of large numbers by which one industry is so closely allied to another that the stopping of one branch may mean the paralysis of nearly all; the vast sums invested in the plants and in the highest developed machinery, these and countless other considerations make the modern strike not only effective but more so than ever before in the world's history.—*From annual report to A. F. of L. convention, Cincinnati, O., December, 1896.*

Show me a country in which there are no strikes and I'll show you that country in which there is no liberty. The state, when it has interfered with industrial affairs, has become the greatest tyrant in the world.—*From address in Faneuil Hall, Boston, April 15, 1901.*

Let those who complain of too frequent strikes ask themselves how much they have done to prevent strikes, to remove the causes which produce them, by discharging their own duties to society.—*American Federationist, July, 1903.*

For the period 1881-1900 the loss to employees in wages through strikes is said to have amounted to $258,000,000, and the loss to employers from the same cause $123,000,000. Lockouts during the same period cost the workmen about $49,000,000 and the employers some $19,000,000.

These, we are told, are the direct losses, and they are tremendous. The inference conveyed is that if no strikes or lockouts had occurred during the period, the above colossal amounts would have been saved and the respective interests be so much richer in consequence.

Now, this inference is subject to heavy discounts, to important qualifications. It is not true that the losses were "pure" losses. It is sheer assumption that in the absence of strikes and lockouts there would have been no stoppages, no interruptions, no enforced idleness. Take the coal mines. There are years when the accumulation of stock is so large that the operators have to suspend production. Where a strike for a few weeks makes such suspension unnecessary, there is no loss in net earnings at the end of the year.

What is notoriously true of coal mining is true of nearly all industries. Business has its ups and downs apart from disputes with labor, and it is the exceptional industry that has no interruptions. Statisticians can not tell what would have happened in any given case if no strike or lockout had occurred and they naturally regard the loss resulting as total and real. But serious thinkers who deal with underlying facts and conditions, and have no preconceived notions to support, take a different view of the matter. . . .

Another fallacy of the statisticians is this—in computing losses, they forget that many strikes result in substantial increases of wages or in reduction of hours. If a certain number of men lose the wages of one month say, in two or three years, and obtain a 10 per cent. increase that is permanent, have they sustained a net loss or have they gained by the strike? It is easy to say that the increase would have come anyway. Perhaps so, perhaps not. In any case, who knows how soon it would have come, how long it would have remained in force without the strike and the fear of another strike? And what about other gains by the workers—moral, physical, social gains in health and leisure, in dignity, in independence, and in authority? Will these be estimated by statisticians and placed on the credit side of the strike account? Altogether, then, the value of the figures on strikes and lockouts is very small and doubtful at best.—*American Federationist, January, 1908.*

Strikes should be avoided whenever possible, but is a strike essentially an evil? As Dr. Lyman Abbott said, in discussing international arbitration treaties:

"What we should be especially interested in, is not that this be a movement for peace, but that it be a movement for justice. Peace has its tragedies, no less than war."

What the right of resistance to injustice is in the political world, the right to strike, to cease work, is in the industrial.—*American Federationist, January, 1913.*

There has never yet been any effort made on the part of the workers for some relief, for some improvement of their condition, but some people have been inconvenienced and others have suffered. If these employers understand their duties to society and to our people they will make arrangements for a satisfactory adjustment between their employees and their companies. The artificial way to do it is a dangerous way, and not only dangerous but ineffective. You will not stop strikes. If they can not strike—that is, if they can not stop work—cannot exercise their rights as American citizens and as free men you will find some explosion somewhere. They will manifest their discontent some other way.

It is a question whether it shall be done in the way of American freemen or whether it shall be done in a measure such as we have seen in revolts. I know that strikes are disagreeable; that they are things that ought to be avoided, and there are no men in all the world who have done more to avoid strikes than these executives of the brotherhood. They are at last driven to the point, not by themselves but by their men, the men they represent. They say, "We are going to have the eight-hour day." They have gone further than I believe their instructions or their credentials warrant them in going, but if they do not stand by their men, if they do not stand by the eight-hour day, depend upon it the men—the rank and file of the men—will relegate them to the limbo of men passé and unrepresentative of the toilers' interests, and instead of these conservative men, who have been driven to this point to represent the interests and rights of their men, they will elect leaders who will be more responsive to deal with their employers in a way to which I would greatly dislike to give even my thought the range.

It is not a pleasant thing, I know. It is one which ought to be avoided and can be avoided. These are the relations between employers and employees. The public is inconvenienced; some suffer, it is true, but, I ask you again, is it the course of wisdom, is it the course of right for any period of time to compel the workman to give involuntary servitude so that the companies may operate their roads and perform their obligations to society? I think not.

If the managers understood definitely that they were to settle their relations with their employees, I doubt if they would hesitate very long or permit the strike to go into force. But even if it were to go into force, with the attendant suffering and inconvenience, bear in mind that it is better, even as awful as that suffering may be, it is better that it be endured rather than the fundamentals of freedom shall be wiped off the guaranties and the statute books of our country.—*From testimony before Senate Committee on Interstate Commerce, on bills in connection with threatened strike of railway employees, August 31, 1916.*

Though better disguised, there marches hand in hand with the idea of the one big union the hysterical and insidious agitation for the general strike of all workers. The general or sympathetic strike is not an innovation. However, as advocated by these promoters of wild vagaries as a means to overthrow existing governmental authority this legal and moral trade union weapon is perverted into nothing less than a revolution-provoking instrument.

Care must therefore be exercised in discriminating between these measures and legitimate collective strikes. In fact, most of the anti-sympathetic strike talk is ill-designed, unwarranted and insincere.

The American Federation of Labor as constituted cannot authorize or direct the calling of any strike—direct, sympathetic or otherwise. Neither are the central labor unions authorized to call a strike of any kind. Strikes, singly or collectively, can only be authorized by the international unions whose members are directly affected.

In a number of instances some of the international unions of closely allied trades or callings have formulated rules and regulations and their agreements with employers have been so designed as to permit of simultaneous action and collective strikes when joint action is required. It is reasonable to assume that as the solidarity of labor finds expression in greater federation of trade unions of kindred and allied trades that the opportunities for greater collective action may develop. Labor will not relinquish in the slightest degree the right to this use of its legal and moral collective weapon to please hostile employers. Neither will it do so to oblige those fanatics who acclaim themselves the workers' saviours and the liberators of the wage-earners of the world.

The strike is a legitimate weapon by which the workers may secure their industrial rights against employers, but when abused and perverted and used to attack the community so that chaos and disruption may paralyze the arm of the government, it then becomes an instrument of anarchy and revolution and carries

INDUSTRIAL WARFARE

with it more harm than good to all concerned.—*American Federationist, April, 1919. (From editorial by Matthew Woll, republished by mutual consent as coinciding with the views of Mr. Gompers.)*

For years and years the members of the police force of the various cities throughout the country have made application to be organized as unions, to have their clubs and their associations transferred from their then existing character to become unions. We have said to them, "Oh, well, to us the question of your being members of the union is immaterial, but we will be glad to aid you as best we can and whenever we can, whether you are organized as unions or whether you are affiliated with the American Federation of Labor or not."

The policemen have appealed to our representatives in various cities, and have appealed to me, coming clandestinely and secretively for fear they might be seen and spotted and victimized, as many of them have been, to try to get them some relief in a way that they cannot get in their existing form of organization. They are not heard, they are not listened to, except one at a time to come before a superior officer, to be chastized rather than to have his grievances remedied; and finally the men have the very heart taken out of them, not daring to have the temerity to present a grievance from which not any one particular policeman suffers, but from which they nearly all suffer in common.

The question came up before the convention of the American Federation of Labor held at Atlantic City just two months ago, in June, 1919, and a resolution was adopted authorizing and directing the executive council of the American Federation of Labor to issue charters to policemen's unions when proper application therefor had been made.

The convention adjourned at the end of June. On July 11 I left the port of New York for Europe. I came back on August 26, and within that period 65 applications were made. Sixty-five unions had been formed of policemen in various cities of the country. Thirty-three charters were issued to policemen's unions throughout the country and others held in abeyance for reasons that I did not know and do not know.

I have been an active member of organized labor for fifty-four years out of my sixty-nine years of life. I have been president of the American Federation of Labor for thirty-six years out of the thirty-nine years of its existence. We began to issue charters to unions in 1883. In all those years I have never seen or heard nor has there come under my observation in any form so many appeals, so many applications for charters from any given trade or calling, business or profession, in so short a time, as were received by the American Federation of Labor from policemen's unions.

Some question the judgment and wisdom of issuing charters to the policemen's unions by the American Federation of Labor or the formation of unions by policemen; but whatever the opinion may be, the fact that it was a real need goes without saying, and the fact of these numbers of organizations springing up all over the country from the farthest west to the east, even to the staid old capital of the United States, and to the city of Boston, shows that the need existed and exists for some remedial agency to secure for the policemen, whose rights and interests have been disregarded, ignored, frowned down upon, the justice which is theirs. They were treated not as self-respecting human beings, but as if they were vassals and who dared not open their mouths, or they would place their livelihood in jeopardy. . . .

As I say, the resolution of the convention was not to organize the policemen, but if applications for charters by policemen's unions should be made, that then the authority is given to the Executive Council to issue such charters. . . .

I make this further statement: The policemen in the District of Columbia or elsewhere in forming their organizations or unions have done so of their own volition. They have not been induced, they have not been urged, either directly or indirectly, to pursue that course. They have the same right to sever their connection with that organization or their affiliation with the American Federation of Labor at their own will. They are free to pursue that course as their own judgment may determine, unrestrained, and without criticism or comment from the American Federation of Labor. It is a voluntary act on both sides, and each can sever the affiliation at its own will. If the policemen shall determine for any reason, or for no reason at all, under duress or of their own will, to sever their connections with the American Federation of Labor, they will receive the unqualified support of the American Federation of Labor in the effort to promote their rights and their interests. . . .

[The CHAIRMAN. Do you make any difference in your conduct applied to these public employers and private ones?]

Mr. GOMPERS. I do, sir.

[The CHAIRMAN. What is the distinction which you make in your conduct?]

Mr. GOMPERS. The distinction that in the last analysis workers giving service to private employers may as a last resort cease work, stop work, quit, strike. In the police I recognize no such right.

[The CHAIRMAN. You recognize no such right. Do you recognize the right in the American Federation of Labor?]

Mr. GOMPERS. I do not. . . .

[The CHAIRMAN. Yes; I understand. In a private service the right to quit, either singly or by concerted action, exists, while in public service, like the police service—I will confine it to the police service in this question—the police do not have or ought not to have that right. Is that correct?]

Mr. GOMPERS. They have not that right, and they do not want to exercise that right.

[The CHAIRMAN. They do not have that right?]

MR. GOMPERS. They do not have that right, and they do not want to have that right, and have so declared in their laws and their rules of conduct.

[The CHAIRMAN. You think they ought to exercise such a right the same as private employees?]

Mr. GOMPERS. I do not; I have already said so several times. . . .

I am not sure, and I am not going to make the charge—I do not know how much part parties and politics have played in the creation of the situation in Boston. I might agree with you, Senator, that there is an opportunity of redressing grievances where the mayor appointed the commissioner of police and where the mayor or the administrator of the force of the municipality may be changed.

In the case before you the policemen of the District of Columbia have no such right. What they want is the right to be heard by a spokesman, the right to be heard by counsel, if you please, not necessarily a lawyer, but by counsel; a right guaranteed by the Constitution of the United States to any of its citizens charged with any crime—the right to be heard through counsel, a spokesman, a man better qualified to present their cause than would be the policeman who has not had the education or the opportunity of speaking for men to men.

They ask to be heard. They are forbidden to organize, forbidden to express themselves for themselves or through any of their representatives chosen by themselves. They came to us and at last we said to them, "Well, if you want to become affiliated we will issue charters." We will try in an honorable, upright, fair manner to present their case or they present their case for themselves and we will supplement it by such moral assistance as we can give them.—*From testimony before Senate Committee on the District of Columbia, September 20, 1919.*

In my letter and the several letters addressed to Judge Gary by the committee, there was not the remotest reference to any question of closed shop or open shop. I assert, without any hesitation or fear of contradiction, that it was not in the minds of the committee and I know it was not in the mind of myself, to discuss the question of the open and closed shop if such conference were had. . . .

[The CHAIRMAN (interrupting). Then you say that the closed shop is not an issue in this strike?]

Mr. GOMPERS. It is not an issue, sir. You can imagine one of the common laborers, unskilled laborers, or skilled workers, if you please, as an individual, going to Judge Gary and presenting a grievance; or, even if not to Judge Gary, to the corporation's counsel, appointed by Judge Gary. You can imagine what chance of presentation would be afforded such poor devil by the representative of this billions and millions of dollars corporation. You can imagine how much courage a man would have in appearing before Judge Gary, or one of his representatives, to present either an individual grievance or a general grievance which the workers may have. . . .

[The CHAIRMAN. Mr. Gompers, Mr. Fitzpatrick stated yesterday, as I remember his statement, that if the conference had been held with Judge Gary, if he had granted a conference, the strike would not have been called. In other words, that the reason for the strike was the failure to secure a conference with Judge Gary. Do you agree to that view of the matter?]

Mr. GOMPERS. With this supplemental reason. I do not think that a mere conference, in which pleasantries might be exchanged —that that was the real purpose of the conference. The conference implied the discussion of the grievances of the men and the effort to reach an adjustment of these grievances, and if that conference had been permitted to take place, in which such a frank discussion could be held, I am firmly convinced that the strike would not have occurred. . . . We do not expect to remedy all the grievances of life in a day. . . .

Men, not impulsive men, but intelligent men, and men conscious of the responsibility of it all, who had declared that they favored the postponement of the date of the strike until after the President's conference was held, when they had come in close contact with the real conditions of the propaganda, of the terrorism, of the corporation's representatives, of the wholesale discharge of men for no other reason than that they belonged to the union, were convinced that it meant either disintegration of the organization because the men would lose confidence, had lost or practically had lost confidence by the mere suggestion that the strike would be postponed. Further, that notwithstanding what any of the officials of the trade unions would have done, regardless of what the committee would have done, the strike would have occurred anyway, a haphazard, loose, disjointed, unorganized strike, without leadership, without consultation, without advice. It was simply a choice whether the strike would take place under the guidance and leadership of men who have proven their worth or under the leadership of some one who might spring up for the moment. . . .

The workers have the right to be heard by counsel of their own choosing, of their own selection. No one underestimates the magnificent guaranty of that right as a citizen before the courts of our country and of our States, but as a matter of fact the working people employed by corporations and large interests, industrial concerns, have more interests involved in their daily vocation, life and work which require representation by counsel than they have before the courts. They want counsel of their own choosing who can speak for them in the common language of our country, and who can present their views as probably the average worker may not have the ability, the courage, or the opportunity to present them. They want for counsel men who can speak as intelligent, constructive citizens, as fellow-workers; men who have felt the wrongs and the injustice of factory life, of mill life; men whom the workers believe have the intelligence (and, if I may say so, a little more polish than we generally have), who can be independent in so far as we are concerned to present and to argue the matters with the employer or the employer's representatives. The right to be heard by counsel is inherent in the political and public life of our country, and we ask for the right to be heard by counsel in our industrial life.—*From testimony before Senate Committee on Education and Labor, September 26, 1919.*

The President made his request that it [the steel strike] should not be inaugurated at that time but should be postponed until after the Industrial Conference which he had called had been held and the opportunity given for that body to determine the course and probably be helpful in an honorable adjustment of the situation. I remind you, my friends, of the fact that in my judgment at that time the strike was untimely, but I had the information given to me in the most direct fashion that the steel corporations had discharged men by the hundreds for no other reason than that they had joined organizations of labor. The fact of membership in a labor organization was the provoking cause for the wholesale discharges and victimizations. Men who remained in these plants were constantly apprehensive of their discharge and victimization. Those in charge could not hold back their strike a day; the workers were determined to go out at the earliest possible moment when they could go out in something like an organized body.

In addition, there were on the ground men who are anti-Americans and anti-progressives in spirit and in action, men who have nothing in common with organized labor or the Republic of the United States, men who would destroy the labor movement of America as gladly and as willingly as they would overturn the Republic. If that strike had not been called on the date set; if there had been an attempt made to postpone it, the men would have gone out just the same and instead of having the counsel and advice and leadership of the constructive trade unionists of America they would have gone under the malicious and malignant influence of the I. W. W. and the Bolshevists. The foreign language press in the United States has long been the medium to prejudice the foreign workers brought into the United States by these corporations and it had been prejudicing the minds of these foreign workmen in the United States Steel Corporation against the men in the American labor movement. We were called fakers, frauds, patrons of capitalism and capitalistic minions, with the money of the capitalistic class jingling in our pockets, and that we were the lieutenants of all the reactionary forces of our day. No wonder the foreign language workers hated us. No wonder they turned away from us. No wonder we found it almost impossible to organize them into American trade unions. These foreign language newspapers were subsidized by financial interests, especially by the United States Steel Corporation.

The I. W. W. agitators and organizers who came into the iron and steel districts during this agitation said: "These men are going to sell you out to the corporations. They do not want you to strike; they want you to work; they want you to be slaves of that corporation, and you will see that they will prove false to you, even at the last moment." If the officers of the twenty-four organizations particularly interested had postponed that strike, it would have given seeming justification to the charges made and the insinuations spread broadcast, and instead of having a strike such as now exists in the iron and steel industry for the past four or five weeks we would have seen the worst conditions possible, and God knows where it would have ended. All the aggression that has led to anything like disorder has been both directly and indirectly under the authority or by direction of the United States Steel Corporation and its subsidiary companies.—*From address at labor demonstration, Liberty Hut, Washington, D. C., October 28, 1919.*

Nation-wide and all other strikes should be unnecessary. But the conditions surrounding the workers makes it impossible for them to secure justice at times unless they do strike. To this the public objects because the strike will cause inconvenience. The comfort of non-strikers is interfered with. When then employers in an industry increase prices nation-wide there is only perfunctory protest from the public. But when labor asks for a sufficient wage to support a family and bring a little joy into the lives of his loved ones the cry goes up that it is un-American, disloyal and every stigma is hurled at them.

A workman must convince his employer that he is entitled to an advance in wages. This can be done only by negotiation, with the right to strike as a leverage and a last resort. If the latter, the public steps in and joins the employer in denouncing the strikers. This is because the public must give up some of its many comforts.

Why should the wage-earner work for less than living wages, which he would have to do if he could not strike. The worker is expected to continue to work at whatever wages his employer is willing to give in order to save the public from inconvenience. The employer is always right; the employee always wrong in the eyes of a misinformed public.

"What is to confine the future demands of labor within the bounds of reason and justice?" you ask. What are the "bounds of reason and justice," when applied to a worker's wages? Is he not entitled to have something to say as to what they shall be? Should he submit his case to the general public for a decision when he knows the general public is exceedingly apprehensive of the slightest inconvenience? A nation-wide strike would not come unless the employers refused to enter into a fair agreement. The worker is always ready to meet his employer half way. The employer refuses to go that far in adjusting disputes unless faced by a strike. The question of "reason and justice" therefore is as much an issue for the employer as the employee. Why should the employer refuse justice and force a strike?

The difference between a strike where the public is not inconvenienced and where it is should have no bearing on the justice of the dispute. The question suggests "compulsory arbitration" as a means of saving the public from being annoyed, otherwise inconvenienced. Where the public is not inconvenienced it does not care how many strikes or how long. Should the public deny justice to those who may have to strike?—*From replies to questions submitted by the "New York World," November 22, 1919.*

THE BOYCOTT

It is well to bear in mind that this weapon of labor [the boycott] is most potent, and one which should be exercised with the greatest degree of care, and with an intense purpose to be absolutely just. An unjust or inconsiderate boycott does more to injure the cause of labor than a hundred victories achieved through its agency. Whenever an application has been submitted to headquarters an investigation was instituted, and the concern complained against given an opportunity to state its version of the matters in dispute. In no case has a concern been placed upon our "We Don't Patronize" list until it has had an opportunity to be heard in its own defense. In each of the letters to employers upon these subjects it was accompanied by the suggestion of an adjustment mutually honorable and advantageous, and tendering, if necessary, our good offices to accomplish that purpose.

At times organizations have objected to the time between submitting the application and the approval of the same by the Executive Council. They have labored under the impression that their simple statement of their complaint should be sufficient, and have, therefore, been impatient with what they regard as unnecessary delay. They fail to realize that we must not only possess the might, but that we must also be in the right. Then again it is pleasing, and especially worthy of your attention, that of the applications submitted fully one-third were adjusted through the intervention of the American Federation of Labor office without the necessity of placing the concerns upon our unfair list.—*From annual report to A. F. of L. convention, Nashville, Tenn., December, 1897.*

Every local organization seems to take upon itself the right to levy boycotts and spread them before the entire country. It seems to me that before people should be asked to taboo a product of any firm, opportunity should be given for investigation, and no boycott recognized unless approved by the conventions, or the Executive Council in the interim of the conventions of the Federation.

The boycott is a very powerful weapon in the hands of the wage workers, but if put on a firm unfairly, promiscuously or without investigation it is likely to react upon us and destroy the usefulness of that method to obtain our rights.

Then again, organizations entirely foreign and antagonistic to the trade unions and the American Federation of Labor have depended in a large degree in carrying out boycotts to a successful termination upon the trade unions affiliated to the American Federation of Labor.

Several boycotts placed on unfair firms by the American Federation of Labor have terminated successfully.—*From annual report to A. F. of L. convention, Birmingham, Ala., December, 1891.*

What is the boycott? There is, fortunately, no reason for any difference upon the right definition of the term. In Anderson's Law Dictionary a boycott is defined as "A combination between persons to suspend or discontinue dealings for patronage with another person or persons, because of a refusal to comply with a request of him or them. The purpose is to constrain acquiescence or to force submission on the part of the individual who, by non-compliance with the demand, has rendered himself obnoxious to the immediate parties and perhaps to their personal and fraternal associates."

The first question to be answered is whether the criminal laws of the United States or of the several component States plainly, directly, and unequivocally declare "A combination between persons to suspend patronage"—the essence of the definition—to be illegal. The answer is a negative one. There is no law in any State or in the nation forbidding any or all combinations to discontinue dealings with obnoxious persons.

In connection with the pending boycott operations in New York and Ohio it has been acknowledged (though not without regret on the part of some) that in neither of the great States named is boycotting a statutory offense. Indeed, it would be impossible to frame a law rendering all forms of boycotting criminal. No one has ventured to advance so absurd and monstrous a proposal, and the courts themselves have had to recognize the perfect legitimacy of at least one form of boycotting. Thus, Judge Spring, of New York, whose decision in the Buffalo Express case, rendered a year or so ago, has recently been given wide publicity on account of its supposed strength, lucidity, and thoroughness, distinctly declared: "The labor organizations had the right to refuse to patronize the Express, or to give support to any patron of that paper."

If words have meaning this sentence establishes the legality of boycotting. We must bear in mind that the difficulty with the Express involved a number of separate organizations—compositors, pressmen, stereotypers—and that they all acted in concert as members of the Buffalo Allied Printers' Unions. If these unions had the right to boycott—that is, discontinue dealings with the Express and all its patrons, it can only be because a combination of any number of men having community of interest to boycott an obnoxious person or persons is not unlawful. So far, then, as the aggrieved workmen were concerned, there was no issue. Judge Spring conceded, then, the right to boycott the Express and its patrons or advertisers and readers.

Can it be contended that the New York judge went too far and erred on the side of laxity or generosity to the boycotters? Not with any show of reason. Any other view is nonsensical on its face. Neither the Express nor its patrons had any vested claim or right to the patronage of the strikers. The strikers were free to bestow their patronage upon whom they pleased, and none could call upon them to assign reasons for their preferences. They were not obliged to purchase the Express, nor were they under obligations to deal with the merchants who used the advertising pages of the newspaper. I take it, therefore, that any court would feel itself bound to affirm the principle laid down in the sentence quoted from Judge Spring's opinion. And that sentence, I repeat, establishes the propriety and legality of simple, passive boycotting by people having a common grievance against one or more persons, even if that grievance be wholly imaginary or trivial.

At what point, then, does boycotting become criminal and a combination to suspend dealings pass into a conspiracy? This is the crucial question.

The Buffalo Express case being typical, I may continue to use it as the basis for my argument. The offense of the boycotters, according to Judge Spring, consisted in this—that they did not limit the combination to members of allied printers' unions, who were directly interested in the dispute, but proceeded to enlist all other labor unions "in Buffalo" in the common undertaking to root out the Express or to coerce it into assenting to the domination of this union. The "other" labor unions joined in the boycott and passed resolutions refusing to patronize the paper and its advertisers, and a special organ was established to push the company and spread the boycott. The consummation of this "scheme," the judge says, was not "insidious, but open, defiant, and unmistakable." In other words, the original boycotters, who acted within their rights in suspending their dealings with the Express and its advertisers, openly appealed, requested, and urged others, not concerned in the difficulty, to become parties to the boycott.

Now, for the sake of simplicity, assume first that this "open and defiant" appeal was accompanied by no threats of any kind. Let us assume that the original boycotters limited themselves to moral suasion and, in the name of such principles as the solidarity of labor, the justice of the demand for fair wages, the economic advantage of strong labor organizations, and so on, they merely requested and exhorted other workmen and elements in sympathy with labor to join in their boycott, would such a course be unlawful? If such appeals and arguments are successful and extend the boycott to outsiders, do we have a case of criminal conspiracy? Are the appellants also guilty of any wrongdoing, and are those who respond to the appeal guilty of some sort of crime?

There is nothing in law or morality to warrant affirmative answers to these queries. There are no decisions upon the hypothetical point raised. We may take it for granted, however, that the most rabid anti-boycott agitator will not venture to assert that boycotters may not resort to moral suasion in trying to enlist others or that outsiders may not heed boycotters' appeals, and of their own free will suspend dealings with persons or firms that had incurred the displeasure of their friends or associates or patrons. Strikers have the right to appeal to their friends to aid them by going out on a sympathetic strike, and their friends have the right to act upon such an appeal. Precisely the same principle applies to boycotters. A sympathetic boycott is as legal and legitimate as a sympathetic strike. Just as men may strike for any reason, or without reason at all, so may they suspend dealings with merchants or others for any reason or for no reason at all. Thus a boycott may extend to an entire community without falling under the condemnation of any moral or constitutional or statutory law. . . .

No one pretends for a moment that it would be proper for a boycotter to approach a merchant and say, "You must join us in suspending all dealings with that employer, or newspaper, or advertiser, on pain of having your house set on fire or of a physical assault." This would be an unlawful threat, and people who would try to enlist others in their campaign by threats of this character would certainly be guilty of a criminal conspiracy.

Do boycotters use such threats? Do they contend for the right to employ force or threats of force? Our worst enemies do not contend that they do. They "threaten," but what do they threaten? They "intimidate," but how? Let Judge Taft, who issued his sweeping anti-boycott injunction, be a witness on this point. He said:

"As usually understood, a boycott is a combination of many to cause a loss to one person by coercing others against their will to withdraw from him their beneficial interests through threats that unless those others do so the many will cause similar loss to them."

This, then, is the threat—this the intimidation. The boycotters threaten third parties to boycott; then, if they refuse, to join them in the boycott of the original subjects of the campaign. In other words, the boycotters say to others: "If you decline to aid us in our struggles, we will suspend dealings with you and transfer our custom to those who do sympathize with us and will support us." The question which the judges and editors who glibly denounce boycotting have never paused to explain is, how a mere threat to suspend dealings can be a criminal threat, like a threat to assault person or property. No man in his senses will dispute this axiomatic proposition, namely, that a man has a right to threaten that which he has a right to carry out. You may not threaten murder, arson, assault, battery, libel, because these things are crimes or torts. But you may threaten to cease admiring him or taking his advice, because he has no claim to your admiration or obedience, and you are at liberty to cease doing that which you have freely and voluntarily done. Similarly, you may tell a man that if he does a certain thing, you will never speak to him or call at his house. This is a threat, but it is a threat that you have a right to make. Why? Because you have a right to do that which you threaten.

The same thing is strictly true of boycotting—of suspension of dealings with merchants, publishers, carriers, cabmen, and others. You may threaten to take your custom away from them and assign any reason you choose. They are not entitled to your custom as a matter of legal or moral right, and you are at liberty to withdraw and transfer it any time and for any conceivable reason. It follows beyond all question that you have a perfect right to threaten to withdraw your custom. The principle is the same whether you threaten one man or a hundred men, whether you are alone in threatening the withdrawal of your custom or a member of a vast combination of people acting together in the premises.

Is not the result coercion of men to do certain things against their will? Very likely, but not all forms of coercion are criminal. Coercion is another term with an ugly and ominous sound which is freely used to intimidate the thoughtless. The legality or illegality of coercion depends on the method used. A man may be coerced by actual force, by the threat of force, or by indirect means which the law cannot and does not prohibit. Coercion by a threat to suspend dealings is, to revert to our illustration, in the same category with coercion through a threat to cease friendly intercourse. . . .

In another New York case we read: "A conspiracy to injure a person's business by threatening persons from entering his employment, by threats and intimidation, is a crime at common law." How clear and forcible! What does "threatening persons by threats" mean? Leave out the terrifying and favorite word "threat" and the proposition is this: "It is a crime to injure a person by telling others that if they do not discontinue dealings with him dealings with them will be discontinued." It is quite possible that this is a crime under the old common law. An agreement to strike for higher wages was a crime in the early days of our Government, under the common law. The common law was vague, obscure, and, as interpreted in less enlightened days, tyrannical. The common law as to strikes has been abandoned, and it will have to be abandoned as to the boycott.

Men have a right to do business, but this is one-half of the truth. The men with whom business is done have the right to withdraw and transfer their custom. This is the other half, which is always ignored in anti-boycott arguments. Keep the two halves in view and boycotting on any scale and for any reason becomes a direct, unavoidable deduction.

Labor claims the right to suspend dealings with any and all who refuse to support what it considers its legitimate demand. The decisions are confused, and the question is new, but ultimately the right of any man to do with his patronage what he pleases must be recognized.

Workmen have a right to say that they will not patronize those who are unfriendly to them and those who support their adversaries. This is all that boycotting implies. There is no aggression here, no criminal purpose, and no criminal way of accomplishing a proper purpose.—*From testimony before Industrial Commission, Washington, D. C., April 18, 1899.*

The union distinctly threatened a sympathetic strike, and called for a general boycott of the plaintiff. It was, undoubtedly, "calculated to injure," and it did injure the plaintiff. But was the injury of a character and kind that the union had no legal right to inflict? Because, said the [Illinois] court:

"The law holds that any person in competition with another may state the truth regarding the business of the other, however injurious to the other that truth may be. This is true of combinations and corporations as well as individuals. The motive in making such truthful though injurious statements, may be to take from the other some of his business and to add to the business of the person making those statements. The motive is a legal one. The act and the motive in this case are both legal."

Had the union threatened to do anything it had no right to do; had it maliciously libeled the defendant and injured him by such libel, a different case would have been presented. But men may "conspire" to do any act which is itself lawful. They may "conspire" to tell the truth. They may "threaten" to exercise their rights. The result may be an injury to the person threatened or denounced or complained of, but such injury is the result of his own conduct, or the incidental effect of ordinary competition, and the law does not undertake to prevent such injuries or punish those who inflict them. If it did, it would destroy individual and industrial liberty.—*American Federationist, March, 1901.*

A certain "master" baker having refused to enter into a union-shop contract with the bakers' local union, that organization, together with the Central Labor Union of the District of Columbia, placed him on the "we don't patronize" list, and by circularizing and otherwise, lawfully urged all workmen and sympathizers with labor to withhold their patronage from him. He appealed to the courts for an injunction to restrain the "boycotters" and declared their peaceable, proper efforts to be a malicious conspiracy to injure him. The lower court granted the injunction "on general principles." There were no precedents in the District of Columbia for such action and no statutes to justify it. The Supreme Court reversed the decision and discussed the question at length. We quote from the clear, logical and convincing opinion:

After all it is a question of individual liberty. It is such a principle that the plaintiff invokes, and it is upon such a principle that the defendants rely for their defense.

The plaintiff has a right to conduct his business in his own way without coercion, without intimidation, exactly as he shall conclude it for his own interest to act. The defendants, jointly and severally, are entitled to the same privilege. They have the right to sell their labor to whom they will and withhold it from whom they will. They have the right to patronize whom they will and withhold their patronage from whom they will. It seems to the court that they have a right to call upon their friends and sympathizers to withhold their patronage from one who refuses to employ them, their friends and sympathizers being left free to answer the appeal as they believe their own interests to dictate. So long as all parties concerned are left free to follow their own choice as they decide their self-interest dictates, it seems to the court that there has been no infringement upon the personal liberty of any one.

But the bakers had demanded a "union-shop" contract! Was that an unlawful demand? "Certainly not," says Justice Stafford. He gives this illustration:

If one manufactures a certain brand of flour, it will be to his interest to convince dealers in flour that they can not afford to be without his brand. It might even be to his interest to convince dealers in flour that they could not afford to deal in any other brand. If he could persuade all consumers of flour to buy only his brand, he could compel dealers to buy only his brand for sale, however much they should prefer to sell some other brand.

Such things are, in fact, done every day in the business world, and our pretended "liberty-loving" friends of the capitalistic press and corporation offices never manifest either pain or horror. Only when labor asks employers to enter into a union-shop contract in the interests of both parties do these gentry take alarm or affect to do so.—*American Federationist, October, 1906.*

It is well known that the term boycott originated in Ireland about twenty-five years ago during the land agitation of the people under the leadership of Parnell, Davitt, and others. An absentee landlord's agent, Captain Boycott, more cruel than the average, incurred the special resentment of the tenantry. They declared that they would "hold no intercourse with him nor deal with him." The incident created world-wide interest, and since then nearly all forms of social ostracism, political opposition (except by regular parties), or commercial discrimination, whether by business men or by labor, have been termed "boycotts." A new phrase was coined for a time-honored method of expressing in practical and effective form the displeasure of one or more persons against unfair opponents.

The coining of the new phrase, however, created no new weapon, no new right, no new wrong.

But to the point, is the boycott in all that the term implies un-American?

All students of American history know that the Boston "tea party" was an American boycott against British merchants and British government.

It is also well known that in various parts of the American colonies there was formed an organization composed of zealous American patriots for the securing of fairer treatment from Great Britain. A large group aimed to achieve American independence.

That organization was known as the "Sons and Daughters of Liberty."

The hopes that they cherished, the aspirations for American independence to which they gave expression, and the acts done to achieve this, were they unpatriotic, un-American? Did they boycott? Let us see.

In the great work of Prof. Woodrow Wilson, president of the University of Princeton, entitled "History of the American People," there are published photographic reproductions of printed boycott posters and circulars issued by the Sons and

A LIST of the Names of *those* who AUDACIOUSLY continue to counteract the UNITED SENTIMENTS of the BODY of Merchants thro'out NORTH AMERICA; by importing British Goods contrary to the Agreement.

John Bernard,
 (In King-Street, almost opposite Vernon's Head
James McMasters,
      (On Treat's Wharf.
Patrick McMasters,
 (Opposite the Sign of the Lamb.
John Mein,
 (Opposite the White-Horse, and in King-Street.
Nathaniel Rogers,
 (Opposite Mr. Henderson Inches Store lower End King-Street.
William Jackson,
 (At the Brazen Head, Cornhill, near the Town-House.
Theophilus Lillie,
 (Near Mr. Pemberton's Meeting House, North-End.
John Taylor,
 (Nearly opposite the Heart and Crown in Cornhill.
Ame & Elizabeth Cummings,
 (Opposite the Old Brick Meeting House, all of Boston.
Israel Williams, Esq., & Son,
 (Traders in the Town of Hatfield.
And, *Henry Barnes,*
 (Traders in the Town of Marlboro'.

The following Names should have been inserted in the List of Justices.

County of Middlesex
Samuel Hendley
John Borland
Henry Barnes
Richard Cary

County of Bristol
George Brightman

County of Worcester
Daniel Bliss

County of Lincoln
John Kingbury

County of Berkshire
Mark Hopkins
Elijah Dwight
Israel Stoddard

WILLIAM JACKSON,
an *IMPORTER;* at the
BRAZEN HEAD,
North Side of the TOWN-HOUSE,
and *Opposite the Town-Pump, in
Corn-hill,* BOSTON.

It is desired that the SONS and DAUGHTERS of *L I B E R T Y*, would not buy any one thing of him, for in so doing they will bring Disgrace upon *themselves,* and their *Posterity,* for *ever* and *ever,* AMEN.

BOYCOTTING POSTER

The true Sons of Liberty
And Supporters of the Non-Importation Agreement,

ARE determined to rësent any the least Insult or Menace offer'd to any one or more of the several Committees appointed by the Body at Faneuil-Hall, and chastise any one or more of them as they deserve; and will also support the Printers in any Thing the Committees shall desire them to print.

☞ AS a Warning to any one that shall affront as aforesaid, upon sure Information given, one of these Advertisements will be posted up at the Door or Dwelling-House of the Offender.

HAND-BILL OF TRUE SONS OF LIBERTY

Daughters of Liberty a few years before the beginning of the Revolutionary War for American independence.

Because of the historic value of these documents and to help dissipate the shallow pretence that labor is guilty of acts un-American in conception and purpose, we herewith reproduce photographic copies of these early American boycott posters and circulars just as they were issued about the year 1775, and just as they appear in President Wilson's history. There are three of them. Read them, names and all. Then ponder over them and let each ask himself whether labor's boycott of to-day is unpatriotic, un-American.

This set of editor-educators—heaven save the mark!—who invoke the eagle's scream in the effort to drown the voice of labor, who clutch at the heavens in the endeavor to becloud the fair name and ennobling purposes of the labor movement, do not know or perhaps remember that even the anthracite coal strike commission felt itself constrained to admit the legality and propriety of primary boycotts, and ventured to criticize only secondary ones. Its logic was dreadfully lame, as we showed at the time, for if we have the right to boycott A, who is unfair, we have the right to boycott B if he persists, in spite of our requests and suasion, in dealing with A. But, waiving this consideration for the present, the aforesaid wiseacres of the editorial sanctum have not even the sense to recognize that primary boycotts, no matter by whom, by how many, or for what reason called and carried on, are entirely legal.

The second set of editors, who are a little more intelligent, we would consider for a moment. This class tries to distinguish between individual boycotts, or boycotts by small groups of persons, and those by strong and powerful unions—locals, central, or national. The latter they profess to regard as illegal and immoral, at any rate, because—because—they hardly know why. Presumably because such boycotts are effective, whereas individual boycotts are negligible.—*American Federationist, November, 1907.*

I saw in a Brooklyn paper an account of widespread meetings of the Ancient Order of Hibernians, locals, which had taken place all over the country, and that they had decided that newsdealers or postal card dealers having on exhibition or for sale cards that caricatured improperly the Irish people should not be patronized, but that they would on the contrary boycott them and give their patronage to others. Of course that was not organized labor.—*From address at Labor Lyceum, Brooklyn, N. Y., April 19, 1908.*

We haven't in all the ranks of agitating and agitated labor a more ardent boycotter than Dr. Eliot. Our evidence? Here it is, at hand (page 36): ["The Future of Trade Unionism in Democracy."]

This all means that in an intelligent and wide-awake democratic society, which does not dread but rather likes the new or novel, and is not the slave of tradition, the consumption of any article which has become subject to a monopoly may be suddenly and effectively reduced. Even the most solid monopolies fear the abstinence of the consumer.

"The abstinence of the consumer!" That's the principle, the gist, the force, the practice of the boycott. The organized wage-worker moves by two cardinal moral principles. The first is: His right, if he is a free man, to dispose of his labor power as he wills. The second is: His right, if he is not a slave, to dispose of his purchasing power as he chooses. And what is the right of one man is the right of many.—*American Federationist, November, 1910.*

Organized labor may claim credit for being in the advance of other institutions in the moralities of this matter of withdrawing patronage. It hears witnesses, attempts conciliation, conserves the rights of both parties to a dispute, and is reluctant to pronounce judgment against even a defiant opponent of trade unionism. Herein it differs from many another class in the community, for we can unhesitatingly say that the boycott, now generally recognized by all classes of society throughout the world as an instrument for remedying grievances, is taken up "instanter" by bodies of people in "highly respectable" circles without giving the persons so penalized any recourse except unconditional surrender. For example, a body of commuters near a large city will in concert quit patronizing a railroad on a day's notice, if another road is at hand to perform their service. Boycotts against men in public life are threatened with a frequency that results in usually leaving them to decide, in their skepticism, which crowd they would rather have boycott them. A President of the United States was not in the remote past menaced by the boycott of one of the large religious denominations for not respecting its Sabbath in its way. The Governor of New Jersey was boycotted last summer by some of the members of the legislature because of his outspoken strictures on their roysterous conduct during the closing hours of the year's session. We have recently had liquor boycotts, neighborhood meat boycotts, the cocoa boycott— to bring about mitigation in the treatment of the enslaved negroes who on the other side of the world gather raw cocoa. Turn which way one will, wherever there is a grievance there is a boycott, or at least talk of the boycott.

In this state of the world's affairs, it is to be recorded that mere dispatronage is now so systematized by the trade unions of America that ultimate boycotts may be reasonably expected to diminish in number and extent. As usual in certain other important moral respects, labor is here in the advanced ranks of reform society, for it gives the possible object of its penalties full time to repent and go scot-free before he be industrially, commercially or financially "singed."—*American Federationist, January, 1911.*

A few days ago I came across a newspaper in which was published a dispatch from a high Catholic priest, in which he took cognizance of a play written by Joseph Medill Patterson. I was exceedingly interested in reading it. In it he says substantially this: that if Mr. Patterson's play advocates divorce and remarriage, it is repugnant to the teachings and the faith of Catholicism, and if that be so the members of the Catholic faith will refuse to witness a performance which is a reflection upon their religion, and they will refuse to patronize a theater in which such a performance will be presented. If not only the prediction but if that advice and suggestion are repeated, however, Bishop Ellis will place himself in exactly the same position where I am, for it is not only a primary boycott upon this production, but it is a secondary boycott upon the theater for permitting the production.—*From address to class in economics, Catholic University, Washington, D. C., May 17, 1911.*

Chief Justice Shepard dissented from the decision of his colleagues in both the injunction and contempt cases and declared that the defendants should not be held as in contempt of court. He held that regardless of the character or purpose of the "We Don't Patronize" list, its publication was protected from restraint by injunction or other process by the First Amendment of the Constitution. His conclusion that the judicial order should restrain acts only, contains the following quotation from Blackstone:

"Every freeman has an undoubted right to lay what matter he pleases before the public: to forbid this, is to destroy the freedom of the press; but if he publishes what is improper, mischievous, or illegal, he must take the consequences of his own temerity. To subject the press to the restrictive power of a licenser, as was formerly done, both before and since the revolution, is to subject all freedom of sentiment to the prejudices of one man, and make him the arbitrary and infallible judge of all controverted points in learning, religion, and government."

Chief Justice Shepard has in all his opinions consistently and undeviatingly upheld the freedom of the individual will as guaranteed under the laws and the Constitution. He has held that abuses of guaranteed rights are subject to punishment by the laws made for that purpose. If a man of the distinguished attainment of this judge and the position of chief justice of the Court of Appeals of the District of Columbia emphatically and unswervingly affirms the contention of labor upon grounds of constitutionality, legality, and expediency, even the most indifferent must conclude that the cause is of consequence and weight. Minority declarations of fundamental principles founded upon truths frequently become the accepted doctrines of a near future.
—*American Federationist, June, 1913, on Court of Appeals Decision on Justice Wright's Injunction.*

PICKETING

What is picketing? It is the stationing of certain members of trade unions near factories or establishments involved in strikes (or lockouts) for the purpose of inducing, persuading, and prevailing upon non-union men to respect the cause of labor and refrain from taking the places vacated by the unionists. How can this be unlawful? It is certainly the right of strikers or their sympathizers to use the public highway peaceably and in a way not obstructive of the equal rights of others. The claim of labor to free exercise of picketing does not include obstruction of the streets and highways, and it cannot be honorably alleged that a few pickets, placed at considerable intervals, interfere with the general liberty of using the highways. . . .

Union labor asserts the legal and moral rights of employing the picket system, just as it asserts the right to strike and to boycott. None of these weapons is necessarily offensive, but they are all clearly defenses. Violence is not a recognized part of labor's plan of campaign. There can be no success for any strike or boycott which defends an assault on person and property.

Labor needs to be strong through numbers, effective organization, the justice of its cause, and the reasonableness of its methods. It relies on moral suasion, because of its conviction that its demands are generally equitable, and picketing is as necessary to the employment of moral influence as the boycott is necessary to the proper use of the moral power wielded by labor and its sympathizers.—*From testimony before Committee on the Judiciary, House of Representatives, March 26, 1900.*

The right to picket is essential to securing an understanding or even a hearing for many an industrial dispute. Coöperation and unity of action among workers must be based upon knowledge of facts and purposes. Only by word of mouth or by some device that appeals immediately to the eye, or by some advertising agency, can workers or strikers disseminate quickly and effectively facts and principles involved in their contest or the justice of their demands upon employers. This proposed measure which denies the workers the right to maintain, carry or transport on any sidewalk, street, public place or private property any banner, sign, transparency, writing or printing denies the workers of their most effective means of getting facts before the public and for placing fellow-workers in a position to decide intelligently upon their attitude toward the strike or lockout.

Employers under the law can secure publicity for their contentions in an industrial dispute through newspapers and other common agencies of publicity which find their way into homes and offices of many citizens. Through their economic power they bar such agencies to the wage-earners. To deny the wage-earners the right to tell their story by word of mouth in the streets, public highways or public places is to deny them a right necessary to carry out the purposes of the labor movement.—*From article prepared for use in the State of Washington with reference to pending bill on picketing, January 11, 1916.*

VIOLENCE AND "GRAFT"

We are citizens of this country, as much interested in it, in its welfare and in its tranquillity, as any men who make up the great citizenship of the United States. We are opposed to riots and riotous conduct, be that during a strike or during industrial peace. But there is a difference between violence and the right of workmen during a strike or lockout of walking on the public streets or public thoroughfares and respectfully approaching workingmen and asking them not to take work in that establishment; trying to argue with them; we claim that is our right. To go beyond that and to enter into any unlawful act, or to make any personal attack, why, of course, it is not lawful and we discourage that. . . .

Our organizations usually have their pickets to patrol the precinct where the strike is taking place and endeavor to persuade the other workmen from taking their places. I know that the terms influencing or persuading are often employed by people in an offensive sense to imply that the persuasion is a club or the fist. That, of course, we do not approve; we do not want that definition to be taken as ours. We shall not pretend to say that under no circumstances does an altercation occur. I do not think that that will be contended even in the best regulated families and communities, not even during the greatest tranquillity between employers and employed; and, of course, all share a like fate occasionally. In the case of men of a peculiar temperament—excitable temperament—when a workman will seek employment in an establishment in which there is a strike, and answer a respectful request or appeal contemptuously or insultingly, he is likely to be met by a remark in kind, leading to—well, a row—blows, perhaps; and when such things occur, come under the observation of well-regulated unions, a man of such temperament, who cannot control his temper, is usually withdrawn and another allowed to take his place. But the right to picket—that, of course, we believe is a lawful right, and it is a right that has been conceded, and conceded generally, until the time when the injunction was employed.—*From testimony before Industrial Commission, Washington, D. C., April 18, 1899.*

I am fully convinced that there is nothing so hurtful to the interests of organized workingmen as the use of physical force in their efforts to secure justice—attacks upon life or property. The men who are active in the labor movement in this country realize that fact and urge it on every conceivable occasion. As a matter of fact it is seldom that a union man on strike makes an attack upon a non-union man. The aggressor is generally an over-zealous sympathizer or an indignant citizen who has a grudge against a corporation; and not infrequently such attacks are promoted by the corporations in order to discredit the men engaged in the contest for wages. . . . We denounce and oppose violence. If any individual in a union commits a crime we expect the officers of the law to enforce the law. Any attempt on our part to apply discipline would be prejudicing his case before it went to the jury. The labor union deals with the economic conditions of work; the Government, representing the whole of society, deals with questions of law and order. Organized labor asks for no exemptions from the law, but it protests against distortions of the law by the courts.—*From interview with James Creelman, New York World, June 7, 1903.*

I have no desire to make so general a statement as to say that there are not dishonest men in the ranks of labor, or that a socalled leader or walking delegate has not proven unfaithful to his trust. But the Sam Parks type has been evolved out of the corruption of the manufacturers. He was corrupted by the manufacturers themselves, and he has been held up as the typical labor leader.

I have the honor of the acquaintance of a large number of business men, public men, and professional men. I am proud to say that I have the friendship of a number of them. I say, with a full knowledge of the responsibility which goes with the statement, that there is as large a number of honest, faithful men in the ranks of organized labor, true to the cause of labor and to our country, as you will find in any walk of life; and I will except none. Mr. Patterson, yesterday, in the course of what was supposed to be an argument against this eight-hour bill, said that the unions are all right if they are only "run right" and if they remain "within the law." The statement was unnecessary except for the purpose of conveying the idea that the labor organizations are not carrying on their work within the law. The same statement that the labor unions are very good so long as they remain within the law applies to every other body on earth. It applies to philanthropic associations. It applies to the churches. I have no desire to excuse or apologize for the improper action of any man or any association.

If a man is guilty of any violation of the law there is provision for his punishment, regardless of whether he is a union man or not; but I resent the insinuation that lawlessness is a part of the work, of the administration, or of the purpose of organized labor. This is a species of the misrepresentation undertaken by the association of which Mr. Parry is the president, and the misrepresentations are not confined to the representatives of organized labor. They have even gone so far as to merit and receive a rebuke from Senator McComas, the chairman of this committee, because of their misrepresentation and misquotation of his statements. They are desirous of making it appear that we are an unlawful association, that we violate the law, and that we are criminal in our conduct because we protest against the injustice, tyranny, and abuse of judicial power; but we are in good company also on that question. Judge Brown, of the Supreme Court of Minnesota, in a recent decision, said:

"Labor organizations or unions are not unlawful, but are legitimate and proper for the advancement of their principles, and it is dependent upon them. The members thereof may singly or in a body quit the service of their employer for the purpose of bettering their condition, and may, by peaceful means to that end, refuse to allow their members to work in places where non-union labor is employed."

Judge Oliver Wendell Holmes, of Massachusetts, said:

"It must be true that when combined they (the workmen) have the same liberty that combined capital has to support their interests by arguments and persuasions and the bestowal or refusal of advantages which they otherwise lawfully control. I rule that the patrol, so far as it confines itself to persuasion and giving notice of the strike, is not unlawful."

—*From testimony before Senate Committee on Education and Labor, 1904.*

Five or six years ago a fierce newspaper wave of indignation, outraged virtue, and denunciation over "labor grafters" passed over the country. It is all quite forgotten now. What did the real substance of it amount to? In New York, one local union official, now dead, was found guilty of extortion in such circumstances that throughout the United States his name was quickly made the synonym for an alleged perfect chaos and carnival of corruption existing in the labor world. In Chicago two or three names of labor men were tacked on to that of the New York convict, to be used in every editorial paragraph written by an enemy of organized labor in the endeavor to show how the unions were dragging the country down to a condition of business peril and established employed-class dishonesty. An assistant district attorney of New York, in the midst of the hubbub over the matter, publicly announced his intention of sending "labor leaders" to Sing Sing by the score. On this point, two years later, District Attorney Jerome, on being asked for the information, wrote to a representative of the American Federation of Labor that up to that time the threatened convictions by the carload had actually amounted to three. In these three cases only one man served his time.

We repeat, that form of crusade against labor's spokesmen and agents has ended. It failed. In spite of the fact that more than 25,000 American labor organizations have officials, the country-wide legal drag-net operated by their actively hostile opponents brought next to nothing to the surface in the way of dishonest administration. Labor had passed through the fire and been found true metal.—*American Federationist, June, 1910.*

Did organized labor properly express its condemnation of violence on hearing of the Los Angeles disaster? It did by interviews, addresses, and publications. The hundreds of union labor papers, in their issues succeeding the event, contained what, taken together, would make volumes, declarative of the sentiments of their editors and of the rank and file of union membership on the subject. All recognized the case as one of mystery, the feeling shown being that of horror at the possibility of any union man being implicated in it. Unions framed resolutions in meetings, declaring that trade unionism was not to be advanced by murderous acts. Union labor officials, and many others, were quoted to similar effect. The president of the American Federation of Labor, the day after the disaster occurred, as published by the St. Louis *Star*, said:

"Labor does not stand for such outrages, nor contemplate such crime. I cannot believe that a union man has done it, and I deeply hope no one who was connected with the labor movement will be found to have done it. It is inconceivable that a union man should have done this thing. And yet, if it is found that a union man has done it, unionism cannot be blamed by fair-minded men for the deed of a man devoid of any human feeling, as the perpetrator of this horrible catastrophe must have been. It was the act of a madman. No one with an ounce of sympathy in his makeup could do aught but contemplate such a crime with the deepest abhorrence."

These facts were further fully presented in the June, 1911, issue of the *American Federationist*, in a seventeen-page article entitled the "McNamara Case," in which the leading facts up to that time were reviewed. Speaking before the St. Louis Central Labor Union on Sunday, October 2, 1910, the day after the disaster, President Gompers asserted he would "immediately turn the dynamiters over to the proper authorities if he could lay hands on them." The *Globe-Democrat* also quoted him as saying: "I only wish I knew the actual perpetrators, and if I did, take my word for it, I would turn them over to justice." The universal condemnation of a murderous deed in labor circles ought to be a fact so far beyond question, so easily ascertainable from accessible records, that no man with any regard for his reputation for veracity could deny it. . . .

Violence, brutality, destruction of life or property, are foreign to the aims and methods of organized labor of America, and no interest is more severely injured by the employment of such methods than that of the workers organized in the labor movement. Therefore, quite apart from the spirit of humanitarianism and justice which prompts the activities of the organized labor movement, policy and hope for success forbid the resort to violence. The American labor movement and its men are loyal Americans and seek to obtain the abolition of wrongs and the attainment of their rights within the law.

Organized labor of America has no desire to condone the crimes of the McNamaras. It joins in the satisfaction that the majesty of the law and justice has been maintained and the culprits commensurately punished for their crime.

And yet it is an awful commentary upon existing conditions when any one man, among all of the million of workers, can bring himself to the frame of mind that the only means to secure justice for labor is in violence, outrage, and murder.

It is cruelly unjust to hold the men of the labor movement, either legally or morally, responsible for the crime of an individual member. No such moral code or legal responsibility is placed upon any other association of men in our country.

In so far as we have the right to speak, in the name of organized labor, we welcome any investigation which either Federal or State courts may undertake. The sessions of the conventions of the American Federation of Labor are held with open doors that all may see and hear what is being said and done. The books, accounts, and correspondence of the American Federation of Labor are open to any competent authority, who may desire to make a study or an investigation of them.

Will the National Manufacturers' Association, the Erectors' Association, and the detective agencies extend the same privilege for public investigation and examination of their books and correspondence?

When we were selected as a Committee on Ways and Means to raise and dispense funds for the defense of the McNamaras and the prosecution of the kidnappers, we were fully impressed with the innocence of the accused men. That impression was strengthened by their written and oral protestations of innocence. We here and now, individually and collectively, declare that the first knowledge or intimation of their guilt was conveyed by the press in their confessions of guilt. From the outset we assured all contributors and the public generally that we would publish an accounting of the moneys received, from whom received, and to whom paid. This assurance will be fulfilled. A report in full will first be made to the Executive Council of the American Federation of Labor, at its meeting to be held at Washington, D. C., January 8, 1912.

The American labor movement has done so much for the workers of our country in improving their condition, in lightening the burdens which the workers have had to bear, bringing light and hope in the homes and in the lives, the factories and the workshops of our country, that it challenges the world of investigators. The organizations of labor of America have been the most potent factors in the establishment and maintenance of the largest measure of industrial peace. Their course is of a conciliatory character, to reach trade agreements with employers, and the faithful adherence to agreements. When industrial conditions become unsettled they are more largely due to the unreasonableness of employers, who regard every effort of the workers to maintain their rights, and to promote their interests, as an invasion of employers' prerogatives, which are resented with consequent struggles. If employers will be but fair and tolerant, they will find more than a responsive attitude on the part of organized labor, but, of one thing all may rest assured, that with existing conditions of concentrated wealth and industry, the organized toilers of our country realize that there is no hope from abject slavery outside of the protection which the organized labor movement affords.

The men of organized labor, in common with all our people, are grieved beyond expression in words at the loss of life, and the destruction of property, not only in the case under discussion, but in any other case which may have occurred. We are hurt and humiliated to think that any man connected with the labor movement should have been guilty of either. The lesson this grave crime teaches will, however, have its salutary effect. It will demonstrate now more than ever the inhumanity, as well as the futility, of resorting to violence in the effort to right wrongs, or to attain rights.

In view of the great uplift work in which the men of the labor movement have been and are engaged, and the industrial problems with which they have to contend, we insist that our organizations of labor should be judged by what they do, and aim to do, rather than to be opposed and stigmatized because one or a few may be recreant to the good name and high ideals of labor, and we appeal to the fair-minded citizenship and the press of America for fair treatment.—*American Federationist, January, 1912.*

He [J. J. McNamara] and every one else assured me that he was absolutely guiltless. McNamara said to me over and over again: "It's all right; you can rely on us." When I left him the last time, he took my hand—he is a tall, broad-shouldered young fellow—and looked me in the eyes and said:

"Sam" (everybody who cares a cent about me calls me Sam; I never cared for "Mr. Gompers" or "President Gompers"), "I want to send a message by you to organized labor and all you may meet. Tell them we're innocent—that we are the victims of an outrageous plot."

I believed him—I had no reason not to at that time—and I delivered his message.

If he had told me in confidence that he was guilty, I will say this: I don't believe I would have betrayed him. I'm willing to stand by that—I don't believe I would have betrayed him. But I certainly wouldn't have declared my confidence in his innocence; and I certainly would not have gone out and helped to collect money for him.

But no one, at any time, gave me the slightest reason to believe these men were guilty. I returned East and went through the arduous work of preparing for the annual Federation convention at Atlanta. It was the most progressive, harmonious, and constructive gathering ever held by labor in America.

Upon my return I was met with this awful thing. These two misguided men were guilty—they confessed that they were guilty. I was horror-stricken and amazed.

I have no intention of adding to the burden and misery of these two wretched men by any statement of mine. What concerns me is the effect of this matter upon the welfare of labor. In my opinion it will not be serious in any way. No former or present enemy can be placated; no true friend of labor will be alienated. . . .

We have been bitterly attacked since the confession of the McNamaras. The newspapers have, with a few exceptions, assailed us. That is nothing more than we expect; we never look for an even break with the newspapers of America. Their managements are employers of labor, in many cases quite large employers, and, with some most honorable exceptions, they seem to believe that their interests as employers must line them up against organized labor, in policy if not in practice.

But the laboring people of this country are not in any way deceived or estranged by this outcry against the organization of labor. They know that the American Federation of Labor has a right, like any other organization, to ask that it be judged by two things—what it has done, and what it aims to do. The workers know what it has done for them in the past, and what they can do under its organization in the future. . . .

Personally I have never received so many words of encouragement and approbation in my career as during these attacks. The men of labor know me. I have worked for long, long years with them. I am one of them. They know that it has been my life's ambition to serve them to the fullest limits of whatever power or ability there is in me. And they know I am neither a dynamiter nor a law-breaker. . . .

Mr. Frank Morrison, Secretary of the American Federation of Labor, was supœnaed by the Federal Grand Jury of Indianapolis to appear before that body and to bring the books of the American Federation of Labor for submission to the experts employed by the Department of Justice for the Federal Government. At headquarters Secretary Morrison and we were exultant when that subpœna was served. He went before the Grand Jury and testified. There was not a question put to him which he avoided or answered except in the most direct manner. All the books, checks, receipts of the American Federation of Labor, of the McNamara Ways and Means Committee, of his personal account, were placed before the Grand Jury and their expert accountants. The books have been returned to the offices of the American Federation of Labor, and on this day, Wednesday, February 14, the following statement was published in the Washington *Times:*

GOMPERS AND MORRISON EXONERATED BY PROBE INTO DYNAMITE PLOT.

President Samuel Gompers and Secretary Frank Morrison, of the American Federation of Labor, have been completely exonerated by the Federal dynamite investigation, according to a positive statement of a Department of Justice official to-day.

Not only were there no indictments returned against these officers, but nothing was brought before the grand juries to indicate that they had any knowledge of the dynamiting conspiracy while the outrages were being perpetrated.

That statement was telegraphed throughout the country and published in many newspapers. Having received telegraphic congratulations and other words of commendation, and asked for a comment, we wrote as follows:

Sincerest appreciation your congratulations that Department of Justice officially has completely exonerated the American Federation of Labor and its officers of any knowledge of or complicity with any alleged dynamite plot or other unlawful conduct. When Secretary Morrison was subpœnaed to appear before Federal Grand Jury and produce all the Federation's books, I was exultant, for I knew that the more thorough the investigation would be made into the affairs of the American Federation of Labor, the more complete would be the exoneration and vindication of the Federation and its officers. In view of present developments I can only express the hope that the men charged with lawlessness may be proved to be innocent. Violence and brutality have no place in the American trade union movement, and now more than ever is it necessary for every earnest, faithful wage-earner to organize, and for all of us to exert our every energy to unite, solidify, and federate the organized labor movement for the establishment of justice and for the common uplift.

—*From "Gompers Speaks for Labor," McClure's Magazine, February, 1912.*

It is easy to blame, condemn, yea, even to pity, but how few try to understand. Perhaps the man who works beside us is going through a cruel struggle and he is all but beaten. The world has him by the throat—we do not try to understand, we call him queer, self-centered, and turn to more cheerful companions. Perhaps our outer cloak of selfishness is but a shield to protect us from the overwhelming burden of the world's sorrow and the bitter wail of those who suffer. Whatever the reason, many of us shut others out of our minds and hearts. We know little of those around, we know little of ourselves, the circumstances that mold our wills and thoughts, the mysteries of our physical and our spiritual selves and the strange relation and the influences between the one and the other. But when we will, we know that every fact, every condition, every person, is the inevitable outcome of determining forces over which individual volition may or may not have control.

With the understanding mind and the spirit taught by the teacher of old, who said, "Let him who is without sin cast the first stone," I would have you consider these men now pilloried by public opinion and adjudged by the court guilty of crimes against society and humanity. I would have you ponder how it is said that among people professing to believe in the brotherhood of man and the gospel of love, men, American citizens, came to look upon violence, dynamite, terror, as the only defense left them against the grinding, conscienceless tyranny of those controlling hours, wages, and conditions of work. That is a terrible charge against society.

There are many ready to heap upon the structural iron workers, not alone the men adjudged guilty, but every member of their union, condemnation and humiliation; many ready to wrap the robes of saintly justice tightly about them lest contact defile them, ready to withdraw from these men every good and uplifting influence and to cast them out to the mercy of whatever interest might profit by their helplessness.

And as to these who counsel harshness and deny mercy—are they the men who have fought the fight in the world of men and conquered without blemish to themselves? Are they men who know the world of work and toil, who have felt or who know the powers pitted against the weaker elements, who have felt or who know the cruelty and heartlessness of the world of profits where men succeed by climbing over and standing upon those they have struck down and defeated? Do these self-appointed censors, so positive and assured of their own virtue that they hesitate not to judge fellow-men, really know this world of toil and fight? Have they themselves been a part of it, and prevailed over it?

These men who are accused of doing these grievous wrongs, of waging a warfare dishonorable and reprehensible, thereby inflicting upon all the workers trouble and heartache—what manner of men are they, and what is their life? Turn to the great cities whose growth has been one of the striking characteristics of the past sixty years. In those cities marvelous structures seem to stretch upward almost touching the cloudland, expressing the infinite ambition of man—structures overwhelming, wellnigh unbelievable in conception and execution, reaching upward twenty, thirty, yea, more than fifty stories, and downward into the depths of the earth. Or turn to the mighty, yet exquisitely delicate structures spanning rivers and chasms that the forces of civilization may conquer every barrier—the bridges, the great engineering achievements in the heart of civilization, or in the lone places of the earth. Watch one of these constructions in the process of erection—the iron skeleton as it rises skyward, the frame about which building materials are to be gathered and fashioned. As the girders and separate pieces are lifted into position, watch the workers moving along narrow places, boldly poised on perilous, dangerous heights, securing bolts and rivets. Watch the human worker as he stands on an iron skeleton of a building thirty stories up from the earth's security and lifts his head upward—there is nothing between him and the vast, bare expanse of the heavens; as he looks out upon the city, the handiwork of his craft and his fellow-workmen, and down, down into the narrow passageways below, there tiny specklike men scurry to and fro like ants occupied with little plans and business. Then ponder well what manner of man is this builder of our modern civilization. He lives a bold, open life; his very breath is danger and conquest.

Or watch him as he goes out, out into the space of the chasm, far from safety, that he may secure for others safety in transportation; as he stands above rushing torrents or floods, or looks down into the crevasses of the earth. Can a man cope with these great elemental powers, fight with the physical powers of the universe for control without daring, courage, recklessness in his heart?

Every day's work he does in building for the safety of others strengthens these natural qualities in himself. No weakling could do such work. The worker comes to exult in his dangers and chances—risk to life and limb is but part of the day's work. Inevitably efficiency in this work brings to the average workman a feeling that results are the ultimate end, that human safety must not weigh too heavily in attaining them.

The structural iron workers perform this kind of service for society. Society accepts the service and thereby incurs responsibility for its effect on the workmen. It is a service that requires a high degree of skill, physical bravery, and the kind of efficiency that feels a responsibility for results. What if the workers did not report to the superintendent each weak place they found, each bolt or rivet that would not hold? Though these workers have done good work—work which is the pride of our civilization—yet did the paymasters begrudge fair terms of compensation and would deny the men in their organized capacity—the only way it was possible—a right to a voice in determining conditions under which they should toil. These paymasters were not single individuals with whom the workers could talk over their claims and perhaps adjust their grievances, but a great corporation connected with the greatest industrial corporation and one of the greatest financial organizations of the world; an organization whose stockholders know nothing of the workmen employed or work done, but entrust all to the managers hired to look after details of operation and responsible to the owners only for producing profits for distribution.

The more profits the managers turn over, the higher is the praise given their management and the greater their reward. Who among them cares if unknown workmen are deprived of a fair share of the wealth they create, in order that profits may be larger? Not only so, but officers in various corporations which alone (the American Bridge Company) were unable to destroy the organizations of these workers, banded themselves together as the National Erectors' Association, and under the banner of the most implacable of labor's foes, the National Manufacturers' Association, and backed by the United States Steel Corporation, declared war to a finish upon the Structural Iron Workers' Union of America.

For six years the fight went on. All of the forces of organized society were used against these men; subtle minds were scheming and plotting that legal authority and practice might aid in the breaking of these men. You say that these men resorted to forbidden methods of violence and even sacrificed lives. You condemn their methods of fighting as elemental, brutal. Of any of those who are guilty, the condemnation is true, but I ask you—were the methods used by the employers less deadly to humanity and freedom? Do you think that one side can play with the forces of injustice and tyranny and not lead to a defensive move on the part of the other? Each will protect its own interests, would anybody else do that for it? Indeed, our very social organization seems to be on trial. And how little does society understand. Even the judge who tried the case, smugly assured of personal irresponsibility, fatuously declared: "The evidence in this case will convince any impartial person that government by injunction is infinitely to be preferred to government by dynamite."

The worthy judge had blindly chanced upon one of the causes, but had failed to realize causal relationship. The words to him were simply a conventional epigram—he does not know that there is a law of life, just as immutable as the law of gravitation, of attraction and repulsion, a law of life which meets tyranny and injustice by resistance. The inaptness, aye, the unwarrantable character of this utterance of the judge, discloses how far afield outside of the case he went to take another slap at labor. If ever the time shall come (and let us hope and work that it never shall come) when government by dynamite shall be attempted, it will have as its main cause the theory and policy upon which is based government by injunction—personal government foisted upon our people instead of a government by law.—*American Federationist, February, 1913.*

RESTRICTIONS ON LABOR ACTIVITIES

There appears to be a tendency on the part of the courts and officers of the government to make all strikes, and particularly those on the railroads, an offense against the laws of the country. Early in the year Judge Ricks issued an order compelling railroad employees to continue their work for a company, and convicted and sent to prison an engineer who had not complied with the order. That such an interpretation of the inter-state commerce law is at variance with its plain intent is held by eminent jurists; and I would cite the fact that when that law was under consideration in the Senate an amendment covering the exact provisions as contained in Judge Ricks' order was defeated. The order of Judge Taft went even farther in its effect upon the denial of the right to cease work in order to obtain fairer conditions of labor than did that of Judge Ricks.

Your attention is called to the fact that the Postmaster-General and the superintendent of the railway mail service recommend in their reports just made the passage of a bill making practically the cessation of work (strike) of employees on railroads an offense against the laws of the United States and punishable by a fine of from $50 to $500 and imprisonment of from six months to two years. The latter-named officer in his report submits a bill framed upon the subject and the former approves it, at the same time adding his definition of a mail train to mean any train even "with a single pouch or a railway postal car." . . .

When nearly every other government of the civilized world is conceding the full right not only of organization, but also the untrammeled right to use every legitimate means for the purpose of securing higher wages, less hours and better conditions for labor, it illy becomes the officers of our Republic to seek further hindrances to intensify and burden the struggles of labor.—*From annual report to A. F. of L. convention, Chicago, Ill., December, 1893.*

We bespeak attentive study for one of the most radical, far-reaching and enlightened decisions ever rendered in the United States by a high court in a labor case. It furnishes a complete vindication of the position of organized labor. It sweeps aside all antiquated notions, so dear to the judicial fossils and the plutocratic enemies of the trade union movement, and invokes modern, rational, progressive principles. It sustains the view expressed in the *American Federationist* in combating the fallacies and half-truths of the pseudo-individualistic press, which has denounced the methods of unions as tyrannical and un-American.

Briefly, what does organized labor claim? This:

1. The right to organize local, central and national unions, and federate all.

2. The right to strike, as a means of enforcing recognition for unions and the principle of "collective bargaining."

3. The right to refuse to work with non-union men.

4. The right to picket establishments involved in a strike, and to employ moral suasion to prevent men from taking strikers' places.

5. The right to boycott, individually and collectively, obnoxious employers and other adversaries of labor, and to induce all friends of unionism to join in such boycott.

Astonishing as it may seem, the decision referred to emphatically upholds each of these claims. It was rendered recently by the appellate division of the New York Supreme Court, a body of five judges, and it was unanimous. There is therefore strong reason for hoping that the Court of Appeals, the highest tribunal in the State, will affirm and indorse the remarkable judgment. The labor question, on its legal side, would then be settled in New York, and settled right. That other States would gradually adopt the same reasonable and just policy, there can be no doubt. The logic of the New York decision is irresistible.

The question presented to the court was this: Has an association of workingmen organized for self-protection and self-help the right to obtain the discharge of one man or any number of men "by threats, intimidation, strikes or otherwise"? In other words, is it lawful for a union to go to an employer and warn him, if he engages certain men, or retains men already in his employ, a strike will be ordered by a combination of other men in his employ? Over-ruling an inferior tribunal, the appellate division of the Supreme Court has answered this vital question in the affirmative. Two opinions were written, one by Justice McLaughlin, the other by Justice Ingraham, distinguished and experienced jurists both.

Justice McLaughlin reasons as follows: It can not be seriously doubted that every workman has the right, in the first instance, to say for whom and with whom he will work, and an employer, of course, has the correlative right of saying whom he will employ or prefer among two or more rivals. Once this reciprocal right is destroyed, liberty is destroyed, giving place to industrial despotism. Now, if one has the right alleged, when acting in his individual capacity, he does not lose it when acting with others clothed with an equal right. Consequently, laborers may combine and say they will not work for employers who engage any but members of labor organizations, and employers may combine and say that they will not employ persons who are (or who are not, as the case may be) members of such organizations. It is true that, as a result of a combination of laborers certain men may lose employment, but that is an incident of industrial liberty and competition.

The fact that organizations cause injury to certain persons does not make their purposes or action illegal. In the words of the supplementary opinion of Justice Ingraham, "It is the illegality of the purpose to be accomplished, or the means used to accomplish that purpose, that makes a combination illegal." The purposes of trade unions are admittedly lawful, and such methods as strikes and threats of striking are not in themselves unlawful, since every man has the right to quit work for any reason and at any time, and this right is not lost when he enters into a combination to exercise it. Hence it is not unlawful for a union to demand and procure exclusive employment, or the discharge of obnoxious workmen, by threats of striking or actual striking.

The principle that whatever is lawful when done by one person is lawful when done by a combination of several, seems almost axiomatic, yet it has been tacitly and openly denied in nearly every labor case previous to that under discussion. That was due to the persistence of old common law notions of "conspiracy"—notions utterly inapplicable to modern conditions. In this age of coöperation and consolidation it is futile and absurd to employ obsolete tests. The advanced position taken by the New York court works a deliberate, intelligent recognition of the doctrine of personal liberty—equal rights—in the sphere of the relations between laborers and capitalists.

A little reflection will show that the boycott is entirely justified in the light of the same guiding principles. There is no question that one man may, for any reason, withdraw his patronage from any person or any number of persons. He does not lose this right on joining an organization; hence any association of men may collectively order and maintain a boycott. Indeed, examine any of the above enumerated claims of organized labor, and it is plainly seen to be valid and proper, if the New York judgment be accepted as well-founded.

Of course, all that labor demands for itself it is willing to grant in equal measure to others. It does not oppose combination among employers. It does not depend on legislation. It asks no special privileges, no favors from the state. It wants to be let alone and to be allowed to exercise its rights and use its great economic power. Workmen must rely on their own strength, the strength resulting from mutualism and organization. —*American Federationist, September, 1900.*

It may be doubted if the extraordinary decision which British unionism has recently received has had a parallel in the development of labor and social legislation since the time of the confiscation by the crown of England of the funds accumulated by the guilds centuries ago. The result is viewed askance by the best friends of labor, and even capitalistic organs of some fairness have not been able to pretend satisfaction with it. The story is most remarkable; for it shows how, under the form of law, rights, and apparently guaranteed opportunities, may be stolen.

It is not, perhaps, generally known that under the English law trade unions are permitted to register and assume a quasi-corporate status. When Parliament enacted this union registration law it was regarded by all, including the members who spoke in its favor, as a valuable concession to organized labor. The avowed intention was to confer a benefit—not to impose a burden or restriction. Mr. Frederic Harrison, the distinguished English writer who has for years been a legal adviser of the

British unions, thus explains the law in regard to registration of unions:

"Until the acts of 1871 and 1875, which legalized trade unions and strikes, the unions were illegal societies, and could be robbed with impunity. The authors of those acts assumed that in making unions legal they did not make them corporate bodies capable of suing and being sued. When some of the unions were asking for power to sue as corporate bodies, some of us on the royal commission told them that, if they had the right to sue, they would be exposed to the liability to be sued, in which case they would soon be ruined. But from that day to this it has been held that trade unions could not be sued as a body and made liable to the whole extent of their funds —benefits to widows and children and all."

But lately the House of Lords (the tribunal of last resort in Great Britain) has rendered a decision which practically makes corporations of unions in spite of themselves, and which exposes the whole of their funds to legal liabilities. The case is known as the Taff Vale case, and grew out of a railroad strike. In the course of this strike the officers of the railway employees' unions circulated documents "calculated to injure" the company and to cause the boycotting of its line. It was the alleged injury inflicted by these circulars that constituted the ground for the company's suit for damages. The House of Lords, overruling the court below, held that unions may be sued in their registered names as though they were full-fledged corporations; that they are responsible collectively for the acts of their respective officers, and that their funds are liable to attachment and may be taken to satisfy all legal claims. This would have been sweeping and revolutionary enough, for the decision violates the intent, spirit, and letter of the registration law. Indeed, the lords, in their opinion, based their conclusion not on legal principles, but on what they were pleased to term "public policy." They *inferred* that parliament, though it did not say so, *meant* to make unions corporate bodies to all intents and purposes; and they argued that the power to own property, to maintain an organization, and act through officers, ought to be accompanied by the liability to be sued and held collectively responsible for injuries caused by the officers. In short, the lords, finding that the law did not go far enough to suit their notion of public policy, *read a new meaning into it*. It was a case of absolute judicial legislation or usurpation.

But this was not all. A second decision, rendered almost simultaneously with that in the Taff Vale case, "filled up the holes" left open by the first. The principle established by this second decision is this, in the briefest possible terms:

That when a trade union seeks to compel or coerce an employer or merchant by "inducing" others not to deal with him, it may be civilly liable in damages. This means that even where no violence or intimidation is used, and unionists limit themselves to means strictly peaceful, employers who are inconvenienced or injured by a strike, and merchants who are injured by a boycott, may obtain damages for such injuries.

Such sweeping law practically destroys the right to advise a strike, the right to persuade men not to work for unreasonable employers, the right to picket, and the right to boycott or circulate boycotting literature. To make injury the test of legality is to revert to the absurdities of the common law of the early years of the struggle of the laborers. As I have repeatedly shown:

Injury does not necessarily imply wrongful action.

A man may injure another without overstepping for a second his proper sphere of action. The question is not whether a man injures another, but how he causes the injury.

A blow is a tort.

A libel or slander is a tort.

A threat to kill or destroy property is criminal.

But injury by means of a peaceful strike or boycott—even when by persuasion and appeal thousands are influenced to join such strike or boycott—does not, morally or legally, entitle the injured party to damages.

The House of Lords has thus minimized the labor of years of effort and progress and reform. Is it possible that these two decisions will be permitted to stand? Will not the House of Commons be called upon by Britain's sturdy workers to annul this judicial legislation and restore to labor the rights thus stolen from it? It is gratifying to know that the British Trade Union Congress has directed the institution of proceedings to determine definitely the legality or illegality of picketing under the new decision.—*From annual report to A. F. of L. convention, Scranton, Pa., December, 1901.*

The injunction granted by the court, in this case, prohibits the officers of the American Federation of Labor, the officers and members of all affiliated unions, their or our agents, friends, sympathizers, counsel, "conspirators or co-conspirators," either as officials or as individuals, from making any reference whatsoever to the fact that the Bucks Stove and Range Co. has ever been in any dispute with labor, or to the fact that the company has ever been regarded as unfair, or has ever been on any unfair list, or upon a "We Don't Patronize" list of the American Federation of Labor, or of any other organization. The injunction prohibits any and all persons from either directly or indirectly referring to any such controversy. Such statement or reference is also prohibited by printed, written, or spoken word. . . .

In my report to the Executive Council, in September, I took occasion to discuss this matter, and I can do no better than repeat the language here:

"Your attention is especially called to a feature of the case of this injunction. If *all* the provisions of the injunction are to be fully carried out, we shall not only be prohibited from giving or selling a copy of the proceedings of the Norfolk Convention of the American Federation of Labor, either a bound or unbound copy; or any copy of the *American Federationist* for the greater part of 1907, and part of 1908, either bound or unbound, but we, as an Executive Council, will not be permitted to make a report upon this subject to the Denver Convention.

"Unless we violate the terms of this injunction, we are prohibited from referring to the case at all, either in our report to the convention or to others. Should a delegate to the convention ask the Executive Council what disposition has been made, or what the status of the case is, we shall be compelled to remain silent. For one, I am unwilling to be placed in such a position. I have neither the inclination nor the intention of violating the process of the court, but I cannot see how it is possible for us to hold up our heads as honest men and still refuse to give an accounting to our fellow-workers and to the public as to the status and outcome of this case."

The Executive Council has been advised that in this report to you I shall fully cover this subject, thus making it unnecessary for duplication in the report which the Executive Council and I will jointly make to you.

As a citizen and a man I cannot and will not surrender my right of free speech and freedom of the press. As president of our Federation, a decent regard for my duty to you and to all our fellow-workers, and to the public generally, requires that a comprehensive report shall be made of these entire proceedings, so that the subject may receive your consideration, to the end that action may be taken to protect the interests of labor and the rights of our people before the courts, as well as before that higher tribunal, the public conscience of the people of our common country.

It is impossible to see how we can comply fully with the court's injunction. Shall we be denied the right of free speech and free press simply because we are workmen? Is it thinkable that we shall be compelled to suppress, refuse to distribute, and kill for all time to come the official transactions of one of the great conventions of our Federation? I opine not.

Now it is the American Federation of Labor and the *American Federationist* which are enjoined from the exercise of the right of free speech and the liberty of the press. In the future it may be another publication, and this injunction will then be quoted as a sacred precedent for future and further encroachments upon the rights and liberties of our people. The contention of labor with the Bucks Stove and Range Co. sinks into comparative insignificance contrasted with the great principles which are at stake. Is it imaginable that inasmuch as the Constitution of our country guarantees to every citizen the right of free speech and free press, and forbids the Congress of our government from enacting any law that shall in any way abridge, invade, or deny the liberty of speech and the freedom of press, that a court by the issuance of an injunction can invade and deny these rights?

I venture to assert that the bitterest antagonists to labor in Congress would not have the temerity to present to that body a bill which would deny to the toilers of our country the right of free expression through speech or by means of the press, and yet this very denial and invasion are attempted by this injunction.

There is no disrespect on my part to the judge or the court when with solemn conviction I assert that this invasion is unwarranted. The wrong has grown from the precedent set by previous injunction abuses, and the judge in this instance has but extended the process. The suppression of freedom of the press is a most serious undertaking, whether in autocratic Russia or in the republic of the United States. It is because the present injunction and the contempt proceedings thereunder suppress free speech and free press, that I feel it my duty to enter a most emphatic protest.

For ages it has been a recognized and an established principle that the publisher shall be uncensored in what he publishes, though he may be held personally and criminally liable for what he utters.

If what is published is wrong, or false, or seditious, or treasonable, it is within the power of the courts to punish him by applying the ordinary process of law.

If what is published is libelous, the civil and criminal laws may be invoked.

The right to freely print and to speak has grown up through centuries of freedom. It has its basis in the fundamental guarantees of human liberty. It has been advocated and upheld by the ablest minds. Tremendous sacrifices have been made in its establishment. These rights must not, cannot, and will not be complacently surrendered—they must not be forbidden by a court's injunction.

Injunctions as issued against workmen are never applied to, or issued against, any other citizen of our country. These injunctions are an attempt to deprive citizens of our country, when they are workmen, of the right of trial by jury. They are an effort to fasten an offense upon workmen who are innocent of any illegal act. They are issued in trade disputes to make outlaws of men, who are not even charged with doing things in violation of any law of state or nation. These injunctions issued in labor disputes are an indirect assertion of a property right in men, when these men are workmen engaged in a legitimate effort to protect or to advance their natural rights and interests.

The writ of injunction, beneficent in its original purpose, has been perverted from the protection of property and property rights, and extended to the invasion of personal rights and human freedom.

It is an exhibition of crass ignorance for any one to assert that we seek to abolish the writ of injunction. The fundamental principles upon which injunctions may rightfully be issued are for the protection of property and property rights only.

He who seeks the aid of an injunction must come into court with clean hands. There must be no adequate remedy at law.

The injunction must never be used to curtail or invade personal rights.

It must never be used in an effort to punish crime. It must never be used as a means to set aside trial by jury.

Yet injunctions as issued against workmen are used for all these purposes and are never used or issued against any other citizen of our country for such purposes, and not even against workmen unless they are engaged in a labor dispute. Such injunctions have no warrant in law, and are the result of judicial usurpation and judicial legislation, which usurp the place of Congressional legislation and are repugnant to constitutional guarantees.

In all things in which workmen are enjoined by the process of an injunction during labor disputes—if those acts are criminal or unlawful—there are already ample law and remedy provided.

Labor asks for no immunity for any of its men who may be guilty of violence or crime. It has no desire to become a privileged class, much less a privileged class of wrong-doers.

Labor protests against the discrimination against workmen which denies them equal justice with every other citizen of our country. If any man of labor be guilty of a violation of any law, we contend that he should be apprehended, confronted with his accuser, and tried by a jury of his peers; that he, like all other citizens, be presumed to be innocent until proven guilty.

This course of justice is reversed by the practice of the injunction in labor disputes; for, as already stated, our form of government and principles of justice maintain that it shall devolve upon the prosecution to prove beyond the peradventure of a doubt the guilt of the accused. In the injunctions issued against workmen, they are required to show cause why they should not be fined or imprisoned. In other words, the burden of proof is shifted from the prosecution or plaintiff, upon the shoulders of the accused or defendant. It is not necessary to prove his guilt. He must prove his innocence. And yet the acts which he is charged with doing may be in violation of no law, though they may be enjoined by a court's injunction.—*From annual report to A. F. of L. convention, Denver, Col., November, 1908.*

There has not been an utterance upon that subject [trade agreements] this afternoon made by representatives of labor or employers that can not be made the subject for a suit under the Sherman anti-trust law, and by which each may be mulcted in damages threefold to the amount claimed, and each man tried and if found guilty sentenced to pay a fine of $5,000 and sent to prison for a year. Indeed, the existence of these agreements—the trade agreements to which we all point with pride and satisfaction—are in themselves all the evidence that is necessary. . . . There is no one who can gainsay the fact that these trade agreements are in violation of the law as interpreted by the United States Supreme Court, and that at any time when any employer of labor or any other man undertakes, upon some whim, to lodge a complaint and bring suit and claim threefold damages, the federal government, through its department of justice, may institute proceedings at any time the administration may so determine rendering every wage-earner prosecuted subject to fine of $5,000 and one year's imprisonment. To say that the administration of to-day has not brought such a suit, is no answer. It may be that the men intrusted with the administration of our affairs to-day are not in accord or are not in sympathy with that view of the industrial situation of the law as applied to it, and if that be so, then the associations of labor exist by the permission, at the sufferance, of the men entrusted with the affairs of government.—*From address before The National Civic Federation, New York, December 15, 1908.*

Here is his [Dr. Lyman Abbott's] entire idea as he wrote it (italics ours): "But the law ought to be, if it is not now, that employees have a legal right to quit their employment in a body for any reason *or for none at all,* and by peaceful measures to induce others to do so, except in those cases in which public safety or public health will be endangered, and in such cases the public ought to provide some other method of redress for the real or fancied wrongs of the employees."

We shall not now discuss the doctor's exception to his dictum.

It would at best include but a small percentage of all employees. His general rule is clear. Wage-workers have a right to quit work for any reason or for none at all.

Our contention for many a year has been that very idea in those very words. It is the only solid base for a true conception of the legal rights of the participants in the trade union movement. . . .

Now, how is it that, times without number, we have observed that audiences which we were addressing refrained from applauding when we said it was clear to us that bodies of workmen had a right to quit work for any reason or "for no reason at all"? How is it that editorial writers and the professors thereupon pronounced us as "radical"—meaning, perhaps, dangerously extreme, or inclined to be riotously revolutionary? How is it that the phrase seemed blasphemous to the reverent, treasonable to the patriotic, unwise to the diplomatic, insulting to the employer? To us it only has appeared a simple fact. It is not necessarily a harmful fact. A workingman with fair common sense might hold it as a truism, valuable in his stock of principles, and yet never be impelled by it to go on strike once in his life. He might regard the joint right of himself and his shopmates (or even his fellow-trade workers) not to go to work if they so willed, thus depriving their employer of their labor, precisely in the light of their common right to set up a coöperative store, thus depriving of their usual custom the storekeepers who had been in the habit of purveying for them. The fact is, an employer has no more legal or property right to a wage-worker's labor than a storekeeper has to a customer's patronage.—*American Federationist, November, 1910.*

Governmental power grows by what it feeds upon. Give an agency any political power and it at once tries to reach out after more. Its effectiveness depends upon increasing power. This has been demonstrated by the experience of the railroad workers in the enactment of the Adamson law. When Congress exercised the right to establish eight hours for railroad men it also considered a complete program for regulating railroad workers which culminated in taking from them the right to strike and the conscription act providing for compulsory service.—*American Federationist, January, 1917.*

If the railroad men undertook to perform any affirmative action that would mean an attack upon life, upon the person, upon property, they are subject to the laws of the country and of the States. If they undertake to do an act that would unlawfully prevent any other workman, a citizen of the country, from going to work, they are amenable to the law and can be made to answer for such action; but when the men working in the railroad service do nothing more than quit their trains and say they will not work under the old conditions, they are within their rights, constitutionally and inherently, and the Republic can not endure if that right is taken from them. You can not make free men of some and compel others to give service or be punished by fine or imprisonment or both.

Look at the disposition of the railroad companies, assuming that the Adamson law is merely a declaration of Congress in the principle that eight hours should constitute a day's work. Take that law, passed by a practically unanimous vote of the Congress of the United States, recommended by the President, and then signed by the President—no consideration is given to it other than to fight it before the courts. Suppose, now, these presidents and the other officials of the railroads should themselves go on a strike, or suppose they should resign their positions and leave all of these institutions without directing boards, without a president, without a general manager, without superintendents, without foremen, and all that sort of thing. How are you going to reach them? Have they not the right to resign? And is not that a strike? . . . Suppose the Members of Congress, the House and the Senate, should resign collectively? . . . They have a legal right to do so. Would they be indicted for conspiracy for resigning from the service of the Congress of the United States? Suppose the House of Representatives refuses to make appropriations until the will of the House is obeyed; and that, after all, is the inherent principle provided in our Constitution, and that is taken from the British law, that appropriations must originate in the House of Representatives. Suppose the House of Representatives should determine that a certain law should pass as a condition precedent to the making of any appropriations for the Government. Would they be haled before the courts for conspiracy and subjected to a fine and imprisonment? The whole element of popular government has its essence right in the power of the appropriations made by the House of Representatives, and it is the old idea of compelling the king to yield.—*From hearing before Senate Committee on Interstate Commerce on "Government Investigation of Railway Disputes," January 11, 1917.*

November 9, 1919, the Executive Council of the American Federation of Labor issued a statement concerning the injunction granted by Judge Anderson ordering the officers of the United Mine Workers to call off a strike of miners. In that statement appears the following:

"Both the restraining order and the injunction, in so far as its prohibitory features are concerned, are predicated upon the Lever Act, a law enacted by Congress for the purpose of preventing speculation and profiteering in the food and fuel supplies of the country. There never was in the mind of Congress in enacting that law, or in the mind of the President when he signed it, that the Lever Act would be applied to workers in case of strikes or lockouts.

"The food controller, Mr. Hoover, specifically so states.

"Members of the Committee having the bill in charge have in writing declared that it was not in the minds of the committee, and the then Attorney General, Mr. Gregory, gave assurance that the government would not apply that law to the workers' efforts to obtain improved working conditions. Every assurance from the highest authority of our government was given that the law would not be so applied."

November 12, former Attorney General Gregory was quoted in the press as having made denial that he had given Secretary Morrison and me the assurances referred to. The press report is as follows:

"Former Attorney General Gregory denied in a statement here to-day that he had given assurances to labor leaders that the Lever Act would not be enforced against their organizations in attempts to better working conditions, as asserted by officers of the American Federation of Labor.

"While Attorney General I did not at any time give assurances to any one that any law would not be enforced against any class of citizens," he said. "I gave no assurances that the government would not seek to enforce the Lever Act."

When the Food Bill was introduced in the House it was thus explained by Representative Lever, its author, in an interview in the *New York Times* of May 20, 1917:

"Never was such a drastic bill drawn. The President has given his word that it is only a war measure and that it ceases to be in effect when the war is over. It is framed simply to safeguard the nation's food supply for its own use and for whatever we can do for our allies while we are *fighting the war out.*"

When the bill came up for action Representative Keating on behalf of labor urged an amendment providing that nothing in Section 4 should be construed as repealing Sections 6 and 20 of the Clayton Act.

June 22, 1917, this debate was held in the House between Representatives Lever and Keating as reported by the *Congressional Record,* page 4396:

Mr. Lever. . . . . We do not believe—and the matter was thoroughly discussed in the Committee on Agriculture—that this section in any wise serves to repeal or amend in the least particular either the Clayton Anti-Trust Act or any other act which deals with the right of men to strike for purposes of increasing their wages or bettering their living conditions. We do not believe that this effects that in the least.

Mr. Keating: Let us get the issue cleared up. Let us get a concrete case. Suppose that men engaged in work on the railroads of the country—we will say, the telegraph operators on a particular line in this country—decided to strike. Is it the object of the gentlemen, and is it the object of this bill that the power shall be vested in some one to compel those men to go back to work? Let us face the issue squarely, and if this is not your purpose, why not adopt this amendment?

Mr. Lever: I am glad to face the issue squarely. If there were such a combination to strike for the purpose of bettering living conditions or increasing wages there is no purpose in this bill, and there is no authority in this bill, to prevent it.

The following day this statement was made by Representative Keating and a letter read from Food Administrator Hoover. (*Congressional Record,* June 23, 1917, page 4515.)

Mr. Keating: Mr. Chairman, this amendment is the one I offered the other day to section 4 of this bill. At that time I made it apply exclusively to section 4. In its present form it applies to the entire bill. When my amendment was before the House the other day the contention was made that I was seeking to have farmers' organizations and labor organizations exempted from the operation of this bill. I want to impress on the members of the House that I am not seeking any exemption for any class. Neither the farmers nor the members of labor organizations, so far as this amendment is concerned, are granted exemption from the provisions of the bill. The sole object of this amendment is to clarify the bill. The chairman of the Committee on

Agriculture has assured us that it was not the purpose of the framers of the bill to interfere in any way with Section 6 and Section 20 of the Clayton anti-trust law. Mr. Hoover, who will be called upon to administer this act, in a conference held a week or two ago with representatives of all the great labor organizations of the country confirmed this view, and suggested the amendment which I have offered. On that point the chairman of the Committee on Agriculture (Mr. Lever) has requested me to read the following memorandum which he has received from Mr. Hoover:

Mr. Hoover's memorandum—" 'Washington, D. C., June 22, 1917.

" 'Memorandum for Mr. Lever. The labor representatives are very much exercised over the possible reading of the food control bill to stretch to control of wages, and they suggest that an amendment may be made providing that the labor provisions of the Clayton Act should not be affected by the proposed bill. I understand that Mr. Keating proposed this amendment and it was defeated.

" 'It appears to me that there is no intention in the bill to interfere and I believe it might silence a great deal of criticism and opposition which might be raised in the Senate if this amendment could be undertaken. I do not wish to impose my views upon you, but simply to suggest that as it is not the intention of the bill to regulate wages, it might do no harm to satisfy this element in the community that they are immune from attack.

" 'Yours faithfully,
" 'HERBERT HOOVER.' "

During the meeting of the Executive Council of the American Federation of Labor June 25-27, I called the attention of the members to the efforts made to have the Lever bill passed. A circular had been sent to all affiliated organizations urging them to appeal to members of Congress. I herewith submit a copy of that portion of the minutes of the Executive Council pertaining to the subject:

"President Gompers informed the Executive Council relative to the action taken by the officers of the American Federation of Labor to secure the enactment of the Lever Bill before the first of July, 1917. He said, in going over the bill, there is a clause which might be construed to be conspiracy if a strike occurred.

"President Gompers informed the members of the Executive Council that an amendment offered by Representative Keating, providing that no part of the Lever Bill should annul Sections 6 and 20 of the Clayton Law, was defeated. President Gompers stated he believes that the amendment could be adopted in the Senate. It was decided that President Gompers draft a statement upon the amendment, to be used to secure its adoption by the Senate."

A letter was sent to all Senators and Representatives urging that this amendment be adopted:

"Provided, That nothing in this act shall be construed to repeal, modify, or affect either Section 6 or 20 of an act entitled 'An act to supplement existing laws against unlawful restraints and monopolies and for other purpose, approved Oct. 15, 1914.'"

Senator Hollis presented this amendment in the Senate and it was adopted. When the bill went to conference it was stricken out. August 6, 1917, Senator Hollis called the attention of the Senate to the danger of eliminating the amendment. He read the amendment and then this colloquy took place. *(Congressional Record,* August 6, 1917, page 6401):

Mr. Sheppard: Does not the Senator think that, if necessary, such an amendment can be enacted subsequently as substantive and independent legislation?

Mr. Hollis: I think it might, but I should dislike to undertake the contract of getting it through both Houses at this time. I think the situation may be so serious that the administration will have to take hold and insist on having it passed. If so, it will go through; otherwise I doubt if it could be put through.

On Monday, August 6, 1917, this statement regarding the right of labor to strike was made in the Senate. *(Congressional Record,* Monday, August 6, 1917, page 6403):

Mr. Chamberlain (Senator in charge of the bill): Mr. President, there is not anything in the act, it seems to me, that would prevent labor organizations from peaceful picketing or the peaceful strike if they see fit to indulge in it; and, while, as I said, I did not vote against the Senator's amendment, and I do not recall having been with the conferees when it was receded from, I would not have hesitated to do so in conference, because I think it unnecessary. It was insisted upon by the Senate conferees for quite a while and finally went out. I really do not know how many days it had been in conference before the Senate conferees finally receded. But Mr. President, I have not any fear that in the administration of the food law anything would be attempted by the President or by the agencies which he has power to create under the Act to prevent any labor or other organization from doing in a peaceful way all that they can now do under the Clayton law to protect themselves and their rights without any saving clause in the bill under consideration. It is not necessary in this bill in order to protect rights.

The defeat of the amendment caused me to call the matter to the attention of the joint meeting of the Advisory Commission and the Council of National Defense held August 6, 1917. Those present at the meeting were: Secretary of Navy Daniels, Secretary of Commerce Redfield, Secretary of Labor Wilson, Mr. Willard, Dr. Martin, Mr. Godfrey, Mr. Rosenwald, Mr. Coffin and Mr. Gompers. The minutes of the meeting show:

"Commissioner Gompers expressed concern over statements that had come to his attention in connection with the pending food bill, indicating that it was the intention of certain elements influential in its framing to prevent all strikes and that it was intended that the enactment of the law should have that effect. Mr. Gompers stated that he brought the matter to the Council for its very serious consideration. On motion of Secretary Redfield it was agreed that the matter should be brought by the acting chairman to the attention of the President."

After returning to my office, August 6, 1917, I dictated to my secretary, among other things, this memorandum of the meeting:

"I stated that I had within a few minutes of the meeting been informed that the amendment, offered by Senator Hollis to the food administration bill, providing that nothing in the bill should be construed to be a repeal or modification of Sections 6 and 20 (labor provisions of the Clayton Act) was defeated.
"The Council of National Defense and Advisory Commission adopted a motion that the acting chairman, Mr. Daniels, be empowered and requested to present the matter, that is, the Hollis amendment and the Lever statement, to the President at the cabinet meeting to-morrow, Tuesday. Each member of the Council expressed the hope and confidence that I need have no apprehension on that score. Mr. Willard arose and stated he was in hearty accord with me on my position upon the subject of the unwisdom of trying to make strikes unlawful.
"I should add that when I made my protest, I also said: 'Gentlemen, I am not going to embellish what I am going to present to you or say an unnecessary word, nor am I going to argue it. I am merely presenting to you my protest, my apprehension in as concise and plain a manner as I possibly can.'"

The same day (August 6, 1917) I had a telephone conversation with Secretary of Agriculture Houston. My stenographer took down my part of the talk with the Secretary, as follows:

Mr. Gompers: This morning while I was in attendance at the meeting of the Advisory Commission, Assistant Secretary of Labor, Mr. Post, called me up and he stated that a senator, whose name he did not mention, had made a similar statement to him in regard to the amendment of Senator Hollis—that is, that the labor provisions of the Clayton Anti-trust law should in no wise be repealed by reason of the enactment of the food bill and the senator wanted to know my understanding and judgment upon the question.

I answered in two parts: One, that in my judgment it was not in good taste for either the Senate or the House to refuse to adopt just that proviso in order to safeguard the interests of the rights of the working people, and that there will be some considerable feeling on account of it. However, that since the Supreme Court of the United States in a recent decision had declared that no private individual or corporation could bring suit under the Sherman Anti-trust law, that it would devolve upon the government, if the senator would make some such utterance in the Senate and base it upon the decision of the Supreme Court, I think it would be all right. In my judgment, of course, the needs of the country at the time require that the food bill be passed and I shall not say a word about it.

The next day, August 7, 1917, I had two telephone talks with Secretary of Labor Wilson, who called me up, one of them giving in detail a conference with President Wilson. Afterward, on that same day, I dictated this memorandum to my secretary:

"Secretary of Labor, Mr. Wilson, called me up saying he was going to have a special interview with the President right away on the Lever bill. He said that after his examination of the provisions of the bill to which I called the attention of the Council of National Defense yesterday he was fully convinced that the interpretation which I placed upon the language was justified; that is, that it would make strikes unlawful and punishable by imprisonment for two years. He said he had made up his mind to try and present the matter direct to the President early this morning and he had made arrangements for that purpose; that he would call me up after the conference with the President. At 1:15 this afternoon Secretary Wilson called me up and stated that he had had the interview with the President and brought the matter to his attention. The President said that perhaps the language of the bill might be so construed as I stated to the Secretary of Labor, Mr. Wilson, and believed by him, but that yet it was with those who were handling products rather than those who were engaged in their production or distribution in the form of labor; that the situation with food products of the country was such that millions were being taken from the people every day unnecessarily and improperly although there is not now a law to prevent it or to regulate it; that the need for the food administration law is imperative, and that any effort now to have the bill recommitted to conference committee for the insertion of the amendment coming to be known as the Hollis amendment would delay the enactment of this, play into the hands of the speculators and exploiters, that after all the prosecution under the bill when it becomes law will depend upon the district attorneys, and that instructions could go forward and would from the Attorney General's office to the various district attorneys instructing them not to bring cases against workmen in contravention to the provisions of the Clayton law; that he believed it would be a wise thing to have the Hollis amendment presented and passed by the Congress as a separate measure after the food administration bill has been passed and become law.

"I asked the Secretary whether we can count upon the assistance of the President in furtherance of such a bill. He said that the President would assist. Secretary Wilson then asked me whether I would help under these circumstances to remove any obstacle in the way of the enactment of the food administration bill and I said that I would.

"At 1:45 the Secretary called me up over the phone and stated that he was called up by Senator Husting in regard to the provisions of the food bill and the provisions in the bill which would make strikes unlawful. The Secretary stated he had talked with me and he had an interview with the President and the Senator expressed the view that he did not believe that the bill when enacted could be interpreted to apply to strikes of workmen, but that in any event the situation was such that the speculators had gotten ahead of the government; that he believed it would be best for the bill to be enacted as it now stands and immediately pushed for passage.... The Secretary told Senator Husting of the result of the talk with the President and with me and that he believed that all objections would be removed to the passage of the bill and he said he had already told him I would place no obstacle in the way of the passage of the bill with that assurance. He asked me whether that statement was correct as he had made to Senator Husting and I informed him that it was."

A conference held with Attorney General Gregory by Secretary Morrison and me brought forth the same information. The attorney general said that he would write the district attorneys not to construe Section 4 as interfering in any way with the normal activities of labor.

The telephone talks between Secretary of Labor Wilson and me were corroborated effectively August 8, when Senator Husting, with whom the Secretary had conversed, told of the statement made by the latter. Senator Husting's statement later in the Senate August 8 also clinches the fact that the President of the United States was quoted correctly when the claim was made that he had endorsed the statement of Attorney General Gregory by saying:

"That after all prosecution under the bill when it becomes law will depend upon the district attorneys, and that instructions could go forward and would from the attorney general's office to the various district attorneys instructing them *not to bring cases against workmen in contravention to the provisions of the Clayton law."*

During the debate in the Senate August 8, the following dialogue took place (page 6481, *Congressional Record*):

Mr. Husting: I voted for the Hollis amendment to the bill, which provided that the provisions of the bill should not be construed to prevent strikes or peaceful picketing or in any way amend or repeal the provisions of the Clayton Act. I would not favor the clause striking out this amendment if I thought it had that effect. I do not think it has that effect. . . .

I was sufficiently interested, however, in the argument made by the Senator from New Hampshire, and by arguments already made upon the legal effect of striking out the Hollis amendment to inquire from those who will have the administration of this law in their hands as to what construction would be placed upon it by them in the event that it became a law in its present form.

I am authorized by the Secretary of Labor, Mr. Wilson, to say that the administration does not construe this bill as prohibiting strikes and peaceful picketing and will not so construe the bill, and that the Department of Justice does not so construe the bill and will not so construe the bill. . . .

Mr. Reed: Will the Senator then say to us why the amendment which would have removed any necessity for construction, or any doubt, was stricken out?

Mr. Husting: I cannot answer that question with authority, but I understand it was stricken out because it was not thought necessary or essential, that it had no effect whatever. I think it would have been wiser to have left it in, but it was stricken out, I understand, upon the argument that it could not legally be construed in that way and that it was surplusage or redundancy.

Mr. Reed: Has the Senator talked with the Attorney General?

Mr. Husting: I will say that I have not. I have not talked with the Attorney General. However, I can say that the Secretary of Labor advised me that this was the opinion of the administration and the Department of Justice. He did not give it merely as a matter of belief on his part, but said that he was authorized to so state.

Mr. Reed: Now may I ask one further question? Suppose that a complaint should be filed in a court of the United States charging a violation of this act, and that the case was lodged in court, and the judge of the court should hold that under the charge made a violation of the law had occurred, is the Senator prepared to say to the country that the Attorney General has stated that under such circumstances as that he would nullify the law and undertake to control the court

Mr. Husting: Mr. President, I cannot say anything further than what I have already said. I do not presume any United States District Attorney will prosecute any person under this law contrary to the interpretation placed upon the law itself by a superior officer.

Mr. Lewis: . . . I am advised . . . that the provisions we placed in the Federal Trade Commission Act in the closing days of its consideration . . . to the effect that there shall not be prosecution of farmers' organizations or members thereof or of labor organizations or members thereof for any of the acts to which we particularly addressed ourselves as criminal concerning commercial bodies, would exclude the prosecutions of which the Senator from New Hampshire had such a sincere fear.

Mr. Husting: Mr. President, that is my belief. I will say to the distinguished Senator from Illinois, that is my view of it; and not only is it my view, but, as I said before, it is the view of the administration, and I am advised is also the view of the Department of Justice and of every eminent and able attorney on the floor.

That a promise had been made that a separate bill embodying the amendment that the law should not "modify or amend or repeal the Clayton Act" is established in the following statement made in the Senate August 8 (page 6482, *Congressional Record*):

Mr. Husting: But it appears here from the debate that many Senators have taken the view that this measure does not modify, or amend or repeal the Clayton Act. So the action of many Senators and their votes will be based upon the assumption that it does not so modify, amend or repeal that Act, and the fact that others do think so will have no other effect than to put their opinion against the opinion of those who believe otherwise. . . . If there is any division of opinion here upon the question of what effect this proposed legislation will have on the anti-trust laws, let a bill be introduced embodying the Hollis amendment, and let it go through both Houses, as I think it will, without much opposition. Then all uncertainty will be swept away. But notwithstanding that this bill is not exactly as I would have it if I had the writing of it, it is necessary to pass this bill at once.

While the discussion over the Hollis amendment was at its height the Supreme Court gave an opinion in the case of the Paine Lumber Company versus Neal. It was held by the court that private individuals could not institute legal proceedings under anti-trust legislation. This encouraged the officials of labor in the belief that the striking out of the Hollis amendment would not work to the injury of labor, as only the Government could institute prosecutions and the Government had given assurance it would not. And as the President and the Attorney General of the United States had said there would be no prosecutions by the Department of Justice, labor felt safe. This feeling was expressed by me in a telegram to Ernest Bohm, Secretary of the Central Federated Union of New York, who had asked for information regarding the anti-strike clause. The telegram said:

"Washington, D. C., Aug. 9, 1917. American Federation of Labor did not delay passage of Food Administration measure for following reasons: Under the interpretation of United States Supreme Court in the case of the Paine Lumber Company versus United Brotherhood of Carpenters it was held that private individuals could not institute legal proceedings under anti-trust legislation. Only the Government could take action. Sundry Civil Appropriation Laws contain provisions that no appropriation for judiciary can be used to prosecute labor organizations under anti-trust legislation. High authority has given assurance that Section 4 of Food Administration Act would not be interpreted to apply to normal and necessary activities of trade unions. The proviso suggested by A. F. of L. that Section 4 should not be interpreted to repeal labor sections of the Clayton anti-trust Act, will be introduced in Senate as a separate measure. This course has the approval of President Wilson, who will assist toward the enactment of proposed measure."

It thus will be seen that every avenue of information gave most emphatic assurances that trade union normal activities would not be a violation of Section 4. The promise to present a separate measure in the Senate providing that Section 4 did not repeal the labor sections of the Clayton Act also had great influence in the decision of the labor officials to cease efforts for the amendment and give their whole attention to urging the passage of the Lever Food Control Bill.

Besides, letters from Congressmen were being received daily. These were all favorable to the contention of labor. One of the many that were significant was from Representative Sydney Anderson, member of the Committee on Agriculture, which prepared the bill. He said:

"It was of course never intended that any provision in the Lever Bill should so operate as to repeal any part of the Clayton Act, and it was the opinion of those who drew the bill that it would not so operate."

Representative Joshua W. Alexander, Chairman of the Committee on Merchant Marine and Fisheries, in answer said:

"As I read the bill there is nothing in it which is in conflict with the provision mentioned in your letter. That was the opinion of the House at the time the bill was under consideration and for that reason the Keating amendment was defeated."

The assurances of the President of the United States through Secretary of Labor Wilson, Attorney General Gregory, the Council of National Defense, Food Administrator Hoover, Representative Lever, and others were accepted as conclusive. They had all been corroborated in Senate speeches by Senators Husting, Chamberlain, Hollis and others. Labor ceased to insist that the bill should be amended and worked whole-heartedly for the passage of the measure. Not a doubt existed that the assurances of the government officials would be carried out.

On Sunday afternoon, September 22, 1918, I delivered an address before the Trades Council of London, England. During the course of that address, referring to the strike of the London policemen which was then on, I said:

"I am not criticizing the strikes. I am merely calling attention to the fact that here you have a law making such strikes illegal. In the United States we have defeated every proposition to make strikes illegal, and yet we are getting results for our people, and we are giving voluntary service."

A few weeks after the enactment of the Lever Bill, in the convention of the American Federation of Labor held at Buffalo, N. Y., in November, 1917, the convention which the President of the United States addressed, the Executive Council of our Federation, in submitting its report upon the question of the high cost of living and the Lever Act among other things, said:

"At the Baltimore convention of the American Federation of Labor, 1916, there were several resolutions introduced and adopted by the convention, directing that efforts be made by the officers of the Federation to secure the passage of legislation which would insure relief from the high cost of living. These resolutions specifically demanded the creation of a Federal Commission empowered to investigate all phases of the subject and recommend to Congress measures designed to remedy the abnormal conditions brought about since the inauguration of the world war, and also to prevent a recurrence of similar conditions in the future.

"Other resolutions were passed, the intent of which was to secure legislation authorizing an embargo upon the exportation of foodstuffs with a view to lessening prices in this country. The Executive Council at its January meeting had these resolutions under consideration and directed President Gompers to carry into effect, so far as possible, the purport of the convention action.

"In accordance with the adoption of the resolution directing the Executive Council of the A. F. of L. to secure a Federal Commission to investigate all phases of the subject, our efforts were directed in assisting to secure the passage of H. R. 4188, known as the Food Survey Bill, which passed Congress and became a law August 10, 1917.

"Upon the designation by the President of Herbert C. Hoover as Food Administrator, a conference was called at the A. F. of L. Building of representatives of the labor organizations having their headquarters in Washington, together with the representatives of the railroad brotherhoods and members of the labor group in Congress, as well as a number of sympathetic Congressmen. Mr. Hoover was invited to attend. At this meeting Mr. Hoover outlined his plans to meet the situation and urged that the A. F. of L. give its support to the Lever Bill, H. R. 4961, known as the Food Control Bill.

"The Federation gave its full support to the principles involved in this legislation, but suggested that the provision which said: 'That any person who conspires, combines, agrees, or arranges with any other person to limit the facilities for transporting, producing, manufacturing, supplying, storing, or dealing in any necessaries; to restrict the supply of any necessaries; to restrict the distribution of any necessaries; to prevent, limit or lessen the manufacture or production of any necessaries in order to enhance the price thereof shall, upon conviction thereof, be fined not exceeding $10,000 or be imprisoned not more than two years, or both,' be added to by the incorporation of an amendment declaring that the intent of this section was not to repeal any of the labor provisions of the Clayton Law. It was feared that the language of this section might be construed to make it unlawful for workmen engaged in food transportation and production to strike.

"An amendment was introduced for the purpose of safeguarding labor's interests in accordance with the above suggestion, and, while Mr. Hoover stated that the section was not intended to prevent workmen from ceasing work, yet acquiesced in the amendment proposed and rendered valuable assistance in an effort to secure its adoption. Upon our failure to secure the adoption of this amendment, the matter was taken up through the Advisory Commission of the Council of National Defense. The Attorney-General concurred in the view that the section was not intended to restrict the right of workmen to strike. As a further precaution, an arrangement was made whereby the Attorney-General was to communicate with all of the attorneys representing the government, informing them of his opinion and directing that no action be instituted against workmen engaged in the industries referred to for ceasing to perform labor.

"During the period that the Food Control Bill was being considered by the administration, the United States Supreme Court rendered its decision in the case of the Paine Lumber Co. vs. United Brotherhood of Carpenters and Joiners, in which the court decided that the conspiracy clauses of the Sherman law could not be made operative by a private party suing for an injunction against another private party or by one corporation against another corporation. The remedy for such a person or corporation is to apply to the Attorney-General of the United States and have him institute a suit for injunction or restraining order.

"Therefore, also in view of our successes since the first session of the Sixty-third Congress in having enacted and reënacted at each recurring session of Congress the prohibitory section of the appropriation provision in the anti-trust section of the Sundry Civil Act, whereby none of the money so appropriated can be used by government officials to prosecute workers in their endeavors to increase wages, decrease hours, or improve working conditions under the general charge of conspiracy or restraint of trade under the Sherman Act, we felt that our position was sufficiently safe not to press further for similar legislation in the Food Control Bill."

At that same convention, the President of the United States delivered an address in which he said:

"While we are fighting for freedom, we must see among other things that labor is free, and that means a number of interesting things. It means not only that we must do what we have declared our purpose to do, see that the conditions of labor are not rendered more onerous by the war, but also that we shall see to it that the instrumentalities by which the conditions of labor are improved are not blocked or checked. That we must do."

—*From address at public mass meeting under auspices of Central Labor Union, Washington, D. C., November 22, 1919.*

If the American people, and in fact a majority of the members of Congress, were awake to the dangers concealed in this bill [Sterling-Graham Peace Time Sedition Bill] a storm of indignation would sweep the nation. It has been widely advertised that this measure protects free speech fully, but prevents advocacy of forcible revolution, bolshevism and anarchy. In fact, it would perpetuate an autocratic censorship over the entire American press. It can be used to kill free speech and free assembly. It strikes a deadly blow at legitimate organizations of labor or any other progressive movement for the betterment of the masses which may be opposed by the advocates of privilege and reaction.

We yield to no man, in public office or out, in our loyalty to the constitution and institutions of this republic; no self-respecting man has questioned or dare question that loyalty. We are for evolution, not revolution; for ballots, not bullets; for a majority rule, not class dictatorship of bolshevism, plutocracy or of the profiteer. We oppose this bill because every legitimate purpose for which it is framed is already covered by existing law. Its illegitimate features, which compose two-thirds of the draft, are utterly autocratic, imperialistic and un-American. . . .

The inevitable result of this bill, if enacted, would be to spread a reign of terror over the United States, fill the country with spies and special agents of the Department of Justice, fill the land with suspicion and heresy hunting would quickly become a national industry. American citizens who love liberty and love America cannot stand idly by and permit this legislation to be enacted. Unless we oppose it our children and our children's children will regard us as cowards and poltroons, faithless to the heritage of our fathers and the struggles of the human race for liberty. If the principles of Magna Charta and the Declaration of Independence and the Constitution of the United States are not worth fighting to preserve, I have wholly misconceived what patriotism and love of freedom mean.—*From press statement, January 19, 1920.*

X

INDUSTRIAL AGREEMENT

ARBITRATION—VOLUNTARY AND COMPULSORY

For a number of years the bill, presumably for the arbitration of disputes between the railroad employees of the country and the railroad companies, was pending in Congress. The American Federation of Labor, at its convention, and its representatives at the Capitol, have from time to time interposed objections against the passage of the bill, on the ground that it interfered with the worker quitting his employment at any time when the conditions of employment became irksome; that in some form or other the bill contained features for the specific enforcement of a contract to labor, or personal service. When the bill was first introduced it had all these objectionable provisions. At each session of Congress the bill, by reason of our objections, has been improved and its direct penal provisions eliminated. At the instance of your representatives, congressmen and senators called attention to the dangerous features contained in the bill, the result of which has been that many of our most important objections have been heeded and rectified. It is true that the brotherhoods and orders of the railroad employees regarded our objection to the passage of the bill with some feeling of asperity; but in the form in which the bill finally became law they will bear willing testimony that, owing to our persistency on this subject, the law is freer from dangers to their interests, their rights and their liberties, and the interests, rights and liberties of the workers of the country, than when the bill was first introduced.—*From annual report to A. F. of L. convention, Kansas City, Mo., December, 1898.*

I believe that there is more real power in the public judgment and public opinion than has been believed. If there be a dispute between workmen and their employers and arbitration ensues when conciliation has failed, and the arbitrators make a public award as their judgment that the workmen are in the right and that the company or employers are in the wrong, such employers could not very long successfully carry on business if they refused to abide by the award. And if the award were publicly proclaimed that the judgment of the arbitrators was that the workmen were in the wrong and that such and such conditions should prevail, the workmen could not long withstand such a public award and judgment.—*From testimony before Industrial Commission, Washington, D. C., April 18, 1899.*

In common with the general trend of organized labor to prevent strikes and lockouts wherever and whenever possible, a sentiment for arbitration has been awakened among the people of our country. There are some, however, who, playing upon the credulity of the uninformed, seek to divert the principle of arbitration into a coercive policy of so-called compulsory arbitration; in other words, the creation by States, or by the nation, of boards or courts, with power to hear and determine each case in dispute between the workers and their employers, to make awards, and, if necessary, to invoke the power of the government to enforce the awards. Observers have for years noted that those inclined to this policy have devised many schemes to deny the workers the right to quit their employments; and the scheme of so-called compulsory arbitration is the latest design of the well-intentioned, but uninformed, as well as the faddists and schemers.

Our movement seeks, and has to a considerable extent secured, a diminution in the number of strikes, particularly among the best organized. In fact, the number and extent of strikes can be accurately gauged by the extent, power, and financial resources of an organization in any trade or calling. The barometer of strikes rises with lack of, or weakness in, organization, and diminishes with the extent and power of the trade union movement.

Through more compact and better equipped trade unions have come joint agreements and conciliation between the workmen and associated employers; and only when conciliation has failed has it been necessary to resort to arbitration, and then the only successful arbitration was arbitration voluntarily entered into.

Organized labor cannot by attempted secrecy evade the provisions of an award reached by compulsory arbitration, and determine upon a strike. By reason of their large numbers their every act would be an open and public act, known to all; while, on the other hand, an employer, or an association of employers, could easily evade the provisions of such a law or award, by modern processes of enforcing a lockout; that is, to undertake a "reorganization" of their labor forces.

It is submitted that the very terms, "arbitration" and "compulsory," stand in direct opposition to each other. Arbitration implies the voluntary action of two parties of diverse interests submitting to disinterested parties the question in dispute, or likely to come into dispute. Compulsion by any process, and particularly by the power of government, is repugnant to the principle as well as the policy of arbitration. If organized labor should fail to appreciate the danger involved in the proposed schemes of so-called compulsory arbitration, and consent to the enactment of a law providing for its enforcement, there would be reintroduced the denial of the right of the workmen to strike in defense of their interests, and the enforcement by government of specific or personal service and labor. In other words, under a law based upon compulsory arbitration, if an award were made against labor, no matter how unfair or unjust, and brought about by any means, no matter how questionable, we would be compelled to work or to suffer the state penalty, which might be either mulcting in damages, or going to jail; not one scintilla of distinction, not one jot removed from slavery.

It is strange how much men desire to compel other men to do by law. What we aim to achieve is freedom through organization. Arbitration is only possible when voluntary. It never can be successfully carried out unless the parties to a dispute or controversy are equals, or nearly equals, in power to protect and defend themselves, or to inflict injury upon the other.

The more thoroughly the workers are organized in their local and national unions, and federated by common bond, policy and polity, the better shall we be able to avert strikes and lockouts, secure conciliation, and if necessary, arbitration; but it must be voluntary arbitration, or there should be no arbitration at all.

It is our aim to avoid strikes; but I trust that the day will never come when the workers of our country will have so far lost their manhood and independence as to refuse to strike, regardless of the provocation, or to surrender their right to strike. We seek to prevent strikes, but we realize that the best means by which they can be averted is to be the better prepared for them. We endeavor to prevent strikes; but there are some conditions far worse than strikes, and among them is a demoralized, degraded, and debased manhood.—*From annual report to A. F. of L. convention, Louisville, Ky., December, 1900.*

All these schemes [compulsory arbitration] are reactionary in their character. They mean simply that the employers of to-day find themselves in a somewhat similar position to the employers of England after the "black death." The king issued a proclamation at that time that any one who would refuse to continue to work for the wages usually paid in a specified year of the king's reign would, by the state, be compelled to labor at such wages, regardless of any wishes that he or she might have. The English Parliament later enacted this into a statute known as the "Statute of Laborers," and reënacted it periodically with ever-increasing penalties, until Henry VIII, finding himself in need of funds, confiscated the guild funds, and by impoverishing the organizations of labor succeeded in enforcing the statute of laborers from that time on.

That law was every bit as fair upon its face as the laws of New Zealand, Indiana, Illinois, or any other of those laws with which I have any acquaintance, because it provided that the judges sitting in quarter sessions should hear both sides and then determine upon a "fair wage" for the year. Readers of "Six Centuries of Work and Wages," by Thorold Rogers, professor at the University of Oxford, will know the results to the English working people. Their daily hours of labor were increased, their wages reduced, until it was necessary to enact the "poor laws," and to quarter the worker upon the occupier, because he was continually being robbed by the employer. It has been stated by others that this law reduced the stature of the British workers by about two inches, and that the poverty—the real, dire poverty —to be found in the back alleys of English cities, even to this day, is largely caused by that species of legislation.—*From address at Arbitration Conference, The National Civic Federation, Chicago, December 17, 1900.*

Mrs. Dwyer of the Women Workers' Union made the following comment (*Australian Worker*, Feb. 11, 1915):

"No girl could get a room in a decent locality for less than 5s; she had to pay her own laundry (2s), she had fares to meet and meals outside to pay for, and was altogether in a most unfortunate position. If the delegates had the morality of womanhood at stake they would send a big deputation to the government, and demand a remedy for this injustice. There were other women workers in a bad position, and the Women Workers' Union did not care to go to the wages boards.
"'You gave up strikes, for what?' asked Mrs. Dwyer. 'To have your conditions decided by a lot of briefless barristers who had secured positions as chairmen of wages boards.'"

The paper for March 11 reported the reversal of the decision of the wages board. Governmental regulation of work relations is subject to all the shifting currents that have influence in politics.—*American Federationist, May, 1915.*

I recall very distinctly that about twenty years ago a Mr. Lusk came from New Zealand to the United States as a crusader and an evangelist for compulsory arbitration of labor disputes between the workers and the employers. He at once undertook a campaign which had been arranged for him to preach his new gospel of compulsory arbitration. Passing from that for a moment, I may say that that good friend of labor and great American, Henry D. Lloyd, who within a year of Mr. Lusk's visit had gone to New Zealand and stayed there for a few months, came back and wrote a book entitled "A Country Without Strikes." I remember very distinctly the rather ill repute that I got myself into by contending against Mr. Lusk's proposition of compulsory arbitration, and I refer to this fact because of the first question submitted for investigation in this resolution.

Now, the newspapers at the time took me to task. I questioned Mr. Lusk in those public gatherings as to what was really meant by compulsory arbitration. I asked him if it did not mean that the workers were to be prohibited by law from stopping work, from quitting employment. I finally pinned him down to the point and he said it did. I asked him that in the event of workmen refusing to abide by an award of a board or a court of arbitration, whether it did not mean that these workers would be fined or imprisoned or both. It was really extracting an answer from him when he finally admitted that that would be the result of disobedience of the court's or board's finding.

I was written down or written up as one who was promoting disorder among the workers, and one who wanted to prevent from being put into operation a very fine method which would prevent strikes.

In spite of any opposition that we could manifest, in the Congress of the United States and in several of the legislatures, bills were introduced for compulsory arbitration, compulsory investigation, and making it unlawful for workmen in concert to leave their employment before a board of arbitration had rendered its award or until a board of investigation had made inquiry and rendered an award.

It required all of the energies and activities of our men to prevent the enactment of this species of legislation. In one of the States it became a law—Colorado—compulsory investigation and forbidding strikes or cessation of work until the court or board had made an investigation and rendered an award. That feature was based upon the Canadian act. From the moment that the Colorado act was on the statute books until the present day there has not been any piece of legislation that has given such general dissatisfaction as that one. A little more than a year and a half ago, in spite of the law the workmen, failing to secure redress at the hands of the commission or the board, simply struck.

They violated the law. They were lawbreakers. But they quit work and got quicker action at the hands of the employers who have recognized since then the proper standards and conditions that should prevail and should have prevailed for a long time previously.

Within ten years of Mr. Lusk's first appearance in the United States as the advance agent for compulsory arbitration, he made another visit to our country. On that visit he took occasion to say that his hopes for the adjustment of differences between employers and employees by a species of compulsory arbitration could not be realized, that compulsory arbitration was a failure, and that he would not recommend it for enactment by the Congress or the legislatures of the States of the United States.

The result of our activities also aroused the employers to the situation, and after we had expended much of our energies in combating this legislation, they too resolved that they wanted nothing of it. . . .

Just about three years ago I had occasion to meet with a committee representing the United States Chamber of Commerce when there was rather a general open discussion of many questions. One of the chief members of the Government of the Australasian States was present, and he, much to my astonishment, because I had not even had the honor of an introduction to him, showed the utter futility of compulsory arbitration in New Zealand or any of the other Australasian confederated States; that strikes had taken place by the hundreds, and by the thousands, and that the law had gone into innocuous desuetude; that it was obsolete; that no one paid any attention to it and that there was now being developed a better method . . . the policy of conciliation and mediation.—*From testimony before Senate Committee on Education and Labor, January 3, 1919.*

I assume that you gentlemen have deemed the proposition of panels as a most just and fair one. I can conceive of nothing that is less suitable to meet the requirements imposed upon the men composing the [regional adjustment] boards than this idea of panels. Except for the right of a few objections, you might as well have proposed the tossing of a coin; it is a matter of selection by lot, by chance. It is true that you provide for a certain number of peremptory challenges, but after the peremptory challenges have been exhausted the men engaged in the controversy may find themselves with a man who is regarded as less fair than another who may have been challenged. The device of panels in the selection of juries in our criminal or civil courts is no doubt the best that can be evolved; but in such cases it is, say, John Jones against Bill Smith, on a matter in which the people subject to jury duty have no personal, private or public interest except to do justice between these two persons. In the criminal matters, the government presents an indictment against a person and there the system of jury selected by a panel is equally fair because the people selected through the panel are supposedly fair and impartial as between the government and the person charged with crime. But in a case between employers and laborers there is not a citizen in our country who is not affected; there is not one of them who is not influenced by his position in life, and to submit to the determination of a board made up by chance, by the panel, is leaving out of consideration the human equation in the affairs of life.—*From remarks before Industrial Conference, Washington, D. C., January 27, 1920.*

COMPULSORY INVESTIGATION

In Canada the reaction has set in against the Lemieux Act. In one of the countries "without strikes" several strikes have occurred, and during this year a general sympathetic strike of all workmen occurred in Brisbane, Queensland. The American labor movement aims to avoid the stress and strain of strikes, but we are not led by glittering generalities or vain hopes. We have some realization of the elements and equation which prompt men to exercise on the one hand the power they possess to dominate for selfish, narrow greed, and on the other hand, the constant hope and aspiration of the toilers to be larger sharers in the wealth they create. The first take advantage of the opportunities which they can create to exercise their power for their narrow, selfish ends. The second, the toilers, realizing that their constant material improvement is necessary for the welfare and progress of the human race, will protest or strike, law or no law, in the effort to accomplish their justifiable purpose. Any attempt by law to curb the right of the workers to sever their relations with their employers, to strike, will be resented, as it should be resented. The American Federation of Labor years ago took a position of antagonism to any such policy, and it is a source of great gratification that I have in some measure aided in preventing, either openly or covertly, the introduction in the industrial affairs of our land of any species of compulsory arbitration or entering wedge that would facilitate such introduction.

We want peace in industry, but we want peace with honor, progress, and freedom. So-called peace, purchased at the price which would shackle the minds and the actions of the workers, is no real peace at all; it is the beginning of slavery.—*From annual report to A. F. of L. convention, Rochester, N. Y., November, 1912.*

Three objections are made to the Lemieux Act [Canadian trade disputes investigation law] by the laborers: (*a*) Necessary delay for action of the board makes quick and effective strikes impossible. (*b*) The wording of the law is so obscure as to furnish a twilight zone which is the delight of the lawyer seeking evasion. (*c*) Public opinion is not that disinterested, immutable judge and champion of the misused that the theory presumes.

These form the specific objections to the operation of the Lemieux Act, the fundamental principal objections are:

Laws must not invade personal rights and liberty. The ownership of a free man is vested in himself alone. The free man's ownership of himself involves his labor power. In fact the only difference between a free man and a slave is the right to sell or withhold his labor power. This precious right must be cherished and guarded against all invasions. It is of greater value than all other purposes or ends. When any workmen or number of workmen are compelled by law to work one month, one week, one day, or one hour against their own volition, then there has ensued and been established slavery.—*American Federationist, February, 1913.*

The workers have not found judicial procedure so effective a means for securing industrial justice that they could advocate the plan you suggest—investigating commissions with power to summons witnesses, to compel the production of documents, and to take evidence under oath. Real, permanent progress in securing betterment for the workers results only from voluntary agreement to terms, because those who agree are persuaded they are doing that which furthers their own interests. Industrial justice cannot be imposed by outside agents, it must emanate from those interests involved in industry.

Governmental investigation, together with its plenary powers, as an agency for securing industrial justice cannot supplant the policy of voluntary conciliation, mediation, or arbitration. The former can never take the place of the voluntary collective bargaining of associated workers and employers. When the stage of a deadlock has been reached in any industrial dispute, whether the workmen are organized or unorganized, when the employer is a single individual or corporation or an association of employers, and when the interruption in the industry or in commerce is of great importance, the good sense as well as the necessity of both employers and employees and the public conscience may be relied upon to find an honorable means of conciliation, mediation, and arbitration voluntarily entered into, and any opinion expressed or award made should be accepted voluntarily by the parties in interest. Unorganized workers have no way to express preference or to judge as to who would best and most faithfully represent them and their interests. Only after a strike of unorganized workers has been in progress for a considerable time are there developed responsible, reliable, and capable leaders to represent them. But by that time the formerly unorganized have become organized and in their organized capacity choose their representatives and leaders. In the inception of organization neither the leaders nor the rank and file have learned the principles and application of industrial justice. If investigations are to be made, and at times they should be, it is better that they be made by public agents, responsible to the people, such as the mediators of the United States Department of Labor, or a committee of Congress, or of the Bureaus of Labor of the States or of the State legislatures.

All investigations depend for their value upon the earnest, fair activity and wise understanding of the individuals who conduct them and their value is largely of an informational nature. The establishment of industrial justice rests upon employers and upon the intelligent activity of employees. . . . An investigation is only a means of securing publicity and in itself has little effect upon securing industrial justice. If investigations are given legal sanction and plenary powers as a method of dealing with industrial disputes, it is more than probable that the findings of commissions will be made obligatory and violations punishable by fines, etc. When compulsion is associated with industrial agreements, then new fetters will be forged for industrial workers and their freedom will again be taken from them. What organized labor wants is not new machinery, new agents for securing industrial justice, but absolute freedom from all fetters and restrictions that have prevented free, normal, and lawful activity in promoting their own welfare.—*From testimony before U. S. Commission on Industrial Relations, New York City, May 21-23, 1914.*

Compulsory investigation legislation is identical in principle with compulsory arbitration; the difference is only one of degree.

Compulsory arbitration makes strikes illegal and strikers criminal for all time instead of for a definite period. . . . Under either, men who refuse to work for any reason, who refuse to perform involuntary servitude may be fined and imprisoned. . . . Stripped of all sophistry and all verbiage, compulsory investigation or compulsory arbitration resolve themselves into compulsory service. . . .

They [Colorado workingmen] know that compulsory investigation of industrial disputes and the restriction of the right to strike take away the power of their economic organization and make the workers dependent upon a commission of three men who are not wage-earners and who do not know the problem of wage-earners from personal experience.

In the name of so-called industrial peace, wage-earners Colorado have been denied the right to exercise their own judgment as to what wages, hours and other conditions of employment they shall present and urge upon employers and when, as a last resort, they shall cease their work to enforce those demands. They have found that the commission can use dilatory methods and delay giving a favorable report upon wage-earners' demands until a time when they can be presented with less inconvenience to employers. They have found that smeltermen who exercised their legal right to quit work when they wished, have been imprisoned and held in jail because they refused to perform increased daily work without corresponding increases in pay. One union found that the demands they presented were lost by the commission. Another group of workers employed by the Lindquist Cracker Company filed demands for increased wages. The cost of living had increased so materially that the cracker workers found their present wages miserably inadequate. The Industrial Commission, after considering the matter, made public its opinion, which contained the following:

"After a most searching investigation we believe there is but one conclusion in this case, that the business will not at this time justify any increase in wages."

The commission further stated that:

"The wages are small compared with those paid in many other industries. We hope that conditions may change in this line so that the employers and employees may reap a fair return from their labor and capital invested. Whenever in the investigation of a wage dispute the commission finds that a concern or industry is in such a state that to increase the wages would drive the concern out of business or into bankruptcy, it is the duty of the commission to refuse to recommend the increase demanded. It is the opinion of the commission that we can not recommend an increase of wages or any changes in hours or working conditions."

The principle which the Industrial Commission endorses in this opinion is a principle which would justify the existence of the most miserable sweatshop conditions. Over and over again it has been held in this country that an industry that cannot afford to pay living wages has no right to exist. The principle which the Colorado commission has endorsed is in direct conflict with this principle of fair business founded upon human welfare.

The experience of the tailors of Colorado is well known. For over three months their demands were delayed for one excuse and then another, and, finally, they found themselves in the same position that they were before they presented their demands to a commission; they must deal with their employers, secure an agreement, or strike. The employing tailors conceded the men's demands and the commission decided in the tailors' favor.

The only real effect that the Colorado law has is to weaken the power and effectiveness of trade unions; to make wage-earners dependent upon a political agency to carry industrial problems into politics. The members of the Industrial Commission are political appointees and cannot dissociate themselves from political issues and political influences. Wage-earners have found it hard enough to establish better conditions of work when the problem is purely an industrial one, but when it is both political and industrial, the difficulties are immeasurably increased.—*American Federationist, October, 1916.*

The workers throughout the entire country are fully aroused to the dangers contained in this proposed "compulsory investigation" plan. These dangers have awakened them to full appreciation of a fundamental principle. Workers cannot delegate to outside authority, even though that authority be the government, the right to regulate industrial relations without creating an opportunity for a continuous infringement upon their rights and freedom. The railroad brotherhoods, like all organizations affiliated to the American labor movement, have opposed the legislative method as the way to secure a shorter workday and higher wages, but the situation was such that the railway brotherhoods yielded to the policy of the government and accepted the Adamson law. But just as soon as the government acquired the right to regulate the hours of work for railway employees, it at once began to augment its powers, to provide regulations for other relations, and to limit the right to quit work. The experience illustrates the danger to which the American Federation of Labor has repeatedly called attention.—*American Federationist, January, 1917.*

Under your proposal, in the event of failure on the part of the [regional adjustment] board to reach a unanimous decision, the majority and the minority may each submit their reasons, which shall be filed for publication. It is predicated, I assume, upon the idea that the public will by force of its opinion compel an adjustment. Has that been borne out by history in industrial adjustments, in industrial disputes? The very opposite is shown. We have had several instances of this character in disputes upon railroads, both steam and electric, in which reports were published and arbitration had and decisions rendered. You cannot reach the people with your official report by a pamphlet; you cannot reach them, and if you reached them, it is doubtful that five per cent of them would read the report. Prominence in the newspapers is during the period when such a controversy reaches its most acute stage so that it amounts to practically a sensation. During that period it appears upon the front pages, and in all likelihood is read by a considerable portion of the people; but after a few days you will find that there are other matters of deep interest to our people and the whole world which take its place upon the front page. Day after day you find it moved back, back, back, until you scarcely find more than a reference to it. That evanescent thing called public opinion is so changeable, it is so concerned with the new important problems which arise in our country and throughout the world, day after day, almost hour after hour. What the public wants is to be let alone, not to be inconvenienced in any way.

Public opinion did not concern itself with the long hours of labor of working people; public opinion did not destroy the sweat-shop system; public opinion did not interpose objection to the eighteen-hour work-day that the men of the street and steam railways had to labor; public opinion did not take the breaker boys out of the mines in the anthracite coal region; public opinion did not bring about compulsory education; the limitation of the hours of labor of women and children. Much as my associates and I look upon strikes as something to be avoided whenever possible, I can say to you gentlemen that the strike of the coal miners in the anthracite region of nearly twenty years ago did more to raise the standard of manhood and womanhood and childhood in the State of Pennsylvania and throughout the country than all other combined associations or groups or government. Attempts were made to take the manufacturing of cigars out of the tenement houses of New York by law; we attempted that, after years and years secured the passage of the law, only to find it vetoed. The bakers, in their effort to secure the shorter workday, secured the passage of a law limiting the hours of labor of bakers to ten per day, and that law was held to be unconstitutional. Did the public protest, or did public opinion secure any change, any remedy? It was the bakers' union, assisted by the American Federation of Labor, that by their voluntary and associated effort secured substantial reductions in the hours of labor. The sweat-shop system no longer exists in the garment making trade in and around New York; was it public opinion that did this? It was the strike of the garment workers which secured the abolition of the sweat-shop system, and now relations between workers and employers are of a practical, mutual character and advantage.—*From remarks before Industrial Conference, Washington, D. C., January 27, 1920.*

INCORPORATION OF TRADE UNIONS

[Q. (By Representative GARDNER.) What would be the objection, from your standpoint, to a trades union assuming a pecuniary responsibility for the keeping of its agreements with contractors or employers? You said you anticipated danger. Would that danger come, in your judgment, from the inability of the union to control its members, or would it not?]—A. Not necessarily, but there are a number of causes that I might put in this way: There is scarcely an act which a union can take but which, in its very nature, by reason of the large number of members, is practically a public act, of which the employers are generally informed. On the other hand, there is scarcely any act that the employer can perform or take which is a public act, or of which information can reach the employees. Contracts are frequently entered into by employers with representatives of organizations. The employer determines upon a change of policy; he does not announce a lockout—simply a reorganization of his forces. The reorganization of his forces is practically a lockout, and the employees have no redress and cannot have any.

[Q. If the labor union were incorporated and as a corporation made contracts with the employer, then it would have redress for the violation of that contract, would it not?]—A. Hardly. There is not an employer who cannot find some means to overcome the terms of a contract, more particularly when labor is poorly organized or insufficiently organized, and he can get others to take their places.

[Q. Then would your objection on that point be that you fear the contract would be binding upon the employees and they would be unable to enforce it against the employer?]—A. Yes, in the courts, to establish it beyond the peradventure of a doubt as legal evidence. Any one who has had long experience as an employee will understand that. Having had an experience of 26 years as a factory operative, I know what that means from my own observation, and I also know that as having come under my observation as one devoting his efforts to the labor movement.

[Q. Is or is not that precisely the evil which the advocates of incorporation seek to remedy? Is the contention not made that if the trade unions were incorporated, so that they were legal bodies, their contracts would have a legal status in the courts; would be legal evidence of what was agreed and would be enforceable?]—A. There are a number of unions that have availed themselves of incorporation under State laws. I do not know whether there is any under the United States law. But the fact of incorporation of a trade union has not added either to its stability or to its ability to enforce the terms of a contract with the employer.

[Q. As a legal proposition, if the union is made a body corporate and the act under which it is incorporated is broad enough, it must be true that such incorporation gives it a legal status to enforce its contract by judgment against the other party to the contract.]—A. If the facts which constitute a practical violation of the terms of a contract could be presented as legal evidence in the courts, that would be true; but as a matter of fact the grievances from which the organized workers suffer, so far as the violation of the terms of a contract goes, are not in its specific violation, but by the surreptitious efforts, by indirect means, to overcome the terms of a contract and practically annul it—as, for instance, determining, say, that for the production of such an article a specific amount of wage shall be paid, and by the introduction of another article precisely the same and simply giving it another name requiring the same amount of work to be performed in the production of the article, yet the terms of the contract are not violated. It is simply called or styled by the employer as something new, not called for by the contract, and in which he insists that that wage is a fair one.

[Q. Then the answer formulates in this way: That the subject is one which can not be covered by contract?]—A. It is, so far as that point is concerned. There is another. In all bodies a certain number are more active for the time being than the larger number constituting the body, and I presume that may be true, too, with all due respect, of the members of this Industrial Commission, as well as it is in the Halls of Congress, as well as it is in the church; and so it is in the organizations of labor. The men who are selected as the representatives of the organization, and true to the interest and the cause of the men they represent, want the terms of the contract lived up to, are good workmen, have been employed for a long number of years by the employer. The employer finds that he would like to nibble at that scale, and he knows that two or three of these men are sticklers for the enforcement of the contract. He will find the means by which these three men have been "neglectful" of their work; he will find the means by which he can demonstrate to a disinterested party that this man has not performed his work as required; he can, through his superintendent or foreman, make his work—his employment—there uncomfortable, make his surroundings unbearable, so that he will, perhaps, in desperation do something that would be a violation of the rule—a violation of a rule that is never punished, and a rule that has become lax by the demonstration of its inutility, and uselessness. This one, recognizing its disuse, doing the same as others, violating that simple rule, gives sufficient cause for discharge. It is good cause, or it is supposed to be good cause, for discharge; it is a violation of the rule, and one, two, or three active men, representative men, are easily disposed of, and the others are conveniently informed that it is best not to be too contentious in the enforcement of the terms of the contract.

[Q. Would not the incorporation of the union relieve precisely the situation cited in the illustration? Neither the active men nor the other men would have anything to say about the contract. It would be the board of that union that made it.]—A. But when the employees of the concern are practically substituted the organization, as such, can take no action. When the spirit has been crushed out of the men the organization cannot take any action, for the reason that they will be compelled to rely for evidence upon the men employed, and they would be either unwilling witnesses or witnesses who would endeavor to shield the violation of the terms of the contract by the employer.

[Q. My understanding, then, is this: That under a corporation, and a contract between the corporate body and the employer, you fear, first, that the contract could and would be enforced against the union in the courts; secondly, that it could not be enforced against the employer because, if a manufacturing business, he is enabled to invent numberless devices for evading it, so that the courts could not protect the union against him?]— A. Yes; there would be so many ways by which he could circumvent it himself.

[Q. Any other reason you want to give?]—A. There was one, yes. The funds of an incorporated union are subject to the union's disposition. The laws of the union define how the moneys can be expended. Usually it requires a two-thirds vote, often a majority vote, to determine; and there is likely to be and is a minority, no matter how small, opposed to any proposed action; and in an incorporated trade union it would be within the power of a minority to enjoin a union from expending its funds even in accordance with its own laws. The effect of it would be disastrous in the case of a conflict between employer and employed. Though an injunction against the expenditure of any money may not be made permanent, yet the fact that the money is not made available at a specified time, the time when the members have a right to look for the benefits to which they have contributed, is in itself sufficient to discourage the men engaged in a conflict. They do not know how long the funds may be tied up. They lose confidence in the ability of the organization to protect them in their contests, and lose heart in the contest itself. Cases may arise when the employer, who frequently has an influence with a number of the men, no matter whether the influence be legitimate or otherwise, may influence a small minority to take such action as will practically do the work of the employer and break the backbone of the contest.—*From testimony before Industrial Commission, Washington, D. C., April 18, 1899.*

One gentleman suggests bonding the union and bonding it before arbitration. Incorporate the unions so that "we can reach (the funds of) the union." A few days ago I had the privilege of addressing myself particularly to this subject while in the city of Boston, and it seemed then as it seems strange to me now, that the gentlemen who discussed this proposition, avowedly upon the high plane of "benefiting the workmen," that they constantly have their eyes upon the few dollars in the treasury of the union. A gentleman stated last week to me that the unions ought to court just such a thing, and that no money that the union could expend could be put to better advantage than the payment of damages in which it might be mulcted by a decision of the court. That is one way of putting it, but, perhaps, like Claude Melnotte, he thought that, assuming the character of a prince, he ought to be generous with other people's property. It is, indeed, strange how many gentlemen are solicitous for the trade union to become incorporated and to be placed within what they call the purview of the law in order that it may be mulcted in damages for any suit that may be brought against the organization. They leave out the opportunity for harassing the unions by interminable law suits. And besides this, the union, attacked from any and from all sides, would be in constant litigation, and it is unquestioned that our organizations could not attempt to retain counsel, either in numbers or in talent comparable to the counsel which is always at the command of wealthy concerns. . . .

Our friend [Louis D. Brandeis] says that the incorporation of the trade union would prevent the emotional action of the men in the organizations—it would tend to obviate the arbitrariness and eliminate the disregard of the unions for law.

Now, I have been connected with the unions of labor since my fourteenth year. The chairman referred to the fact that at ten years of age I entered a factory. I was a journeyman workman at fourteen. The unions at that time prescribed no age limit as to either youth or old age, and I became a member then.

I think I have had about as much access to the unions of labor in the United States as our friend who addressed you just now. I think that I have had as much means of knowing what transpires in the unions of labor as he has, and I say to you in all candor, without any mental reservation whatsoever, that I have yet to hear the first threat or declaration or address or speech made by any man in a union that implied lawlessness, much less threatened it, and that I have never known of a union of labor either advising, consenting to or conniving at violence or lawlessness.

To every student, and particularly to those who are active in the labor movement, it is a fact known beyond question and so easy of demonstration that I am astounded to find that it should escape the attention of the average man, and it is this: That there is no strike of workingmen so bitterly conducted, in which there is such hostility, in which there is so much lawlessness or violence as the strike of the non-union men, the strike of the unorganized men. The union of labor implies, first, a mutual interdependence. The unions of labor instil dignity, a strength of character, a self-restraint, and the restraint of one member upon the others. . . .

As a matter of fact, in numberless instances where violence and lawlessness have been laid at the door of organized labor the corporations and the employers, through their own emissaries, have been guilty of lawlessness, intending to provoke the public indignation against and upon the heads of men engaged in the organized labor movement.—*From address before The National Civic Federation, New York City. (American Federationist, February, 1903.)*

COLLECTIVE BARGAINING

Only two objections have been raised to this claim for recognition of so-called "third parties"—a term which must be rejected as a misnomer. The first, and most serious one, is that it is somehow alleged to be opposed to the "freedom of contract." The employer is free when he treats with his own men, and does so through any agency of his own choosing, but he is a poor victim of dictation when compelled to receive and treat with "outsiders" appearing as authorized spokesmen of his men. Was ever a more preposterous and fallacious distinction drawn by presumably intelligent persons? Do we not confront the pretense in a new guise? Not many years ago it was violently asserted that the right of a man to manage and regulate his own business negatived the demand of labor for the recognition of limited local unions. We believe that a few fossils still tenaciously cling to this absurdity.

Freedom of contract is not violated when employers are represented by "outsiders" any more than it is violated when twenty-five men in a factory send a "committee of three" to lay grievances before their employer. The employer originally contended that, if he was not permitted to deal with his men as individuals, hire and discharge them at will, fix wages in each individual case without reference to any standard, he was robbed of his "constitutionally guaranteed" freedom. Now he contends that his freedom is jeopardized when he is "coerced" into recognizing an "outside" body which, however, has the credentials and authority of his own employees. . . .

The objection that such organizations are strangers and do not understand the circumstances attending local controversies is too flimsy to be considered at length. The question of fitness is for the men to determine, and if they, who have everything at stake, are willing to be represented by national officers—the employers can certainly afford to recognize these.—*American Federationist, October, 1900.*

It should be our constant aim to make the collective bargains, that is, agreements with our employers, as advantageous to our fellow-workers as it is possible to obtain in the course of negotiations; but when these agreements are made, it should be no less our steadfast purpose to faithfully abide by and live up to their terms for the full time of their existence. As an individual earns and receives the confidence of his fellows by self-respect, self-restraint, and absolute faithful adherence to his plighted word, so does organized labor in its collective capacity deserve and win the respect and confidence, first of all, of our own members; second, that of the community in which we live, thus gaining the commendation of an enlightened public opinion. But we also compel the respect and confidence of employers to more readily recognize our unions, by which negotiations are opened up, and the best opportunities presented for agreements for stipulated periods.

If we strictly adhere to this course, we shall gain constantly greater successes; there will be an appreciable diminution in strikes and lockouts, and we shall take away from the enemies of our cause the only pretence they have for special and hostile legislation, one feature of which was the spasmodic and bitter demand for compulsory arbitration, with its attendant features of mulcting the workmen, the unions, or the threat of the imprisonment of our toilers for the exercise of their natural and lawful right to leave or change their employment at will.—*From annual report to A. F. of L. convention, Scranton, Pa., December, 1901.*

We have heard employers say that "if any employees have any grievance to present I will hear them and try to rectify it, but I want them to come to me." As a rule in practice, if the employees of any particular plant or establishment shall have the temerity to appoint a committee to present to an employer a list of grievances or requests for improved conditions, there are two elements which enter into it—either the committee have made up their minds that their fate will be discharge and hence will become brusque, will become overbearing and entirely impracticable, or, on the other hand, they will be docile and not present the real grievances, or requests of the employees, and either view perverts the real purpose for which the committee or representatives of employees make their presentation to the employers.

For that reason we ask for the right to be heard by counsel, and, if you please, not the counsel which the employers may designate for us, for, like you, if you have a case in court, we resent the attempt of the party of the second part to decide for us who shall represent the interests of the party of the first part. As a matter of fact in the interests of peace, in the interests of a better feeling between the employers and the employed, I recommend to your very serious and very careful consideration the suggestion of the right of labor not only to be organized but to be heard by counsel, the counsel of the organization, not those who may be honored with a diploma in the legal profession, but those who have the diploma granted them by the confidence which has been reposed in them by their fellow-workers organized with them and who have made common cause with them.—*From address in Buffalo, N. Y., January 9, 1903.*

Two facts should be emphasized. One, that it is the aim and purpose of the organized labor movement of our country to have employers and workmen faithfully carry out the terms of an agreement or contract in regard to labor and the conditions of employment. The other is that such an agreement or contract is not specifically enforceable by employers or by workmen.

In all the land there is no law by which any one is bound to specifically perform the service specified in any agreement or contract. Indeed, in any agreement or contract between workmen and employers, were the specific terms of the agreement or contract enforceable by law, men would, by the force of law, be compelled to perform work which they might find onerous, unjust, and unfair, and that moment involuntary servitude, a form of slavery, would be established. In no agreement or contract entered into between two persons in America has any one ever been required specifically to carry out its terms. The alternative has always been held, that unless a party to the contract fulfills the specific terms of the contract he may be called upon to respond in damages. The mere fact that workmen may not be in a position to respond in damages is no reason why they can be bound by the agreement or contract specifically to perform the services stipulated.—*American Federationist, August, 1912.*

The American Federation of Labor has repeatedly declared and emphasized the principle that agreements entered into between organized workmen and their employers covering a specific period, with provisions for wages, hours, and conditions of employment, should be sacredly kept. I think that perhaps the most conspicuous instance where there was provocation to break a contract not on the part of the employers themselves but by reason of the interests involved was the case of the United Mine Workers. During the anthracite strike a general clamor went up for the United Mine Workers to hold a special convention to declare a general sympathetic strike of all the coal miners of the country. Despite the great desire that all had to help their fellow-workers, yet to the great credit of the United Mine Workers they refused to take any action that would violate their agreements with their employers. They kept the faith and their pledged word. Instead of giving the employers the right to say that it was useless to enter into agreements with an organization that would break agreements at any convenient time the United Mine Workers established an additional argument for entering into new agreements. Nevertheless the anthracite miners' strike terminated with considerable improvement in their condition.—*From testimony before U. S. Commission on Industrial Relations, New York City, May 21-23, 1914.*

Even if the charge be true that the unions violated contracts, none do more than the men in the American labor movement to discountenance it, to prevent it, to try and overcome it, to try to adjust it and to chastise and discipline their own people, and this requires some courage, which I have not so often seen displayed on the other side. You do not know what it means for a man in his national or international trade union to rise up and say: "You shall not and dare not, within the confines and under the jurisdiction of this international union, pursue the course you have; and unless you return to work within an hour or within 24 hours, as the case may be, your charter, your affiliation to this international union, part of the American Federation of Labor, shall be severed and severed at once." Men in the American labor movement have that courage to say those things, and they do it. They have done it. They have done it within the past few days in three instances of my personal knowledge.

Read the proceedings of the conventions of those national and international unions. Read the declaration of the American

Federation of Labor, and read the declarations of the departments affiliated to the American Federation of Labor. Read the proceedings of the chiefs of the brotherhoods, of the railway service, and you will find that there is not anywhere any set of men who are so on guard to protect the rights of agreement, to maintain the principle that there can be no success in the labor movement so long as there shall be violations of agreement and contracts with employers. If you know of any other influence anywhere that accomplishes the same result I would like to know it, because we would want to copy it.—*From address before National Industrial Conference, Washington, D. C., October 17, 1919.*

The labor group proposed the following: "The right of wage earners to organize, without discrimination, to bargain collectively, to be represented by representatives of their own choosing in negotiations and adjustments with employers, in respect to wages, hours of labor, and relations and conditions of employment, is recognized."

That declaration carries with it the thought that there are questions of a divergent character which often arise between employers and workers, and upon which in an orderly, rational and natural way an effort may be made by the employers in conference with the representatives of the workers to reach an adjustment. It is a recognition that though the interests of employers and employees are not necessarily harmonious there are some conditions, relations and interests in common.

Earlier in these proceedings I took the opportunity of stating that the employers, by the attitude they have assumed in this conference, are placing themselves exactly in the same position as the I. W. W. The employers' group represented in this conference have put themselves on record as against agreements with wage-earners as such. The I. W. W. in its propaganda, in its declarations, have taken the position that workers should not enter into agreements with employers. The position in which the employing group has placed the employees of America is not an enviable one.

The preamble of the I. W. W. organization has in its essence this: The working class and employing class have nothing in common. Having nothing in common, they do not seek agreement, they do not seek a conciliation, they do not seek collective bargaining. They seek the opportunity of taking advantage, in every opportunity which may present itself at any moment to break an existing arrangement or understanding, to fight for another, and to declare as a fundamental principle of its tenets the confiscation of the property of the employers.

I admit that our trade union movement is not perfect, but I submit that there is not a single voluntary organization in this or any other country which has contributed so much to a constructive policy within rational lines. The declaration which we have proposed is rejected and repudiated by the employing group. They want shop organizations, the employers' union. They are building upon quicksand. They are resting their hope upon flimsy ground, in their benevolent and solicitous attitude toward the workers in their employ. An organization means something. It means that any group of workers shall have the free opportunity to express themselves, and that in the course of time and experience they will become, as every labor organization in America and throughout the world has become, more considerate and under the obligation of duty and responsibility. . . .

If the workers maintain their organization, time makes them realize their responsibility, and the employers experience a change in the mental attitude that they are masters of all they survey, and sit down and discuss in conference means and methods by which these adjustments and agreements and collective bargainings are brought about.

The shop organization, the employers' union of workers, never brings any one anywhere. It may be held by employers that their workmen are contented. Perhaps in so far as they are concerned they know the workers are contented; but the contentment is something like the contentment of the people of Poland. They were content at the point of the bayonet, and in the industrial plants they are content at the point of starvation. I do not mean the starvation of wanting bread. Hunger is a relative term after all. We may satisfy our hunger for food and clothing, but there comes a hunger for better food, for better clothing, for better homes, a hunger for better opportunities for themselves and their wives and their children and for those who shall follow them. There is no man so thoroughly starved as the one who has his aspirations destroyed.

My associates and I in this labor group in this conference are not here by sufferance; we are here, as are the employers, at the direct request of the President for our representation. . . . Is it imaginable that we, as the representatives of the organized workers of America, including, with the railroad brotherhoods, four and a half million wage-workers in the United States, can enter into this conference and remain members of it, with a refusal on the part of the employers' group to admit the right of the wage-workers to organize for collective bargaining? Is it possible that such a construction can be placed upon the President's call? I doubt it. Is there anything that any man can say is unfair or improper in the declaration that we have submitted, and which the employers' group, by their vote, defeated? We hear this talk of the individual workers. Do we not say in that declaration, "the right to organize without discrimination"?

If this were a new proposition, mild as it is, it might be understood why the opposition; but during the war, with the governmental departments the agreement existed recognizing the principle, and carrying it out in practice with employers, thousands and thousands of them, in the United States. A system of collective bargaining obtained without question, when our representative labor men, both local and national, met with the employers, unheralded and unknown, except to them and to the employees, and brought about results to the mutual advantage of both. There are some who will say: "But look, here is a strike, and here is a lockout, and does not that disprove your claim for collective bargaining?" And I say: "No, it does not; no more than when we read that a burglar has entered the home of a peaceful sleeping citizen it proves that we are a nation of burglars." The strike or the lockout is an incident, and compared to the great mass of workers and employers an inconsiderable and insignificant incident.

The word spoken here by the vote of the employers' group settles nothing. You have defeated labor in its declaration here, but we will meet you again, and we will meet you in conference, and you will be just as glad as we shall be to meet you in that conference for collective bargaining.—*From address at the National Industrial Conference, Washington, D. C., when the Labor Group withdrew, October 22, 1919.*

It is of interest to know that the public representatives [in National Industrial Conference] in their report to the President gave unqualified support to the principles of collective bargaining as presented by the labor group. It is interesting also to know that in the group of representatives of the public there were a larger number of employers than were contained in the group representing employers and that these employers in the public group were the employers of more workers than were the employers of the employers' group. In its report to the President, the public group made the following declaration relative to collective bargaining:

> We believe that the right of workers to organize for the purpose of collectively bargaining with their employers, through representatives of their own choosing, can not be denied or assailed. As representatives of the public we can interpret this right only in the sense that wage-earners can be free to choose what organizations or associations they will join for this purpose.
>
> In the recognition of the right of workers so organized to be represented by representatives of their own choice difficulties will from time to time arise. We believe that it would be possible for a properly constituted arbitral authority to adjust such difficulties with justice and fairness to all parties concerned.

—*American Federationist, December, 1919.*

To make the employees equal in power and influence to the employer they must be organized and, through regularly chosen representatives, meet the employer on a common footing. By conceding points on each side an agreement can be finally reached that will maintain better relations and therefore greater industrial peace.

In no other walk of life does the idea exist that a man must arbitrarily accept any offer that may be made by another. There are two sides always to an agreement. Each side ought to have equal chances to propose and insist upon what it considers a fair agreement.

Industrial peace can be secured only by the righting of wrongs suffered by the workers. If a body of workers has a grievance it can be adjusted only through conferences with the employer or his representative. As all can not meet the employer at one time it is necessary for them to select representatives to carry out their will as expressed collectively. This right is identical with that always held by the employer and never challenged by the law or the public.

In all spheres of activity in which employers, business men, public men and citizens generally have any matter in which their interests are involved, they not only avail themselves of appearing by their own representatives and counsel of their own choosing, whether in litigation before the courts or in business relations, but they are guaranteed even by the constitution of our country the right to be heard by counsel. The claim of the workers in this respect is founded upon the same fundamental beneficial principle—the right of the workers to be represented by counsel (not lawyers), representatives of their own number and of their own choice. . . .

Collective bargaining in industry does not imply that wage earners shall assume control of industry, or responsibility for financial management. It proposes that the employees shall have the right to organize and to deal with the employer through selected representatives as to wages and working conditions.

Among the matters that properly come within the scope of collective bargaining are wages, hours of labor, conditions and relations of employment, the sanitary conditions of the plant, safety and comfort regulations and such other factors as would add to the health, safety and comfort of the employees, resulting in the mutual advantage of both employers and employees. But there is no belief held in the trades unions that its members shall control the plant or usurp the rights of the owners.

Collective bargaining takes into consideration not only mutually advantageous conditions and standards of life and work, but also the human equation, a desideratum too long neglected.
—*From pamphlet, January, 1920, on "Collective Bargaining: Labor's Proposal to Insure Greater Industrial Peace."*

It is not often given to me to participate in jubilees and festive occasions where employers and employees agree. For me it is sufficient unto the day to try to bring about the relations that so happily now exist between your employers' association in the building industry and the workers in the building trades. I am quite content that others shall share and enjoy the wonderful results of the new relations which are brought about by workers and employers who understand each other and try to reach honorable adjustments of all their differences. . . . Out of the dispute which existed between men having honest differences of interest and of judgment you have reached a conclusion that it is best as men engaged in this great industry to unite and mutually work for the best interests of all concerned in the great community in which you are privileged to live. It is this understanding for which the American labor movement is striving; it is recognition of the principle that while your interests are not always harmonious they are frequently mutual and that each can be of service to the other, and that in any conflict where one seeks the mastery over the other there is not a possibility of recognition of the mutuality of interests.—*From address at dinner of Boston Building Trades Employers' Association, Boston, Mass., January 7, 1920.*

Man forgets the roughness of the struggles in the ideality which he hopes to attain. And so in the labor movement of the past and of to-day, whatever roughness there may be attached to it, the future will forget and forgive in the ideal to establish better relations and better standards for the great mass of the people of our country.

The time has gone by when employers of labor can assume for themselves the position of absolutism, of autocracy. Industry and commerce must become more democratic in their initial as well as their continued operations.

Last night I was honored by being present at a gathering of organized employers and of organized workers, and found that as the result of years of experience an entire important industry has come to an agreement with the workers in their representative organized capacity. It rarely has occurred that such congenial companionship and friendship and real understanding of the position of the other party have been so well exemplified as on the occasion last evening.

What we aim to do is not, as some people attribute to us, the overthrow of government or the destruction of anything that is worth while maintaining. The movement of American organized labor is constructive, not destructive. It is to make to-day a better day than yesterday, to-morrow a better day than to-day, and to-morrow's to-morrow, each of them a better day than the one that has gone before, not by tactics or policies that are destructive but by a constructive, rational and natural policy. If error occurs during this great, inspiring and constructive work, who will throw the first stone?—*From address by invitation before Chamber of Commerce, Boston, Mass., January 8, 1920.*

I regard the human equation as the largest concern of business and I think that the only way to acquire the truly personal relation on a man-to-man basis is to arrange the basic hours and pay through a bargain with a responsible union body, for then there is no question of goodness on the part of the employer or of contentment on the part of the employee. The parties meet as buyers and sellers on a level plane and because each has something that the other wants there is no reason on earth why their bargain can not be carried through with the same dignity, with the same mutual satisfaction, and with the same fairness of aim on the part of both sides that makes a present-day bargain between business men the beginning of a relationship.

Nobody in these days would employ a salesman who would come back after having sold a customer and declare triumphantly, "I did that fellow up all right. I got the best of him." Any sales manager would discharge that salesman on the spot, for he would know that such a man would destroy and not build up trade. It is quite the same way in dealing with workers, and I am speaking not merely from a hypothetical position but as an actual employer.

We have one hundred people or so in the headquarters of the American Federation of Labor, all of whom are working under my general direction and I do not think that it would be possible to have a more cordial relation than exists between us. They not only do everything that I ask them to do but they endeavor to anticipate my wishes in every respect and quite frequently do more than I want them to do.

If I were an employer of general labor I should expect to bargain in the fairest possible spirit and I believe that I should receive fair service in return. Once we remove the union's suspicion of the employer and the employer's suspicion of the union there is nothing in the world to prevent the most cordial relation—the sort of relation that we all like to have with everybody with whom we come in contact. The bargain would settle the questions of hours and wages and with them out of the way, the road would be open for truly personal contact. . . .

The interests of the employer and the employee are in no sense identical. Do not confuse that point. They have not an identity of interest, but they have a coöperation of interest—that same coöperation of interest which exists between a manufacturer and his best customer. No intelligent manufacturer will sell so much or at such a price that his customer must lose money. It is just as much his concern to see that his customer makes money as it is to see that he manufactures—for without the one there can not be the other.

Exactly this same kind of relation between the employer and the employees promotes good work and fair wages on the part of the employees and consequently a good output at a fair profit on the part of the employer. This manly relation is not possible with company unions or with any organization which ultimately depends upon the will of the employer for then the necessary independence of spirit will not be present; deference is very apt to turn into servility.—*From interview with Samuel Crowther on "What I Should Do If I Were an Employer," in "System Magazine," April, 1920.*

XI

THE LABOR VIEW OF PROFIT-SHARING, "EFFICIENCY" MANAGEMENT, AND INDUSTRIAL DEMOCRACY

PROFIT-SHARING AND COÖPERATION

Judging from the history of such efforts in the past, I would look upon such propositions [profit-sharing or coöperation] with a very great deal of suspicion. There have been few, if any, of these concerns that have been even comparatively fair to their employees. The average employer who has indulged in this single-handed scheme to solve the social problem has gotten out of the workers all that there was in them and all their vitality, and made them old prematurely, to the tune of five or ten years of their lives. They made the worker work harder, longer hours, and when the employees of other concerns in the same line of trade were enjoying increased wages, shorter hours of labor, and other improvements, tending to the material progress of the worker, the employees of the concern where so-called profit-sharing was the system at the end of the year found themselves receiving lower wages for harder work than were those who were not under that beneficent system. . . . So long as our present social system shall last, it is positively ludicrous for any concern or few concerns to attempt to solve the social problem for themselves. It is just as ludicrous and ridiculous as it is for a number of well-meaning people, well-meaning workmen, to make up their minds to enter upon a colonization scheme of coöperation. They isolate themselves from the world—even if their purpose is a success, if their scheme is a success, they have simply emancipated themselves from the world, and are contributing nothing toward the solution of the struggle; yes, they have hindered the struggle, for, as a rule, these people are discontented with the wrongs that exist, but, though manifesting some little thought and ability, deprive the people who are struggling from the benefits of that knowledge and discontent; so in the sum total, it is depriving the movement for social improvement, economic advancement, of the intelligence, and independence, and manhood, and character of these people who isolate themselves from the rest of the world. And so it is with those profit-sharing concerns, perhaps prompted by no other cause than that of philanthropy or desire to solve the problem. That is not the way it must be solved; you can not solve the social problem without taking into consideration the human family. . . .

We are operating under the wage system. As to what system will ever come to take its place I am not prepared to say. I have given this subject much thought; I have read the works of the most advanced economists, competent economists in all schools of thought—the trade unionist, the socialist, the anarchist, the single taxer, the coöperationist, etc. I am not prepared to say, after having read, and with an honest endeavor to arrive at a conclusion—I am not prepared to say that any of their propositions are logical, scientific, or natural. I know that we are living under the wage system, and so long as that lasts it is our purpose to secure a continually larger share for labor, for the wealth producers. Whether the time shall come, as this constantly increasing share to labor goes on, when profits shall be entirely eliminated, and the full product of labor, the net result of production, go to the laborer, thus abolishing the wage system; or whether, on the other hand, through the theory of the anarchist, there should be an abolition of all title in land other than its occupation and use, the abolition of the monopoly of the private issuance of money, the abolition of the patent system—whether we will return to the first principles; or whether, under the single tax, taxing the land to the full value of it—I am perfectly willing that the future shall determine and work out. I know that as the workers more thoroughly organize, and continually become larger sharers in the product of their toil, they will have better opportunities for their physical and mental cultivation instilled into them, higher hopes and aspirations, and they will be the better prepared to meet the problems that will then confront them. For the present it is our purpose to secure better conditions and instill a larger amount of manhood and independence into the hearts and minds of the workers, and to broaden their mental sphere and the sphere of their affections.—*From testimony before Industrial Commission, Washington, D. C., April 18, 1899.*

We have good reason for not believing that one of the [Steel] corporation's employees in five earning under $1,500 a year ever owned a share of its stock, the requisite preliminary to this "profit-sharing." It is to be doubted that the ratio now reaches one in ten.

As to the "generosity" of the corporation's acts in this respect, here are the main facts: This special stock issue, a fixed amount from time to time, was to all employees, from the top down, the highly salaried as well as the wage-earning class. The shares were sold the employees at the market rates, at which any outsider could buy. The benevolence of the company was to be recognized in taking payment on the installment plan and in a $5 bonus per year given to the holder of each share of the allotted stock, which was not to be paid, however, until the end of five years. As the first issue was of 25,000 shares, the bonus on it would amount to $125,000 a year. This amounted to considerably less than $1 a year per employee, of whom in 1902 there were 168,000.

To equal a 10 per cent raise in wages an employee earning $700 a year would have to buy at least fourteen shares, which the share allotment did not permit him to do, to say nothing of the impossibility of his ability ever to pay for that number of shares out of his wages. Up to the present time it is to be doubted that 1 per cent of the total capital of the corporation has gone to all the employees, in every class, under the scheme. To the wage-earners receiving under $1,500 a year, how much has been allotted? A mere slice of a fraction of one-half of 1 per cent.

Meantime, numerous trade unions in other industries have advanced the wages of their members 10 per cent or more. Besides, union conditions are of themselves worth another 10 per cent in any establishment, not in sentiment, but in cash for the year, through protection against the aggressions and tyrannies of foremen and the constant encroachment of employers upon those shop rights and civic rights of the men which a union maintains.—*American Federationist, February, 1910.*

In looking over notes and clippings concerning the moves and opinions of the new profit-sharers, or proposed profit-sharers, the expressions of altruism and philanthropy seem to be "lugged" into the discussion, while the language of calculating business comes to the front frequently and forcibly. The profit-sharers are considering "the various methods by which employers may bind their employees closer to them"; they are seeking in a deceptive annual dividend to labor "a sound business move"; they wish "the employee to be governed by the same motives that animate the employer"; they invariably "seek efficiency." This language has a purely business-like sound. But wherein it indicates an increased happiness for the masses of labor is not convincing.

Not only on behalf of organized labor but on the part of the general public, one test of its social efficacy may at the outset be offered to the advocates of profit-sharing. It is this: Will the employing profit-sharer take as a basis the union scale of wages and hours in his occupation and the working conditions deemed fair by law and union custom and proceeding from that level offer in addition any of the forms of profits which have been recommended by the professed upholders of profit-sharing? How many names this question would eliminate from the list of its advocates is an estimate which any observer of the movement may make for himself.

Union wages, hours and conditions form convincing evidence to the masses of wage-workers that the employer is fair and square. He stands before the community simply as a man, not bidding for the doubtful commendatory appellation of philanthropist or apostle of a new society. His actions are above suspicion. He is also a man of business sense; he has all the wage-workers in his line to choose from as employees. His "labor troubles" are, if not at an end, at least plainly confined to a well-known area.

The nomenclature of profit-sharing is singularly rich in equivocal terms. "Loyalty." Is the employee to be wholly loyal to his employer and not first of all loyal to himself? How loyal is an employer to his furnishers of raw material? He is loyal to them only so long as they sell him what he wants at the lowest market rate. "Efficiency." Never to be missed in any lecture or discourse on profit-sharing, this term points to push, grind, and hurry to the exhaustion of the employee, despite its admitted legitimacy up to the point of average physical abilities. "Profits." Is the withholding of 5 or 10 per cent from an employee's wages during the year and returning it to him at an appointed annual date a sharing of profits or a mere restitution of withheld earnings?—*American Federationist, May, 1916.*

To attain the greatest possible development of civilization, it is essential, among other things, that the people should never delegate to others those activities and responsibilities which they are capable of assuming for themselves. Democracy can function best with the least interference by the state compatible with due protection to the rights of all citizens.

There are many problems arising from production, transportation and distribution, which would be readily solved by applying the methods of coöperation. Unnecessary middlemen who exact a tax from the community without rendering any useful service can be eliminated.

The farmers, through coöperative dairies, canneries, packing houses, grain elevators, distributing houses, and other coöperative enterprises, can secure higher prices for their products and yet place these in the consumer's hands at lower prices than would otherwise be paid. There is an almost limitless field for the consumers in which to establish coöperative buying and selling, and in this most necessary development, the trade unionists should take an immediate and active part.

Trade unions secure fair wages. Coöperation protects the wage-earner from the profiteer.

Participation in these coöperative agencies must of necessity prepare the mass of the people to participate more effectively in the solution of the industrial, commercial, social and political problems which continually arise.—*From American Federation of Labor Reconstruction Program, adopted by A. F. of L. Executive Council, December 28, 1918. (Excerpt republished by mutual consent as expressing the views of Mr. Gompers.)*

"EFFICIENCY" EXPERIMENTS

It is a conceded fact that the working people of our country are the hardest worked and the largest producers of wealth, both per man and in the aggregate, as compared with any workmen in the entire world. And yet these doctrinaires of so-called efficiency imagine that by still further burdening the toilers of America they can make them work harder and produce more; produce more, aye, even to the extent of trebling the quantity of their product. Perhaps they have not heard or read the warning of that keenest of observers, Herbert Spencer, who, on the occasion of his last visit to the United States, when he noted the intensity with which the toilers of our country were working, declared that in the interest of the country and of its people, the time had arrived to preach and practice "the gospel of relaxation."—*American Federationist, April, 1911.*

The year has witnessed a discussion on a national scale of the doctrines and practice of "Scientific Management." This new economic gospel has its prophets and its policies, and for a brief time had its crusade. While its leaders professed that its objects comprised many reforms in management, arguments in favor of what came to be popularly called "efficiency" principally turned upon the idea of getting more product out of the toil of the laborer. The phases of efficiency presented to the wage-workers were those of systems long known, both to indoor and outdoor workers. Included in the scheme were the bonus and piece systems, together with methods of contracting and of fining which have long been fought by trade unionists, and also a method of sweating, by which if a stated task were not completed the promised bonus for it was entirely lost and wages fell to a point at which they would have stood on the ordinary day's production.

Many absurd or unfounded claims were for a time advanced in support of the so-called "Scientific Management." It was said, for example, that in the course of its application, now extending over more than a decade, it had never occasioned a strike. The truth is that only during the last year its attempted introduction has brought on a series of labor disputes, the employees in the navy yards and on other government work having struck against it by the means immediately at their hand, namely, an appeal to Congress against the changes, and especially the sweating, the system brings into practice.

As one book after another, or one pamphlet after another, was issued on the subject, numerous public addresses being made meantime by its supporters, it became more and more evident that the men whose names were chiefly associated with it were not in agreement as to the principles of "efficiency" and its application. It is to be said to-day that the system has been far from uniformly successful. It has been abandoned in some of the largest works where some years ago it was adopted. The fallacy in the statement that wages were increased by the application of scientific management is now generally recognized. For the time being, after its adoption, the wages of a small proportion of a force may be raised, whereas much of the work usually done by skilled men is turned over to unskilled helpers, working far below the wages usually paid to mechanics. It is plain that the system is not adaptable to most of the work done on time. It has been said that in America 50,000 persons were working under the system. If so, the fact cannot be proven by any detailed statistics taken by any census, so far as trade unionists have been able to ascertain. It originated in, and has been chiefly confined to, the workshops of certain large companies which have been notorious employers of non-union and freshly-arrived foreign labor. In large shops it has long been known that certain operations which are performed without variation day after day may only require a low-wage machine attendant, and if the preliminary stages of the work have been systematized, of course the output will be large at a low cost. In small shops, however, and in industries in which the shopwork is not the main factor, the field for the pyramidal labor arrangement, or organization, of scientific management is small. Moreover, the promoters of the system have so extravagantly advertised its claims, and especially their charges of wilful loafing against American laborers, that the general conclusion is that they are mere discoverers of a "mare's nest." They have expected the public to give credence to the absurdity that workmen in general "soldier" to the extent of "one-third or even one-half of a proper day's work." The public has refused to believe this slander on the American workingman, and the workers themselves have everywhere challenged these traducers to bring forward proofs of their assertions. In view of the fact that America's workers are the greatest producers per man and in the aggregate in the whole world, it is an offense against the common sense of men to ask them to believe that, in shops where foremen are ever on the alert, where the penalty for loafing is discharge, where all the men strive to be among those kept on in dull times, where the great majority of them are responsible fathers or supporting members of families, the workers would by common consent endeavor to deceive and defraud their employers by delivering only half a day's work for a full day's work. All of "Scientific Management" which is built upon this basis of detraction must obviously be disbelieved.

As the discussion now stands, the wage-workers have by far the best of it. The system has not been taken up by employers in general. The number that have shown much interest in it form a very small proportion throughout the country. Railroad managers have treated the estimated possible savings to industry by "efficiency" prophets with contempt. It may also be said that employers have been slow to believe that such wonderful improvements could be made in management as they have proclaimed. In a book issued by one of the authors supporting the system, the statement is made that where one point relating to the wage-earner was to be improved, nine points relating to the employer could be improved. Inasmuch as the advocates of "efficiency" have failed to make much of a success on the one point pertaining to the workshop, we respectfully invite their attention to the nine points in the office department which await their labors.

The verdict on efficiency has been pronounced by society. It has already been relegated to a place on a shelf among the nostrums, sensations, and paraphernalia of magic workers of the past. The American public has not welcomed the spectacle of steel works where, under an inspector, stop-watch in hand, one man is carrying five tons of pig iron where he formerly carried one, or of a bicycle shop where one girl does the work formerly done by three, when she is not carried out fainting, or where in a textile mill a girl is paid for the ordinary day's work after she has striven and strained and almost completed the allotted bonus task of doing two days work in one.—*From annual report to A. F. of L. convention, Atlanta, Ga., November, 1911.*

Sometimes efficiency experiments have been tried in institutions not of an industrial nature. The New York *Nation* comments editorially upon two such experiments as follows:

"Just now the University of Wisconsin is being subjected to an 'efficiency' survey, which must make any true scholar feel strongly tempted to hand in his resignation. Subpoenas are even threatened, and a New York researcher is reporting to be attending class-rooms with a stenographer by his side—doubtless to count the words the professor utters, to measure the attention of his listeners, to put a stopwatch on him, as if he were a bricklayer or a pig-iron handler. When an efficiency test was tried at Harvard last year, the whole faculty rose in arms, and the president withdrew the proposal; at Wisconsin, they must obey what the state decrees, when it decrees, or get out. To any one who thinks at all, this method of 'bringing a university up to date' is destructive of the very best for which it should stand. It is the beginning of an intellectual thraldom likely to stifle any great soul, to reduce a college to the basis of a factory, and to ignore entirely its priceless spiritual values."

In time, and that not far distant, thinking men and women will realize that what applies to these two universities is equally true of the "bricklayer and the pig-iron handler"; that the conditions and the distinctive tendencies which justified a strike on the part of the Harvard faculty also justify a strike by the Westinghouse employees; and that a factory should be conducted with the same high regard for souls as colleges and universities. Factory workers have souls—often just as big souls as university workers. Besides there are many more factory workers than university workers, and therefore national and social welfare make necessary the conservation, protection, and real development of the masses of the people if the nation is to realize the greatest possibilities.—*American Federationist, August, 1914.*

An investigation of scientific management was made for the Federal Commission on Industrial Relations. This investigation was conducted by Prof. Robert F. Hoxie of the University of Chicago, with the advice and assistance of Mr. John P. Frey, editor of the *Molders' Journal,* and Mr. Robert G. Valentine, representing the employers' interests. The report, which was signed by all of these investigators, points out the following defects that were observed:

"(a) Failure to carry into effect with any degree of thoroughness the general elements involved in the system.

"(b) Failure to adopt the full system of 'functional foremanship.'

"(c) Lack of uniformity in the method of selecting and hiring help.

"(d) Failure to substantiate claims of scientific management with reference to the adaptation, instruction and training of workers.

"(e) Lack of scientific accuracy, uniformity and justice in time study and task-setting.

"(f) Failure to substantiate the claim of having established a scientific and equitable method of determining wage-rates.

"(g) Failure to protect the workers from over-exertion and exhaustion.

"(h) Failure to substantiate the claim that scientific management offers exceptional opportunities for advancement and promotion on a basis of individual merit.

"(i) With reference to the alleged methods and severity of discipline under scientific management the 'acrimonious criticism' from trade unions does not seem to be warranted.

"(j) Failure to substantiate the claim that workers are discharged only on just grounds and have an effective appeal to the highest managerial authority.

"(k) Lack of democracy under scientific management." ...

The wage-earners know that a truly scientific plan for securing efficiency must be a comprehensive plan that involves all of the processes of production, one that does not expend itself on the application of labor power by the workers, but gives proportional consideration to an adjustment of the materials and the scheme of production over which the employer has control.

Real scientific efficiency in production must have regard for the human factors in production and must find a place in the scheme for principles of human welfare. Science places a high value upon human life, and everywhere makes the human effect the paramount consideration.

Scientific management as found in most instances has to do only with time and motion studies, ostensibly to establish new standards and bases for wage compensations. However, time or motion studies so far made are all based upon averages and make no attempt scientifically to establish principles that could be termed just standards for compensation.

Time and motion studies fail to make any consideration for human fatigue. They are only crude methods for establishing the work that can be done under highest pressure in the shortest period of time without any pretense of conserving human creative power. The whole emphasis is put upon the quantity of material output. Merely mathematical maximum of production is not the desirable scientific output.—*American Federationist, June, 1916.*

The American Federation of Labor has achieved a tremendous victory of far-reaching consequence in protecting workers in certain trades against a pernicious system that threatened the manhood, the independence and the initiative of the workers of those trades. Particularly the workers in the metal trades have felt the impending danger of efforts to fasten upon them systems of so-called "scientific management." These systems are endeavoring to establish a new standard for paying wages, a standard that would inevitably undermine the health and mentality of workers, for it is a standard that aims directly to speed up workers to the exhaust point and to instill mechanical habits of work.

In order to protect the lives and health of workers, Congress incorporated into the Sundry Civil bill and Fortifications bill the following proviso:

"*Provided,* That no part of the appropriations made in this act shall be available for the salary or pay of any officer, manager, superintendent, foreman, or other person having charge of the work of any employee of the United States while making or causing to be made with a stop-watch, or other time-measuring device, a time study of any job of any such employee between the starting and completion thereof, or of the movements of any such employee while engaged upon such works; nor shall any part of the appropriations made in this Act be available to pay any premium or bonus or cash reward to any employee in addition to his regular wages, except for suggestions resulting in improvements or economy in the operation of any government plant."

These bills were approved by both houses of Congress and have been signed by the President. The same proviso is included in the Naval and Army bills. Thus the workers have secured congressional approval for their opposition to systems that have sought to give to a new exploiting scheme the sanction of science and of efficient production.

Workers have proven by their actual experiences that stop-watch time-measuring systems are neither scientific nor are they in furtherance of most effective production. The workers are not opposed to methods or devices that facilitate production, but they are opposed to methods that dehumanize the workers.

The so-called scientific efficiency systems that have been thus far proposed are neither scientific nor efficient. The workers are in favor of methods that will enable them to become more effective, intelligent, resourceful participators in production. Such methods must necessarily be educational in nature.

The labor movement declares that efforts to promote production in quality as well as quantity must have as their primary consideration the development of the creative power of the human agents.—*American Federationist, August, 1916.*

Only out of production can we all grow prosperous, and every aid to production that does not involve human waste is a benefit to society. If the added production is gained at the cost of a human being, then it does not help society, because even from a cold standpoint of economics it tends toward over-production by destroying in the very making of the product those who would directly or indirectly buy that product. Whatever are the evils in the distribution of the products of work (and there are many of them), those evils are not going to be cured by producing less. That will not solve the problem of distribution. That will only provide humanity with one bone instead of two to snarl about. As I said before, I am in favor of every possible device which will increase the productivity of human labor and increase its standards. This is best done with the assistance of science. There can be no objection to really scientific management (not the so-called scientific management with its stop-watch methods and bonuses), that which is for the benefit of all the parties to industry and not only of one. As an employer I should know that it would be shortsighted to expect to get steadily more from my workers and at the same time give them steadily less.

The better industrial engineers who are interested in improving industry and not merely in coddling employers know this to be a fact, and they regard an inequality in pay—that is, a pay which is less than the performance—as a waste of human resource and pursue such wastes as belligerently as they pursue any other wastes.

I think that scientific industrial instruction can best be given and possibly can only be given in coöperation with the workers and with committees of the workers, so that none will have to work blindly. I am quite sure that the assurance that the improvement of methods will be for all will invite the most active coöperation on the part of the union officers. The old "ca'canny" methods originated by the Scotch, the limitation of production, the idea that there is only a certain amount of work in this world to do and that it must be spread out thin, are dead and ought never to be revived, and will never be revived. As an employer I should discriminate between the union organized for work and the organization falsely called a "union" which is organized to prevent work.

I should not only endeavor to have all of my employees organized but I should want to have them organized in such a way that I might, as an employer, consult with their representatives on constructive policies and not confine the consultation merely to differences. This constructive side has undoubtedly been neglected. It has been neglected because the suspicion between the employer and employees has commonly been so intense as to confine their activities to watching each other. Once they get together along the lines that I have outlined and check their suspicions, then there is room for that vast amount of constructive work which will so greatly improve industry in its every phase. Fighting produces battle leaders and it may well be that the conditions surrounding union organization have produced a number of leaders who have been compelled to be militant rather than constructive. This is undoubtedly a question of circumstance and not at all of fundamentals. . . .

In order to obtain increased operating efficiency I should call in the union heads just as I should call in an industrial engineer, but even more frequently and on a more intimate basis. This would prevent dissatisfaction among my men by making wages always the last reduction instead of the first. I would know as an employer that high wages do not mean increased cost of production but, on the contrary, are the greatest possible incentive toward the invention of better machinery and tools in order that the worker's power may be extended to an almost indefinite degree. I would know that cheap men do not mean a cheap output. Wherever the human element is cheap you will find the methods and means of production in the most backward condition. I would pay high wages and I would endeavor by every possible means to eliminate the wastes from my plant, and to gain the maximum of efficiency without brutal driving.

There is an impression that the unions are against machinery, are against the better ways of doing business, are against scientific management, and in favor of stringing out every job to the greatest possible extent. That, it is true, was the English attitude of the old country. It is not the attitude of the American labor movement.

The unions at one time opposed the introduction of machinery because both the workers and the employers saw labor-saving machines not as aids to production but as substitutes for men. I am in favor of every possible mechanical device that can substitute for human labor, but if the employer looks at the machine solely as an instrument to take employment from men he is bound to fail just as are the workers who oppose the machinery because apparently it is going to cost them their jobs. That is the shortsighted view. The workers can break the machines, and they can destroy the blue prints, but the idea remains and if it is a good idea it will be put into force. Otherwise, we bar the economic progress of the world and encourage instead of prevent waste.—*From interview with Samuel Crowther on "What I Should Do If I Were an Employer," in "System Magazine," April, 1920.*

THE TRUE "DEMOCRATIZATION OF INDUSTRY"

Perhaps the following might be regarded as a summary of demands to be satisfied in the pending readjustment of conditions:

No wage reductions.

No lengthening of the working day.

Opportunity for suitable, regular, remunerative employment.

A workday of not more than eight hours; a work week of not more than five and a half days.

Protection for women and children from overwork, underpay and unsuitable employment.

Increased opportunity for both education and play for children.

The elimination of private monopolies and protection from the extortions of profiteers.

Final disposition of the railroads, telegraph, telephone and cable systems to be determined by consideration of the rights and interests of the whole people, rather than the special privileges and interests of a few.

Comfortable, sanitary homes in wholesome environment, rather than elaborate improvements of no special benefit to the masses of the people.

Heavier taxation of idle lands, to the end that they may be used for the public good.

A government made more responsive to the demands of justice and the common good by the adoption of initiative and referendum measures.

In a word, any and all measures shall be taken tending toward constant growth and development of the economic, industrial, political, social and humane conditions for the toilers, to make life the better worth living, to develop all that is best in the human being and make for the whole people a structure wherein each will vie with the other in the establishment of the highest and best concepts and ideals of the human family.—*From "Labor Standards After the War"; Annals of the American Academy, December, 1918.*

Two codes of rules and regulations affect the workers; the law upon the statute books, and the rules within industry.

The first determines their relationship as citizens to all other citizens and to property.

The second largely determines the relationship of employer and employee, the terms of employment, the conditions of labor, and the rules and regulations affecting the workers as employees. The first is secured through the application of the methods of democracy in the enactment of legislation, and is based upon the principle that the laws which govern a free people should exist only with their consent.

The second, except where effective trade unionism exists, is established by the arbitrary or autocratic whim, desire or opinion of the employer and is based upon the principle that industry and commerce cannot be successfully conducted unless the employer exercises the unquestioned right to establish such rules, regulations and provisions affecting the employees as self-interest prompts.

Both forms of law vitally affect the workers' opportunities in life and determine their standard of living. The rules, regulations and conditions within industry in many instances affect them more than legislative enactments. It is, therefore, essential that the workers should have a voice in determining the laws within industry and commerce which affect them, equivalent to the voice which they have as citizens in determining the legislative enactments which shall govern them.

It is as inconceivable that the workers as free citizens should remain under autocratically made laws within industry and commerce as it is that the nation could remain a democracy while certain individuals or groups exercise autocratic powers.

It is, therefore, essential that the workers everywhere should insist upon their right to organize into trade unions, and that effective legislation should be enacted which would make it a criminal offense for any employer to interfere with or hamper the exercise of this right or to interfere with the legitimate activities of trade unions.—*From American Federation of Labor Reconstruction Program, adopted by A. F. of L. Executive Council, December 28, 1918. (Excerpt republished by mutual consent as expressing the views of Mr. Gompers.)*

Industry, like government, can only exist by the coöperation of all. Like government, industry must guarantee equal opportunities, equal protection and equal rights and benefits to all. Every edifice, every product of human toil is the creation of coöperation of all the people. In this coöperation it is the right of all to have a voice and to share in an equitable proportion of the fruits of these collective enterprises. Wherever men co-exist in industry not less surely than in politics, the principles of freedom, justice and democracy must and will prevail. Wherever the wage-earners are not permitted to organize, these rights of free men are denied and those who enforce this denial do violence to the most sacred principles of American society. This is government without consent of the governed and those who believe such an arbitrary and autocratic relation in industry can continue are the idlest of dreamers. Those who persist in such practices are our nation's most dangerous enemies. It is they who plant the seed of anarchy and bolshevism. . . .

Democracy must be progressive or die. The old political democracy is the father of this new industrial democracy. The trade union movement is the potential new industrial democracy. Trade unions develop the reason, the conscience and the civic sense of the wage-earners. Trade unions should be encouraged because they appeal to reason and not to the destructive passions of man. By combining into trade unions, in acting collectively, deciding questions by debate and majority vote, making sacrifices of opinion and individual superiority for the common good of all, the workers receive an education and training which eminently fit them to take their rightful place in industry and in organized society. Indeed, it is only by this education and training that democracies can live and grow and develop.—*American Federationist, May, 1919.*

Democracy in industry is a very real thing toward which human society is advancing. But since that remote day in which some wise person learned the gentle art of deception there has never been a noticeable lack of devotees. Someone is always ready to try a hand at producing "something just as good," or something which will pass for the genuine.

So it is with industrial democracy. The past month brought a dozen reports of "industrial democracy" in practice. The lesson in deception has been handed down from generation to generation. The modern practitioner has lost none of the finesse of his forbears. On the contrary, there are indications that in many cases he excels, going so far as to deceive himself. It is possible that some of the employers who are putting "industrial democracy" into effect are themselves deceived into the belief that their article is genuine.

This manifestation is, in a way, a sign of the times. Employers who realize that the industrial autocrat has had his day strive, from one of two motives, to set up something in place of industrial autocracy that will look like that for which the new day calls. Employers may do this from a genuine desire to better the lot of those working people who operate the plants, or they may do it out of a desire to halt progress half way by means of a decoy.

The superficial movement toward "democracy" as embodied in the various schemes devised by employers is given a fresh impetus by the host of men and women released from war service in Washington. This host of men and women, having had something in an emergency capacity to do with production during the war, now step forth as industrial experts ready to pour advice into the ears of employers—ready and eager to devise for them attractive and beneficent schemes for "model" shop "government" of one kind or another. Dozens of these "expert" advisers are at large in the country. Some of them did get a real insight into the problems of industry. Some of them may have been little more than filing clerks. Others were employed in various capacities, ranging from letter writing to inspection of output. Practically none of them ever labored in their lives, in the strict sense of the word, and many of them never had a liking for the laboring classes except as producers of wealth in which they are not expected to share. Most of them are self-imposed authorities. Some may have attained scholarship and perhaps chairs in institutions of learning. Others again may have amassed fortunes and find it a peculiarly interesting and profitable pastime to play with the lives and conditions of the wage-earners. These men have yet to learn, however, that the workers are humans like themselves, capable of self-expression and self-determination and that the wage-earners of America can not be treated by the yard-stick or moved about in a cold, academical, statistical and mechanical fashion like so many pawns on a checker board.

The war is over and everybody is talking about labor. Casting about for some outlet for their energies, many of these men pick on the "labor situation" and become labor or industrial "experts" or "adjusters."

Many an employer is being "experted" or "adjusted" into some new channel by a highly skilled benefactor who served ten months at a desk in Washington and is now ready to reshape the world!

In this ferment it is not surprising that there should be a rapid increase in the number of employers who are willing to experiment under the kindly—and perhaps costly—tutelage of the mentor from Washington.

Generally these proposals are variations of the "company union" idea. Sometimes they comprise a "shop committee" plan. Then again they may embrace the more elaborate and elusive "government" organized into "house," "senate," "cabinet," etc. In some cases stock ownership is a feature, while in others representation on the board of directorate is conceived as the panacea for industrial democracy. Sharing in excess profits also seems to be a popular plan which has been urged as another method of industrial democracy.

The one kindly word that could be said for these schemes is that they might prove their own futility to labor, if they could be tried out without destroying the labor movement, and thus lead to something fundamental in the way of approach to democracy. But there has been proof enough—proof to spare; no more proof is needed to demonstrate that labor's future must be worked out for labor through its own trade union organizations, directed by labor, without the patronage of employers or so-called industrial experts.

There has yet to appear the first employer or industrial-expert-made "industrial democracy" plan which contemplates the existence of trade union organization as the expression of the workers' desires in the plant.

There is present in every case subtle efforts to delude the workers into the belief that they are exercising a voice in industry when as a matter of fact the employer holds the veto and deciding power. It is quite apparent that the underlying motive in all these schemes is to prevent the workers from organizing or joining a trade union or to weaken the trade union where it may exist and thereby disable the workers from entering into an effective strike to force the employer beyond his veto and deciding power.

The workers are not satisfied to sell their right of combining and striking for any plausible or partial participation in management. The American workers distrust the latter because it is in keeping with the old oligarchic strategy by which democracy has been defeated in detail. The triumph of employers heretofore virtually consisted in granting popular control in such small quantities that the control could and has been controlled.

The question that concerns men who want orderly progress instead of revolution is whether business and industry will collaborate with labor or will take an attitude that will drive labor to wrest from them, by revolutionary methods, a new order in industry.

Workers organized in trade unions need not accept without protest the arbitrary ruling of an employer. They have the means and the independence and the machinery with which to make effective protest. History is written largely by the protests that have been made against the arbitrary rulings of those entrenched in authority. When the employers' decree marks the limit of progress, then the hope that burns in the breast of thinking men and women will have come upon sad and evil times.

Industrial democracy is the great goal of the future. It is the thing to which the eyes of men are turned. It must and will be a real democracy of industry. No sham will do. And not all the advice of "experts" will serve to inflict upon the working people anything labelled "just as good."

Doubtless many of these "experts" and experimenters are imbued with a fine zeal and actuated by the best of motives. Many an honest man has bought fakery from many an honest man. To be deceived and harmed by a friend, though well-intentioned, is as painful and harmful as deliberate and intentional wrong-doing by a foe.

The outstanding feature of it all is that there is a growing consciousness of the determination on the part of the workers to put an end to all that savors of industrial autocracy. With this object in view, the workers of America will continue to agitate, educate and organize into trade unions and through their trade unions fight their own battles for industrial freedom, industrial justice and industrial democracy.—*American Federationist, September, 1919. (From editorial by Matthew Woll, republished by mutual consent as expressing the views of Mr. Gompers.)*

Existing high and excessive prices are due to the present inflation of money and credits, to profiteering by those who manufacture, sell and market products, and to burdens levied by middlemen and speculators. We urge:

The deflation of currency; prevention of hoarding and unfair price fixing; establishment of coöperative movements operated under the Rochdale system; making accessible all income tax returns and dividend declarations as a direct and truthful means of revealing excessive costs and profits.

The ideal of America should be the organization of industry for service and not for profit alone. The stigma of disgrace should attach to every person who profits unduly at the expense of his fellow-men. . . .

Credit is the life blood of modern business. At present under the control of private financiers it is administered, not primarily to serve the needs of production, but the desire of financial agencies to levy a toll upon community activity as high as "the traffic will bear."

Credit is inherently social. It should be accorded in proportion to confidence in production possibilities. Credit as now administered does not serve industry but burdens it. It increases unearned incomes at the expense of earned incomes. It is the center of the malevolent forces that corrupt the spirit and purpose of industry.

We urge the organization and use of credit to serve production needs and not to increase the incomes and holdings of financiers. Control over credit should be taken from financiers and should be vested in a public agency, able to administer this power as a public trust in the interests of all the people.—*From declaration of general Labor Conference in Washington, D. C., December 13, 1919, presided over by Mr. Gompers: excerpts reproduced as expressing his views.*

America's workers stand ready in the new year as in the past to do their full duty as American citizens. We have always placed our obligations as citizens above all else. As citizens we are true to the American ideal of equal opportunity for all.

In the past we have found it necessary to fight for that ideal against agencies that sought to establish special privilege. Those fights have not been in defense of class advantages, but to assure to wage earners the rights and opportunities that all should possess. Our struggles may have brought discomfort to others, but they prevented a greater evil—deterioration of the virility of a part of the nation.

The great struggle of labor in the past has been to assure to workers in their industrial relations the rights of free citizens. We have fought to give the ideal of America dominating influence in shops and factories.

Our militant struggle has won general recognition for our demands, but our work is not all militant. We are in a position to contribute to the improvement of production processes and organization.

The immediate problem of the world is to develop a production organization that will benefit directly those who are the real producers and will also serve the needs of starving nations. When assured of just dealings America's workers are able to coöperate in freeing production from the grasp of speculators and influences that manipulate industry to enrich a few who gain unfair advantage, thus preventing production.

This is a big job, but it is essential for well grounded development in the years to come. It is essential to that ideal which is American—equal opportunity for all. America's workers will do their full share in working out all our country's problems.—*New Year's statement, January 1, 1920.*

It has been my pleasure to work with the American labor movement nearly all my life, from my young boyhood up to this hour, and I can recall with the greatest satisfaction its consistent, progressive, liberty-loving, patriotic course. When I shall have done my work, whatever it may be, if the world will remember me for five minutes after I am gone and say, "He tried to be of service to his fellows in life," I shall be content.—*From address, by invitation, before Chamber of Commerce, Boston, Mass., January 8, 1920.*

INDEX

A

"A Country Without Strikes," by Henry D. Lloyd, 263
Abbott, Lyman, 192, 242
Accidents, industrial, 42
Adamson law, 243-245
Advisory Commission, 248, 256
Agents-provocateur, 51
Alexander, Joshua W., 254, 255
Alien workers, 34; predominate in steel industry, 164
American Bridge Co., 231
American Federation of Labor, achievements, 27; affiliated organizations, 17, 18; Bolshevism, attitude toward, 35; Buffalo convention (1917), 255-257; Bucks' Stove and Range Company's suit against, 238-242; child labor, attitude toward, 121; component parts, 6, 14, 15, 26; conventions, character of, 25, 26, 28, 29; dues, per capita, 27; eight-hour movement (1888), inauguration of, 84; executive council, 17, 18, 28, 177; expenses, publicity of, 50; federal labor unions, 161; federation, efforts to secure, 6; foundation of, 13, 26; funds, 50; government, democratic character of, 27; growth, reasons for, 5; negro workers, efforts to organize, 166-170; officers, authority of, 27; policemen's unions, attitude toward, 195; president of, 16; railroad strike (1894), attitude toward, 188; "scientific" management, protects workers from evils of, 299; social insurance, attitude toward, 147; steel workers, efforts to organize, 164; strength, 31; strikes, has no authority to call, 194; toleration in, 2; unemployment, efforts to mitigate, 157, 158; union label, attitude toward local unions' right to issue, 177-178; unity, trade union, efforts to secure, unskilled workers, efforts to organize, 163, 164, 165, 166
American Federation of Labor Union Label, 175
American Labor Union, 35
Ancient Order of Hibernians, 214
Anderson, Sydney, 254
Anti-Boycott Association, 52
Anti-trust laws, 253
Apprentices, employers' demand for, 134; regulation of, by trade unions, 133
Arbitration of industrial disputes, 259, 260; in railroad service, 259
Arbitration of industrial disputes, compulsory, 260-262; Canada, 266, 267; Colorado, 264, 269, 270; New Zealand, 262, 263; compulsory investigation, 268, 269, 270, 271; compulsory investigation in Colorado, 269, 270; regional adjustments, 271
Arbitration of industrial disputes, voluntary, 267, 268
Assumption of risk for industrial accidents, 135; legislation modifying, 139

B

Ballard, S. Thurston, 174
Battleships, relative cost of, in government and private yards, 99
Bohm, Ernest, 254
Bolshevism, 35, 37
Bonus system, 299
Boston building trades, 287
Boston Chamber of Commerce, 288

313

INDEX

Boston tea party, 211
"Boston Transcript," 110
Boycott, 50, 203-217; "Buffalo Express" case, 204-206; definition of, 204, 207; criminal, 206; Catholic boycott of divorce plays, 216; editor-educators' opposition to, 214; efficiency of, 203; legal, 204-209, 210, 216; morality of, 215; origin of term "boycott," 211; political boycotts, colonial period, 211-213; regulation of right to issue, 203; "We Don't Patronize" List, 203
Boycott, Captain, 211
Brandeis, Louis D., 111, 277
British goods, boycott of, 211-213
British Trade Union Congress (1887), 1
Brotherhood spirit in trade unions, 144
Bucks' Stove and Range Company, suit against American Federation of Labor, 238-242
Bureau of War Risk Insurance, 154
Budapest, Hungary, 36
Business patronage, 50

C

Capital, combinations of, 41
Captains of industry, 85
Chamberlain, George E., 248
Charlatans, 11
Chattel slavery, 13
Child labor, 118; evils of, 119, 120, 131; in the South, 122; influence of, on child conservation, 129; legislation, 121, 126, 127; opposition of organized labor to, 121; organized labor's work to abolish, 124, 126
Child labor products, boycott of, 127
Children, 125
Choate, Joseph H., 133
Cigarmakers, effect of 8-hour day on longevity of, 105
Cigarmakers' International Union, 105
Cigarmakers' Union No. 144, New York, N. Y., 2
Class feeling, 21, 22

Clayton law and the Lever Food Control Act, 245-257
Closed shop. *See* Union shop
Collective bargaining, 116, 278-289; control of wages by, 74, 75; keeping contracts, 280, 281; organized labor's demands from National Industrial Conference (1919), 282-284
Colorado, 103
Company stores, 61, 62
Competition, 38, 39
"Connecticut" (battleship), cost of, 99
Contempt of court, 216
"Contributory negligence," responsibility of, for industrial accidents, 135; legislation modifying, 139
Coöperation, 294
Coöperative commonwealth, 33
Cost of living, 79; report of Executive Council, A. F. of L., on, 255-257
Council of National Defense, 248, 249, 256
Courts, The, 50, 51
Cramp, 94
Credit, 309, 310
Currency, inflation and deflation of, 309

D

Damage suits against trade unions, 235-237
Darrow, Clarence S., 64-66
Davis, David, 15
Death benefits, trade union, decrease of due to 8-hour day, 100
Detective agencies, 39, 40, 51
District of Columbia Supreme Court, 210
Distribution of wealth, 3
Dual federations of labor. *See* Western Labor Union
Dwyer, Mrs. (Australia), 263

E

"Economic and Social Importance of Eight-Hour Movement," by George Gunton, 91
"Efficiency," industrial, 294-303

INDEX

Eidlitz, Otto M., 183
Eight-hour day, advantages of, 81, 94, 99-101; criticisms of answered, 94-97; effect of on cost of production, 99; effect of on foreign markets, 96; effect of on longevity of workers, 100, 105; effect of on output, 98, 100, 106, 107; effect of on wages, 105; employers' opposition to, 94-97; results in shipbuilding industry, 94
Eight-hour day by law, 101; criticisms of, 100-104, 106
Eight-hour law in Colorado, 103
Eight-hour movement (1886), 82; (1888), 84
Eliot, Dr. Charles W., 214
Elston, Josephine W., 174
Emigration, 155
Emigrants, international protection of, 155
Employers, 287; interest in workers, 53, 54; not eligible for membership in trade unions, 32, 33; opposition to shorter workday, 93; responsibility, lack of industrial sanitation and hygiene, 54; risks of, 41; wages, attitude toward, 62, 63, 64
Employers' liability for industrial accidents. See Workmen's compensation.
Employers on arbitration boards, 48, 49
Employers' organizations, 38
Employers' "trade unions," 55, 283
Employment, waiving risks to secure, 135
Employment agencies for migratory workers, 143, 162
Employment agencies, federal, 145; labor exchanges, state and national, 143
Equal pay for equal work, 118
Europe, trade union movement in, 1
Executive Council, American Federation of Labor, authority in jurisdiction disputes, 178; statement by, on power of local unions to issue union labels, 177; minutes of consideration given anti-strike clause in Lever Act, 247; statement by, on attitude toward Lever Act, 255-257; statement by, on coal miners' strike (1919), 245

F

Federal Labor Unions, 32, 33, 161
Federation Française des Travailleurs du Livre, 1
"Fellow servant" responsibility for industrial accidents, 135; abrogation of by States, 139
Ford Motor Co., effect of shorter workday on output, 108
Foreign markets, 96
Francs, 98
Frankenheimer, John, 111
Freedom of contract, 278
Freedom of the press, 50, 216, 238-242
Free speech, 50, 238-242
Frey, John P., 298

G

Gardner, 273, 274, 275, 276
Gary, Judge Elbert H., 198
Gerry, Elbridge T., 123
Gladden, Washington, 173
Gladstone, William E., 47
Glass Bottle Blowers' Association, 146
Gompers, Samuel, incidents in career of, 7, 9, 131, 311
Gorgas, William C., 104, 105
Government work, 8-hour day on, 98-101
Great Britain, 1
Gregory, Thomas W., 245, 251, 257
Gunton, George, 91

H

Hand production, 11
Hanna, M. A., 47
Harvard University, 298
Havemeyer, John C., 66
Heine, 18
"Hilfee," German periodical, 98
Hiring and firing. See Labor turnover.

INDEX

Hollis, 248
Hoover, Herbert C., 36, 245, 247, 256
Hours of labor, minimum, 39
Houston, David Franklin, 249, 250
Hoxie, Robert F., 298
Hubbard, Elbert, 63, 64
Housing, 31, 32
Hungary, 36
Husting, 251, 252, 253

I

Immigration, 155
Impossibilists, 30
Individuality, workers', 16, 18
Industrial accidents, 135; employers' responsibility for, 136, 140; employers' liability for, State laws, 139; increased by machine production, 138, 140, 148; inherent in modern industry, 137; responsibility of drink habit for, 148
Industrial cripples, vocational rehabilitation of, 154
Industrial democracy, 303-311
Industrial depression (1893), 85
"Industrial Depressions," report on, 81
Industrial education, 15, 16
Industrial freedom, 102
Industrial peace, 48
Industrial relations, human equation in, 288; regulation of by law, 102
Industrial sanitation and hygiene, 54, 55-57
Industrial stagnation, 68, 69
Industrial unionism, 183
Industrial Workers of the World, 165, 281; in 1919 steel strike, 201
Industries, regulation of, 304
Ingalls, Melville E., 46
Ingraham, 234
Initiative and referendum, 103
Injunction against American Federation of Labor (Bucks' Stove and Range case), 238-241
Injunction against United Mine Workers coal strike (1919), 245, 257
Injunctions, 240, 241

Intemperance, 89-91
International Brotherhood of Stationary Firemen, 17
International Labor Conference (1919), 157
International Typographical Union, 58, 59, 146

J

Jurisdiction disputes, 178-184; industrial unionism does not prevent, 183; menace to trade union movement, 180-182; not limited to trade unions, 183; origin and development of, 179
Justi, Herman, 43
Justice, 13

K

Keating, 24
Kilbourne-Jacobs Manufacturing Co., 40
Kilbourne, James, 40
Kirby, 45, 49, 50
Knights of Labor, 15, 32, 35
Kun, Bela, 36

L

Labor conferees, 48, 49
Labor disputes, public opinion in, 271, 272
Labor "grafters," 221
Labor leaders, 16
Labor movement, 29
Labor representatives, qualifications, 24, 25
Labor-saving machinery, effect on glass bottle blowers and printers, 146; effect on production, 92; displacement of labor by, 81, 82; introduction of on a large scale, 92; effect on workers, 92, 93; increases unskilled labor, 161; trade union measures to relieve distress caused by, 82
Labor standards, post-war, 157, 158
Labor supply, monopoly of, 21, 23

INDEX

Labor turnover, 55, 158, 160
Labor, rights of, 50, 233
Labor, risks of, 41, 42
Laughlin, J. Laurence, 21
Leisure, use of by workers, 89
Lever, 246
Lever Food Control Act, 245-257; Former Attorney General Gregory's statement with regard to its enforcement, 245; limited to duration of war, 246; Lever-Keating debate in House of Representatives regarding anti-strike provision of, 246, 247; minutes of A. F. of L. executive council regarding, 247; Senate adopts A. F. of L. amendment, 248; conference committee rejects A. F. of L. amendment, 248; does not prohibit strike, 248; action of Advisory Commission and Council of National Defense relative to, 248, 249; memorandum of conference of Samuel Gompers with Secretary of Agriculture Houston relative to, 249-250; memorandum of conference of Samuel Gompers with Secretary of Labor Wilson relative to, 250-251; Attorney General Gregory agrees not to apply it in violation of Clayton anti-trust law, 251; debate in Senate on "anti-strike provisions" of, 252, 253; attitude of American Federation of Labor, 254; report of Executive Council, A. F. of L., on, 255-257
Lewis, 253
Liberty, 18, 19, 44
Limitation of output, 21, 23, 170-175
Linotype, the, 58, 59
Living wage, 39, 58, 60
Lloyd, Henry D., 263
London, Meyer, bill providing for social insurance, 149-151
Los Angeles *Times* disaster, 49, 222-228; organized labor's condemnation of, 222
"Louisiana" (battleship), cost of, 99
Lusk, 263, 264

M

McBride, John, 7
McElwain Company, 107
McLaughlin, 234
McNamara, J. J., 225
McNamara case, 223, 224, 225-228, 228-232
Machinery, labor saving, effect on wages, 58, 59
Manning, Cardinal, 47
Manufacturers, denunciation of trade unions by, 44
Manufacturers' Information Bureau, 40
Migratory labor, 143, 145, 162, 163
Minimum wage, definition of, 58, 59, 60, 62; legal, 76, 77, 78
Minimum wage legislation, 77, 78
Modern industry, 133
Money, inflation and deflation of, 309
"Monthly Review," 110
Morrison, Frank, 227, 251
Mosely, Albert, 95
Motherhood, 123

N

National Association of Manufacturers, 47, 49, 50, 51, 52, 53, 221, 231
National Civic Federation, 110, 277
National Council for Industrial Defense, 52
National Erectors' Association, 231
National Industrial Conference (1919), 200
National Industrial Conference (1920), 265, 272, 281-285
National Labor Union, 15
Negroes, disfranchisement of, 122
Negro workers, attitude of organized labor toward, 166-170; organization of, 166-170
Negro workers' trade unions, opposition of employers to, 166; representation in central labor bodies, 168
New York *Nation*, 297
New Zealand, 262, 263, 265

INDEX

Nine-hour day, disadvantages of, 94; in French mines, 98
Non-unionists, 109, 112, 113

O

Old-age pensions, 147
"One big union," 34, 35, 194
"Open" shop, 112, 114, 115
Organizations of capital, 42, 43, 44, 45
Otis, Harrison Grey, 41, 42
Overproduction, 85, 92
Overtime, 59

P

Packing industries, organization of, 166
Paine Lumber Company vs. United Mine Workers, Supreme Court decision, 253, 257
Palmer, Potter, 46
Parks, Sam, 220
Parry, David, 15, 51
Parsons, John B., 111
Patten, Simon N., 75, 76
Patterson, Joseph Medill, 216
Peace treaty, 37
Perkins, George W., 105
Phillips, Wendell, 47
Picketing, 217, 219
Policemen, organization of into unions, 195-198; action of A. F. of L. relative to, 195
Political action, 33
Pope Leo XIII, 46
Potter, Bishop, 24
Poverty, 18
Preferential union shop, 116
Prices, high, 309
Private gunmen, 39, 40
Production, competitive, 56, 57; improved methods cause unemployment, 133; machine, 85, 92, 93
Products of labor, right to own, 21, 22
Profit sharing, 290-294
Profiteering, 309
Public expenditures, retrenchment in, 147
Public interest in strikes, 201
Public opinion in labor disputes, 271, 272

Public peace, maintained by trade unions, 185
Public works, 147

R

Railway Brotherhoods, 31
Railway employers, 243-245
Railway strikes, 232
Railway strike (1894), attitude of A. F. of L. relative to, 188
Ralston, Jackson H., 111
Reconstruction, 303, 304
"Reconstruction of Economic Theory," by Simon N. Patten, 75, 76
Redfield, William C., 174
Reed, James R., 252
Revolution, 30, 31
Revolutionary policies, 33, 34
Ricks, 232
Riots, 45
Rochdale system, 309
Rooker, William V., 111
Russia, 35, 36

S

Schwab, Charles M., 172
"Scientific" management, 300
Sedition legislation, peace-time, 257, 258
Saloons, 89
Seasonal labor, 79, 80, 162
Shepard, Chief Justice, 216, 217
Sheppard, Morris, 248
Sherman anti-trust law, 52, 242
Shorter work-day, effect on wages, 86-89; effect upon social wellbeing of workers, 86-91, 97; relation to unemployment, 82, 85; relation to intemperance, 89, 90; workers' use of leisure resulting from, 89
Sinclair, Upton, 146
"Six Centuries of Work and Wages," by Thorold Rogers, 262
Social insurance, compulsory, 149-153; in Germany, 152; limitations and defects of, 152, 153; influence upon poverty, 152; old-age pensions, 147
Socialism, 21, 222

INDEX

Socialists, 33, 146; labor legislation, policy of, 101-104
Soldiers and sailors, vocational rehabilitation for, 154
Sons and Daughters of Liberty, 211
Stafford, Wendell P., 210
"Statute of Laborers," 262
Steel industry, organization of workers in, 164
Steel workers' strike (1919), 98-201
"Store order" wages, 61
Strikes, 30, 31, 185-202; American Federation of Labor cannot call, 194; attitude of courts toward, 232; averted by trade unions, 187, 189; coal strike (1919), 245-257; criticism of, 186, 189; damage suits against trade unions for strikes upheld by British House of Lords, 236; efficiency of, 189-191; general strike, 194; legal in United States, 255; "losses" in wages due to, 191; prevention of, 192-194; right to strike, 50, 233-235, 243-245; Taff Vale strike, litigation, 235-237
Strike-breakers, 112
Structural iron workers, duties of, 228-231
Structural Iron Workers' Union of America, 231
Subdivision of labor, 92
Supply and demand, 67, 68

T

Taff Vale case, 235-237
Taft, William H., 45, 46, 207, 232
Teachers, right of to organize, 127
Teachers' trade unions, 127, 131
Time-measuring devices, 299
Time wages, 60
Trade agreements, 30, 48, 49, 242
Trade union employment bureaus, 134
Trade unions, aims, principles, 2, 3, 7, 45-47, 287, 310; autonomy, 4; benefit funds, 12, 19, 20; brotherhood in, 144; criticisms of and objections to, 21-23, 34, 44, 45, 46; democracy of, 36; dues, 9, 10, 11, 12; efforts to mitigate distress caused by labor saving machinery, 82; form of, 3, 4; growth, 34; individuality, influence upon, 16; justice, relation to, 13; legality of, 221; liberty, relation to, 19; loyalty of, 37; membership limited to wage-earners, 32, 33; necessity of, 3, 285; non-unionists, attitude toward, 109; officials, 23, 24, 34; official journals, 15, 16; capital, organization of, attitude toward, 42, 43; percentage of workers belonging to, 31; progressiveness of, 37; right to organize, 116, 273-277, 282, 284; shop unions, 283; trade unions, national, origin, need of, 4, 12
Turner, J. K., 40

U

Unemployment, 69, 70, 141-143; increased by inventions, 133; increased by immigration, 155; insurance against, 147, 156; determination of, 154; prevention of by Government, 157, 158; public works to mitigate, 148, 157; trade union efforts to mitigate, 82
Union Advocate, 2
Union label, 175-178; A. F. of L. label, 175; first label, 176; local unions not permitted to issue, 177; results of, 177; significance of, 176
Union shop, 112; justice of, 114; rests on freedom of contract, 113
Union shop agreements, legality of, 108, 112
Union shop contracts, 210
United Mine Workers of America, 103, 104
United States, the, 54
United States Commission on Industrial Relations, 268, 281, 298, 299; report on efficiency, 298, 299
United States Steel Corporation, 231, 292

INDEX

United States Supreme Court, 253, 257
University of Wisconsin, 298
Unskilled workers, 161; increase of by introduction of labor saving machinery, 161; organization of by A. F. of L., 164, 165; organization of by I. W. W., 165; predominance of alien workers among, 163

V

Valentine, Robert G., 298
Van Cleave, W., 52
Violence, 21, 23, 219-232; opposition of trade unions to, 221
Vocational rehabilitation, 154

W

Wage-earners, 30, 31
Wage reductions, 62, 63, 66, 67, 68-73, 76; wage scale, sliding, 59, 60; wage system, 291
Wages, 58-79; and circulation of money, 71; and prices, 64, 65, 78; control of by collective bargaining, 74, 75; determination of, 66, 67; high wages, 78; increased wages and prices, 78; influence of trade unions, 74; iron law of, 72; limit to, 66, 74; low wages, 105; store order wages, 61, 62; time wages, 56
Wages fund, 72, 73, 74, 75
Walking delegates, 10, 11
Welfare work, employers', 55
Western Labor Union, 33
Westinghouse Company, 55
Wilson, William B., 250, 251
Wilson, Woodrow, 200, 211, 257
Woll, Matthew, 309
Women in industry, 118, 120, 127, 129; effect on wages, 123; trade union organization of, 130, 132
Women workers, registration of, 131
Women Workers' Union, 263
Workingmen, comparative protection of in Europe and the United States, 54
Workmen's compensation for industrial accidents, 135; effect of litigation on net compensation, 137
World war (1914-1918), 257

American Labor: From Conspiracy to Collective Bargaining

AN ARNO PRESS/NEW YORK TIMES COLLECTION

SERIES I

Abbott, Edith.
Women in Industry. 1913.

Aveling, Edward B. and Eleanor M. Aveling.
Working Class Movement in America. 1891.

Beard, Mary.
The American Labor Movement. 1939.

Blankenhorn, Heber.
The Strike for Union. 1924.

Blum, Solomon.
Labor Economics. 1925.

Brandeis, Louis D. and Josephine Goldmark.
Women in Industry. 1907. New introduction by Leon Stein and Philip Taft.

Brooks, John Graham.
American Syndicalism. 1913.

Butler, Elizabeth Beardsley.
Women and the Trades. 1909.

Byington, Margaret Frances.
Homestead: The Household of A Mill Town. 1910.

Carroll, Mollie Ray.
Labor and Politics. 1923.

Coleman, McAlister.
Men and Coal. 1943.

Coleman, J. Walter.
The Molly Maguire Riots: Industrial Conflict in the Pennsylvania Coal Region. 1936.

Commons, John R.
Industrial Goodwill. 1919.

Commons, John R.
Industrial Government. 1921.

Dacus, Joseph A.
Annals of the Great Strikes. 1877.

Dealtry, William.
The Laborer: A Remedy for his Wrongs. 1869.

Douglas, Paul H., Curtis N. Hitchcock and Willard E. Atkins, editors.
The Worker in Modern Economic Society. 1923.

Eastman, Crystal.
Work Accidents and the Law. 1910.

Ely, Richard T.
The Labor Movement in America. 1890. New Introduction by Leon Stein and Philip Taft.

Feldman, Herman.
Problems in Labor Relations. 1937.

Fitch, John Andrew.
The Steel Worker. 1910.

Furniss, Edgar S. and Laurence Guild.
Labor Problems. 1925.

Gladden, Washington.
Working People and Their Employers. 1885.

Gompers, Samuel.
Labor and the Common Welfare. 1919.

Hardman, J. B. S., editor.
American Labor Dynamics. 1928.

Higgins, George G.
Voluntarism in Organized Labor, 1930-40. 1944.

Hiller, Ernest T.
The Strike. 1928.

Hollander, Jacob S. and George E. Barnett.
Studies in American Trade Unionism. 1906. New Introduction by Leon Stein and Philip Taft.

Jelley, Symmes M.
The Voice of Labor. 1888.

Jones, Mary.
Autobiography of Mother Jones. 1925.

Kelley, Florence.
Some Ethical Gains Through Legislation. 1905.

LaFollette, Robert M., editor.
The Making of America: Labor. 1906.

Lane, Winthrop D.
Civil War in West Virginia. 1921.

Lauck, W. Jett and Edgar Sydenstricker.
Conditions of Labor in American Industries. 1917.

Leiserson, William M.
Adjusting Immigrant and Industry. 1924.

Lescohier, Don D.
Knights of St. Crispin. 1910.

Levinson, Edward.
I Break Strikes. The Technique of Pearl L. Bergoff. 1935.

Lloyd, Henry Demarest.
Men, The Workers. Compiled by Anne Whithington and Caroline Stallbohen. 1909. New Introduction by Leon Stein and Philip Taft.

Lorwin, Louis (Louis Levine).
The Women's Garment Workers. 1924.

Markham, Edwin, Ben B. Lindsay and George Creel.
Children in Bondage. 1914.

Marot, Helen.
American Labor Unions. 1914.

Mason, Alpheus T.
Organized Labor and the Law. 1925.

Newcomb, Simon.
A Plain Man's Talk on the Labor Question. 1886. New Introduction by Leon Stein and Philip Taft.

Price, George Moses.
The Modern Factory: Safety, Sanitation and Welfare. 1914.

Randall, John Herman Jr.
Problem of Group Responsibility to Society. 1922.

Rubinow, I. M.
Social Insurance. 1913.

Saposs, David, editor.
Readings in Trade Unionism. 1926.

Slichter, Sumner H.
Union Policies and Industrial Management. 1941.

Socialist Publishing Society.
The Accused and the Accusers. 1887.

Stein, Leon and Philip Taft, editors.
The Pullman Strike. 1894-1913. New Introduction by the editors.

Stein, Leon and Philip Taft, editors.
Religion, Reform, and Revolution: Labor Panaceas in the Nineteenth Century. 1969. New Introduction by the editors.

Stein, Leon and Philip Taft, editors.
Wages, Hours, and Strikes: Labor Panaceas in the Twentieth Century. 1969. New introduction by the editors.

Swinton, John.
A Momentous Question: The Respective Attitudes of Labor and Capital. 1895. New Introduction by Leon Stein and Philip Taft.

Tannenbaum, Frank.
The Labor Movement. 1921.

Tead, Ordway.
Instincts in Industry. 1918.

Vorse, Mary Heaton.
Labor's New Millions. 1938.

Witte, Edwin Emil.
The Government in Labor Disputes. 1932.

Wright, Carroll D.
The Working Girls of Boston. 1889.

Wyckoff, Veitrees J.
Wage Policies of Labor Organizations in a Period of Industrial Depression. 1926.

Yellen, Samuel.
American Labor Struggles. 1936.

SERIES II

Allen, Henry J.
The Party of the Third Part: The Story of the Kansas Industrial Relations Court. 1921. *Including* The Kansas Court of Industrial Relations Law (1920) by Samuel Gompers.

Baker, Ray Stannard.
The New Industrial Unrest. 1920.

Barnett, George E. & David A. McCabe.
Mediation, Investigation and Arbitration in Industrial Disputes. 1916.

Barns, William E., editor.
The Labor Problem. 1886.

Bing, Alexander M.
War-Time Strikes and Their Adjustment. 1921.

Brooks, Robert R. R.
When Labor Organizes. 1937.

Calkins, Clinch.
Spy Overhead: The Story of Industrial Espionage. 1937.

Cooke, Morris Llewellyn & Philip Murray.
Organized Labor and Production. 1940.

Creamer, Daniel & Charles W. Coulter.
Labor and the Shut-Down of the Amoskeag Textile Mills. 1939.

Glocker, Theodore W.
The Government of American Trade Unions. 1913.

Gompers, Samuel.
Labor and the Employer. 1920.

Grant, Luke.
The National Erectors' Association and the International Association of Bridge and Structural Ironworkers. 1915.

Haber, William.
Industrial Relations in the Building Industry. 1930.

Henry, Alice.
Women and the Labor Movement. 1923.

Herbst, Alma.
The Negro in the Slaughtering and Meat-Packing Industry in Chicago. 1932.

[Hicks, Obediah.]
Life of Richard F. Trevellick. 1896.

Hillquit, Morris, Samuel Gompers & Max J. Hayes.
The Double Edge of Labor's Sword: Discussion and Testimony on Socialism and Trade-Unionism Before the Commission on Industrial Relations. 1914. New Introduction by Leon Stein and Philip Taft.

Jensen, Vernon H.
Lumber and Labor. 1945.

Kampelman, Max M.
The Communist Party vs. the C.I.O. 1957.

Kingsbury, Susan M., editor.
Labor Laws and Their Enforcement. By Charles E. Persons, Mabel Parton, Mabelle Moses & Three "Fellows." 1911.

McCabe, David A.
The Standard Rate in American Trade Unions. 1912.

Mangold, George Benjamin.
Labor Argument in the American Protective Tariff Discussion. 1908.

Millis, Harry A., editor.
How Collective Bargaining Works. 1942.

Montgomery, Royal E.
Industrial Relations in the Chicago Building Trades. 1927.

Oneal, James.
The Workers in American History. 3rd edition, 1912.

Palmer, Gladys L.
Union Tactics and Economic Change: A Case Study of Three Philadelphia Textile Unions. 1932.

Penny, Virginia.
How Women Can Make Money: Married or Single, In all Branches of the Arts and Sciences, Professions, Trades, Agricultural and Mechanical Pursuits. 1870. New Introduction by Leon Stein and Philip Taft.

Penny, Virginia.
Think and Act: A Series of Articles Pertaining to Men and Women, Work and Wages. 1869.

Pickering, John.
The Working Man's Political Economy. 1847.

Ryan, John A.
A Living Wage. 1906.

Savage, Marion Dutton.
Industrial Unionism in America. 1922.

Simkhovitch, Mary Kingsbury.
The City Worker's World in America. 1917.

Spero, Sterling Denhard.
The Labor Movement in a Government Industry: A Study of Employee Organization in the Postal Service. 1927.

Stein, Leon and Philip Taft, editors.
Labor Politics: Collected Pamphlets. 2 vols. 1836-1932. New Introduction by the editors.

Stein, Leon and Philip Taft, editors.
The Management of Workers: Selected Arguments. 1917-1956. New Introduction by the editors.

Stein, Leon and Philip Taft, editors.
Massacre at Ludlow: Four Reports. 1914-1915. New Introduction by the editors.

Stein, Leon and Philip Taft, editors.
Workers Speak: Self-Portraits. 1902-1906. New Introduction by the editors.

Stolberg, Benjamin.
The Story of the CIO. 1938.

Taylor, Paul S.
The Sailors' Union of the Pacific. 1923.

U.S. Commission on Industrial Relations.
Efficiency Systems and Labor. 1916. New Introduction by Leon Stein and Philip Taft.

Walker, Charles Rumford.
American City: A Rank-and-File History. 1937.

Walling, William English.
American Labor and American Democracy. 1926.

Williams, Whiting.
What's on the Worker's Mind: By One Who Put on Overalls to Find Out. 1920.

Wolman, Leo.
The Boycott in American Trade Unions. 1916.

Ziskind, David.
One Thousand Strikes of Government Employees. 1940.